Inflation and the Personal Income Tax:
An International Perspective

Inflation and the Personal Income Tax:

AN INTERNATIONAL PERSPECTIVE

VITO TANZI

Assistant Director, Tax Policy Division
International Monetary Fund,
Washington, D.C.

CAMBRIDGE UNIVERSITY PRESS

CAMBRIDGE
LONDON   NEW YORK   NEW ROCHELLE
MELBOURNE   SYDNEY

CAMBRIDGE UNIVERSITY PRESS
Cambridge, New York, Melbourne, Madrid, Cape Town, Singapore, São Paulo

Cambridge University Press
The Edinburgh Building, Cambridge CB2 8RU, UK

Published in the United States of America by Cambridge University Press, New York

www.cambridge.org
Information on this title: www.cambridge.org/9780521229876

© Cambridge University Press 1980

First published 1980
This digitally printed version 2008

A catalogue record for this publication is available from the British Library

Library of Congress Cataloguing in Publication data
Tanzi, Vito.
Inflation and the personal income tax.
1. Income tax – Effect of inflation on.
I. Title.
HJ4637.T35   336.2′42   79–52667

ISBN 978-0-521-22987-6 hardback
ISBN 978-0-521-06870-3 paperback

To my children
VITO LUIGI
ALEXANDRE BRUNO
GIANCARLO OLIVIER

Contents

Preface

L'inflation est l'oeuvre du diable parce qu'elle respecte les
apparances et détruit les réalités.

André Maurois

Whether inflation is, or is not, the work of the devil is an issue on which I
would rather not make a pronouncement; however, it *is* the theme of this book
that inflation respects appearances while destroying reality. Inflation distorts
tax systems and, in the process, affects the level of taxation and its incidence
among taxpayers. But these distortions are often not obvious and, at times,
are so subtle that not only unsophisticated observers but even highly
sophisticated ones may be deceived into concluding that nothing has changed
in reality. This book deals with these distortions, with respect to income
taxes, and with what can be done, or has been done in various countries, to
deal with them. As the subject is of considerable interest to policymakers
around the world, I have preferred to emphasize the practical, rather than the
purely theoretical, side of the problems. This, however, does not imply that
this book will be of no interest to academic economists or to students of
taxation. The problems are simply too important and complex to be left just to
policymakers. This book includes thirteen chapters ranging from fairly
theoretical to eminently practical ones. In all cases, the perspective is an
international one, although because of greater availability of data for the
United States, some issues are illustrated with examples for that country.

Chapter 1 outlines the nature of the problems and the solutions. Chapters 2
and 3 deal with the impact of *progressivity* on real tax burdens when the price
level changes. Chapter 2 discusses the way in which the distortions come
about, the analytical schemes for carrying out the adjustment, the choice of
the index, and so on. These issues have received considerable attention in the
literature. Chapter 3 deals with actual countries' experiences. It identifies
many countries – both developed and developing – that have introduced
indexation and shows the considerable variety in pursuing a policy of
indexation.

Chapters 4 through 6 deal with incomes from capital sources for which the
major problem is not progressivity but the proper definition of taxable
income. For these incomes, inflation will "destroy reality" by distorting
taxable bases. Chapter 4 deals with capital gains; Chapter 5 with interest

income; and, Chapter 6 with business incomes. In all cases, the problem is first presented and possible solutions are discussed. Then countries' experiences are reviewed. Chapter 7 deals with another type of distortion that has hardly been recognized in the literature, namely, that due to differential lags in the collection of taxes. These lags are very significant when the rate of inflation becomes high. Chapters 8 and 9 deal with the sensitivity of income tax revenues with respect to real and inflationary changes in income. The latter of these chapters proposes an indexation scheme that accounts for inflation as well as real growth.

One of the channels through which inflation destroys reality is by the creation of fiscal illusions; in other words, through the people's inability to pierce the fiscal veil in order to see what is happening to their real tax payments and, therefore, to their real incomes. Especially when inflation is a new phenomenon, individuals may not be sophisticated enough to appreciate fully the extent to which inflation and taxation interact to increase their real tax burden. Thus, for example, wages may increase enough to neutralize the price change but not enough to neutralize the effect of tax progressivity on the wage increases. If inflation persists, taxpayers may in time become more sophisticated so that they will begin to demand before-tax increases that take into account not only the erosion of the value of the monetary unit but also the effect of the tax. This reaction may lead to what has at times been referred to as a tax-push inflation. When this happens, one could argue that inflation adjustments are no longer required on ground of equity but they would certainly continue to be required on ground of stability and, perhaps, efficiency.

Chapters 10 through 12 deal with some of these issues especially in relation to interest incomes and wages. Some tax-push is likely to exist also in relation to incomes such as capital gains, profits, and so on. However, no theory has yet been developed in connection with these other incomes. Chapter 13 is a concluding chapter that briefly touches on some issues not discussed in previous chapters.

At various stages in the preparation of this book, I have received advice, comments, and/or specific information from various individuals. It would not be feasible to mention all of them but I would like to thank my colleagues within the Tax Policy Division, as well as Milka Casanegra-Jantscher, Ke-Young Chu, Andrew Feltenstein, Richard Goode, Michèle Guerard, David Morgan, and Leif Mutén. My thanks also go to Miss Carmelita O. Eugenio for her competent typing of the manuscript and to Mrs. Chris Wu for statistical assistance. I would also like to acknowledge that some material used is based on previously published articles in Banca Nazionale del Lavoro *Quarterly Review* and in International Monetary Fund *Staff Papers*.

V.T.

1

Inflation and personal income taxation: an introduction to the main issues

Inflation affects individuals in myriad ways: as consumers, wage earners, savers, asset holders, borrowers, lenders, taxpayers, and so forth. This book will not deal with all of these effects but it will, instead, concentrate on the relationship between inflation and personal income taxes. That taxes and prices are somehow related has, of course, been known for a long time. In 1945, Colin Clark caused quite a stir with his controversial thesis that a high level of taxation sets in motion forces of an economic, political, and psychological nature that inevitably lead a country toward inflation.[1] Clark's thesis sounded plausible in 1945, a year of high (for that time) taxes and inflation. But then, with the end of the war, inflation became a problem of the past and interest in Clark's thesis eventually subsided. That thesis, and much of the public-finance textbooks' discussion of tax shifting, dealt with the effects of taxes on prices. Today, however, inflation is no longer seen as a temporary aberration or as a disease of a few irresponsible countries, but, rather, it has become a more or less permanent condition in a universal context. As a consequence, it was inevitable that there should be a growing interest in the reverse of the above-mentioned relationship. The focus of interest now is less on the effect of taxes on prices than on the effect of changes in price levels on tax systems.[2] The reason is that inflation inevitably brings about distortions in tax systems and especially in income taxation: the burden of taxation as well as its distribution among the taxpayers are changed and not necessarily in desired directions.

The nature of the problem

If the tax system were truly inflation-proof, neither the tax burden (i.e., the ratio of tax revenue to national income) nor the distribution of that burden among the taxpayers would be affected by inflation. No country has, so far, managed to develop such a system; in fact, there are reasons that argue against even the theoretical existence of such a system. However, much can be done, and in some countries has been done, to introduce corrective mechanisms that reduce, if not eliminate, these inflation-induced distortions. For these mechanisms to be successful, it is necessary that the nature of, and the causes for, these distortions be clearly understood.

Inflation distorts the personal income tax in many ways but mostly through its effects on (1) the base for the assessment of the tax; (2) the real progression of the rates; (3) the significance of the collection lag; (4) the size of the collection lag; (5) the legal structure of the tax; (6) tax evasion; (7) fiscal illusions. These factors are, of course, of varying importance although they are all relevant with respect to the personal income tax. The more important among them – mainly the first three – will receive considerable attention throughout this work. The others will be discussed in various places but will receive less attention. For the moment, a few brief remarks on each of these will suffice.

Inflation and the tax base

If all statutory income increased at the same rate and at the same time as the general price index, and if the legal definition of income were identical with the economic definition, inflation would not distort the base on which the tax is assessed: that is, income, when deflated for the change in the price index, would remain constant. However, in reality, inflation inevitably brings about changes in the real value of income. Some of these changes are due to the inevitable leads and/or lags in the adjustment of some types of incomes, such as wages, to price changes; for these, no generalization is possible, so they will be largely ignored. More importantly, however, inflation makes incomes from capital sources – interest, capital gains, profits, and so on – *as defined for tax purposes* diverge from their economic definition.[3] Profits may be inflated if, in measuring the excess of receipts over costs, the latter (especially depreciation and inventory) are calculated at their historical (and thus lower) values.[4] Capital gains are inflated, because they are calculated on the difference between the resale value of the asset, which reflects current and thus inflated prices, and the acquisition cost, which reflects lower historical prices. Interest income is inflated because part of it compensates the lender for the erosion that he suffers in the value of the loan. In most of these cases, the problem is that between the time when the expense is incurred or the money is lent, and the time when the receipts are received, or the loan is repaid, the value of the monetary unit may have changed con-

siderably. Consequently, different yardsticks are used to measure outlays and receipts.

The real progression of the rates

Inflation changes the real progression of the personal income
tax in two basic ways. First of all, it reduces the real value of those
exemptions, deductions, credits, and so on, which are fixed in nominal
amounts. Second, it distorts the progressivity of the tax by reducing
the real width of the brackets to which the tax rates apply. As inflation
progresses, the real width of those brackets becomes narrower and the
tax becomes more progressive. Therefore, a taxpayer will find himself
climbing the tax ladder of the progressive rates even when his real income has not changed. Furthermore, different individuals are affected
differently, depending on their initial position and their family status.

The significance of the collection lag

Although, for some incomes, the lag between the time when
the income is earned and the time when the tax payment is made (the
collection lag) is very short (as it is for incomes subjected to withholding at the source), for others it can be sizable (mostly for capital incomes). As the rate of inflation speeds up, the loss in the real value of
the tax liability caused by this lag becomes more significant. Or, putting it differently, the gain to the taxpayer associated with the postponement of the tax payment increases. This factor introduces inequities among taxpayers: those who cannot postpone the payment end
up paying more taxes in real terms than those who can, even when their
income is the same. The overall tax burden is also affected as the real
value of tax revenue received by the government falls.

The size of the collection lag

The size of the collection lag is partly determined by legal considerations as the law or, more often, the directives issued by the tax
administration, prescribe when tax payments have to be made. However, in most countries, the taxpayer has some discretion over the tim-
ing of the payment, especially when he is willing to pay some interest
surcharge or penalty. If these penalties and/or surcharges are not adjusted in line with inflation, or are adjusted with a lag, as is often the
case, they may become low or even meaningless when compared with
the rate of inflation. In such cases, postponing the tax payment will
become the cheapest source of credit available to taxpayers, so the
inducement to delay paying taxes will become strong indeed.

The legal structure of the tax

Some writers have argued that the legal structure of the income tax is what it is because of inflationary expectations. In other words, in the absence of inflationary expectations the legal structure of the tax would have been somewhat different. Examples that have been cited in this context are the following: depreciation charges that the enterprises have been allowed to take may have been made more liberal by the fear that, in the presence of inflation, using historical costs as bases for the calculation of depreciation would leave the enterprises with insufficient funds to replace the depreciated asset; the rates at which capital gains are levied may have been reduced on the expectation that, with rising prices, part of the gain may be fictitious; investment credits themselves may have been introduced because of inflationary expectations.[5]

This type of distortion is very hard to verify, as one would need to know the intentions of the policymakers when they enacted the tax laws. However, since the future rate of inflation was obviously unknown at the time of that enactment, it is hard to see how the legislators could have changed the law to neutralize a rate of inflation that, in theory, could range from zero to infinity.[6] What is disturbing about this type of argument is that, carried to its extreme, it precludes any discussion about inflation-induced distortions and about corrections for those distortions. Since the *status quo ante* is not known one cannot discuss *adjustments for inflation* without discussing more basic reforms of the tax system.[7]

Tax evasion

In some countries, it has been argued that taxpayers' resentment against being pushed by inflation into higher marginal tax rates, even when their real, before tax, income has not changed, has led to lower degrees of tax compliance. In some cases, the reduction of the real value of exemptions, deductions, and credits has led to a significant increase in the number of taxpayers, and this has placed inevitable strains on the tax administration. Thus, the greater willingness on the part of the taxpayers to evade tax has been met by a lesser ability on the part of the tax administration to detect evasion. The result has been an increase in tax evasion.

Fiscal illusions

It is not clear to what an extent taxpayers suffer from fiscal illusions in a period of inflation. It is likely that when inflation is a new phenomenon, individuals may not fully appreciate the extent to which the interaction of inflation and taxation is increasing the tax burden on them and is thus reducing their after-tax income. For example, when fiscal illusions exist, wages or interest payments may not increase sufficiently to neutralize the above-mentioned interaction. However, in time, if inflation continues and comes to be anticipated, people will begin to see through the fiscal veil and will attempt to recover the losses in real income. In such cases, workers as well as lenders may require and get increases in wages or in interest that compensate them not only for the change in prices but also for the induced change in real tax payment. If this happens, inflation adjustments will no longer be justified on the ground of equity but may still be required by reasons of efficiency or stability. There is evidence from some countries that wage earners may no longer suffer from these illusions. There is less evidence of this as far as receivers of capital incomes are concerned.

The nature of the solution

Faced with the distortions of the income tax structure brought about by inflation, governments can react in three basic ways: they can do nothing; they can introduce periodic and discretionary adjustments, hoping to neutralize the more serious distortions; or, finally, they can introduce more permanent, automatic adjustment schemes. These automatic schemes are often referred to as indexation. Which of these alternatives will be chosen depends on various factors, of which the most important are the rate of inflation, the expectation about its permanency, the ideological coloring of the party in power, and the facility with which tax laws can be changed.

When the rate of inflation is relatively low – say less than 5 percent per year – its distortional effects will be limited.[8] It will thus be easier for a country to do nothing, at least for some time. However, as the rate of inflation rises, the need for some sort of action will soon begin to be felt. Often the reaction of the government will be to resort to periodic tax cuts aimed at neutralizing in part the effects of inflation.[9] This, for example, has been the policy followed by countries such as Belgium, Germany, Japan, and the United States.[10] On the other hand, as we shall see later, various countries have chosen to introduce permanent adjustment schemes. These schemes have often been opposed by leftist political forces on the ground that a discretionary policy of tax reduction could be better adapted to a policy of income redistribution.[11] They have also been opposed on the ground that discretionary adjustments give the government a freer hand in formulating the correct fiscal policy. However, this is doubtful as long as economic agents anticipate those changes. The rational expectations hypothesis is clearly relevant in this context.[12] When the rate of inflation becomes permanently high

– say, above 20 percent per year – the question of whether a country should introduce automatic adjustment schemes becomes somewhat academic. In this situation, the only practical alternatives may be indexation (Argentina, Brazil, Chile), or abolishment of personal income taxation (Uruguay) unless the tax laws can be changed with such rapidity, and at such low cost (in terms of time and effort) to the policymakers, that yearly ad hoc adjustments remain feasible.[13]

In passing, it ought to be mentioned also that if a country relies significantly on excise duties levied with specific rates, which in an inflationary situation suffer revenue losses, the government may welcome the increase in revenue associated with the income tax as this increase may compensate for that loss. But the problem of the redistribution of the burden among taxpayers will still remain significant.

Both the periodic discretionary adjustments and the more permanent schemes (indexation) have more often than not dealt with only some of the many distortions outlined above. In fact, with the exception of very few countries, they have, for the most part, dealt only with the issue of the real progression of the rates. Therefore, one should not assume that indexing the income tax means removing all the distortions brought about by inflation.

In order to use a consistent terminology throughout this work, we shall distinguish four types of indexation which to varying degrees have been used in different countries. We shall call *indexation for exemptions* the automatic adjustment of exemptions, deductions, credits, and so on, which are expressed as fixed monetary amounts by the tax laws of a country. This type of indexation attempts to neutralize the impact of inflation on these amounts.[14] We shall call *bracket indexation* the automatic adjustment of the width of the brackets to which the progressive tax rates apply. This can also be called rate-structure indexation. This adjustment, together with the previous one, attempts to maintain a constant rate progression for the income tax.

Both of these automatic adjustments can be related to inflation alone, or as will be shown later, they can be related not only to inflation but to some index of productivity change. In such a case, the indexation could be done with changes in nominal income, average wage of industrial workers, minimum wage, and so forth. These particular indexation mechanisms are required because of the progressivity of income taxes. They would not be necessary if the income tax were strictly proportional.[15] Furthermore, the same type of indexation mechanism can be used for any progressive tax, be it in the form of income, wealth, expenditure, capital transfer, inheritance, and so on.

The third type of automatic adjustment will be called *indexation for capital-income adjustment*.[16] Another name for it is indexation of the tax base. The objective of this adjustment is to modify the definition of income used for tax purposes in order to remove inflationary distortions in costs and/or outlays and to make it consistent with a proper economic definition. This type of adjustment normally concerns capital gains, interest incomes, and interest deductions, depreciation charges, and inventory profits. In a proper adjustment scheme, this type of adjustment must precede that related to exemptions and brackets. Furthermore, indexation for capital income adjustment is not necessitated by the progressivity of the tax but, as long as there is inflation, it would be required even if the tax were strictly proportional. Most of the really thorny problems with inflation adjustments relate to this type of indexation. This explains why fewer countries have introduced it.

Finally, we shall also discuss the *indexation of taxpayers' liabilities*, which is an aspect that has received very little attention. This relates to the effect that the lags in tax collection have on real revenue when the rate of inflation becomes high. Indexation of liabilities attempts to maintain that real value, regardless of the size of the collection lag.

The introduction of these indexation mechanisms is not without difficulties. These will be discussed at some length in the relevant chapters. On the other hand, there has been considerable discussion about the effects of indexation on (1) the distribution of the tax burden, (2) the stability of the economy, (3) the rate of inflation itself, (4) the size of the public sector, (5) the efficiency of the economy, and so forth. For some of these, there is very little consensus, for others there is more. The problem is that quantification of these effects requires the building of econometric models as, for example, was done by Bosson and Wilson for Canada, and by Pierce and Enzler for the United States.[17] But, of course, these models are themselves based on specific assumptions and on the data from particular countries, so their results are not beyond controversy and cannot be generalized to all countries.

One point that perhaps needs to be emphasized before concluding this introductory chapter is that the arguments for neutralizing the effects of inflation on the tax system are not based on the assumption that the existing real tax system is correct or optimal, so that any deviation from it is necessarily undesirable. Rather it is based on, perhaps, a romantic or, should one say, complimentary view of the tax policy process that assumes that changes in the real tax system are, or, better, should be the result of explicit policy decisions rather than of haphazard events. The fact that the real tax system does not, often, reflect one's view of what an optimal system should look like – and the fact that inflation-induced deviations from it may, at times, even move that system in the "right direction" – may reduce the strength of some of the arguments for indexation but does not make them incorrect.

This book deals only with income taxes. However, other taxes are also affected by inflation. For completeness' sake an appendix to this chapter briefly discusses other taxes.

Appendix: problems and adjustments in relation to other taxes

Other taxes, besides those on incomes, are also affected by inflation but the issues involved, as well as the solutions that can be adopted, are generally simpler. Although this book deals with income taxation, it is appropriate to discuss briefly some of those issues. We shall consider: (1) social security contributions; (2) taxes on goods and services, including customs duties; (3) taxes on real property; (4) taxes on net wealth; (5) taxes on transfers of wealth; and (6) direct taxes on expenditure.

Social security taxes

The reaction of these taxes to changes in prices depends mainly on the way in which they are levied, because they are normally collected without much of a lag. When these taxes are levied on total income from employment with proportional rates, the situation is similar to that of proportional personal income taxes when the tax base is not distorted. In the absence of lags in payments, revenues will increase at the same rate as prices as long as the employment incomes keep up with price changes. Therefore, no corrections are needed. Italy, Norway, and Sweden are among the countries where social security taxes are basically proportional.[18] In spite of this proportionality, over the 1965–75 period these countries managed to increase sharply the ratio of social security contributions to GNP through increases in the rates.[19]

If social security charges are levied on nominal incomes below a ceiling, and if this ceiling is not raised in line with inflation (or if it is raised only with a lag), then revenues are likely to fall in relation to employment income. In this case, the increase in current income, regardless of whether it is caused by real growth or by inflation, will not lead to a proportional increase in revenues. Countries that tax wages only up to a given limit include Canada, Belgium, France, Germany, the Netherlands, and the United States. In this case, the simplest solution is to adjust the ceiling in line with the change in the price index. All the above-mentioned countries increased the ratio of these taxes to GNP over the 1965–75 period. Thus, either the ceilings were more than adjusted or the rates were increased.

If, as it has been true in some countries (Ireland, Denmark, and the

United Kingdom[20]), the social security charges are levied as specific taxes (so much per worker), revenues will not respond to changes in current income (unless the latter is associated with higher employment). Therefore, revenues will not react to price changes, and, unless discretionary changes are made, they will decline in real terms. In Denmark the ratio of social security taxes to Gross Domestic Product (GDP) did decline between 1965 and 1975, but it did not in the United Kingdom and Ireland.

Excise and sales taxes

For excise taxes, the important distinction is between specific (or unit) and ad valorem taxes. With specific taxes, the product is levied on the basis of weight, volume, quality, alcoholic content, and so on, but not value. Consequently, when the price rises, the nominal tax payment remains unchanged and the real value falls. On the other hand, if the excise is imposed on the value of the product, the tax will increase with the price of the product. As long as the price of the product rises in line with the general price level, an ad valorem excise tax will be neutral with respect to inflation. However, some of the most important excises – including those on alcoholic beverages, tobacco, and gasoline – are often specific duties. Furthermore, they are often collected with significant lags. Statistical data for the OECD countries for the 1965–75 period show that the ratio of excises to GNP and to total taxes did in fact fall for most countries and especially for those which experienced higher rates of inflation, such as Denmark, France, Italy, the Netherlands, and the United Kingdom. In a prolonged inflationary situation, there would be little scope for specific taxes unless the rates were adjusted often or were indexed for price change.

For general sales taxes, the situation is somewhat different. These taxes are imposed at ad valorem rates, and because they affect a broad range of products, they can be expected to respond automatically and proportionately to price changes.

Countries that rely on customs duties levied with specific rates face the same problem as those with specific excises: inflation will normally bring about a fall in real revenues. Once again, the solution is the substitution of specific rates with ad valorem ones, or, alternatively, the indexing or frequent adjustment of specific duties.

Real property taxes

The impact of inflation on real property taxes is threefold: (1) it affects the potential tax base – that is, the market value of the property; (2) it accentuates the divergence between the market and the assessed or taxable value of the property; (3) it affects the real value of revenue because of collection lags, which are often substantial for these taxes. There is no reason why the market price of real assets should move closely in line with the change in the cost of living. If individuals antici-pate continued inflation, they will come to see these real assets as hedges against the erosion in their net worth associated with holding cash balances and other financial assets.[21] Consequently, the market price of real assets may increase faster than the rate of inflation. This factor, per se, would tend to increase real revenue. However, assess-ments often lag behind changes in market prices, so the tax rates may be applied to outmoded values thus leading to a fall in real revenue. Only with frequent assessment and with reduced collection lags can countries be able to prevent the erosion in the tax base. And only with short collection lags will they be able to maintain the real value of rev-enue. For the 1965–75 period, the share of property taxes in GDP fell in most OECD countries, indicating that the two negative factors more than compensated for the positive one.

Taxes on net wealth

Net wealth is defined as the difference, at a specified date, be-tween the value of all the assets in the possession of an individual and the sum of his liabilities. Net wealth taxes are often levied with prog-ressive rates above a tax-free exemption. In a period of inflation, in order to preserve the real progressivity of the tax, there is a clear need to escalate (i.e., increase) the tax-free level, as well as the brackets, in line with the price index.[22] One example of this type of adjustment is provided by the net-wealth tax introduced in Argentina on April 9, 1976 (Law No. 21282). The adjustment in the exemption and in the five brackets is made on the basis of the change in the wholesale price index for nonagricultural products. Thus, the marginal rates, that vary be-tween 0.50 percent and 1.5 percent, are levied on constant real val-ues.[23]

Taxes on transfers of wealth

For taxes on transfers of wealth, it is wealth transferred, either as a gift or as an inheritance, that forms the base on which the tax is levied. If the tax is proportional without any exemption, no adjustment is required. If the tax is proportional above an exempted amount, then the amount needs to be increased by the change in the relevant price index. If the tax is progressive, the brackets need to be adjusted, just as was the case for the net wealth tax. If the progressivity is related to the total cumulative transfer over the donor's lifetime, then not only the brackets must be adjusted every year for the change in the price level in order to maintain their real progressivity, but, before they are cumulated, past transfers must be adjusted by the increase in the price index since the time the transfer was made.[24]

Direct taxes on expenditures

For direct taxes on expenditures, the issues are exactly the same as for income taxes when the problem of capital-income adjustment (i.e., the problem of the proper definition of income) is ignored. An expenditure tax levied with a proportional rate, and without an exempted portion, is inflation-neutral. If there is an exemption expressed as a fixed monetary amount, the exemption should be adjusted yearly for the change in the price index. If the tax is progressive above an exemption fixed in monetary units, the exemption, as well as the brackets, must be adjusted annually for the price change. This adjustment will keep the real progression constant in real terms.

This appendix has provided a cursory view of the inflation adjustments needed for taxes other than those on incomes. Some of these adjustments will become somewhat simpler to understand after the indexation of income taxes has been discussed in detail. Some of the problems left out of this discussion (such as the choice of the index, the relevant period over which the index is observed, etc.) will also be understood. The main point is that once the issues and the solutions concerning income taxes have been discussed, the problems and the adjustment mechanisms related to other taxes appear much simpler.

BIBLIOGRAPHY

Aaron, Henry J. "Inflation and the Income Tax: An Introduction." In Henry J. Aaron, ed. *Inflation and the Income Tax.* Washington, D.C.: Brookings Institution, 1976, pp. 1–31.

Allen, Richard, and Savage, David. "Indexing Personal Income Taxation." In Thelma Liesner and Mervyn A. King, eds. *Indexing for Inflation.* London: Institute for Fiscal Studies, 1975, pp. 41–60.

Fellner, William, et al *Correcting Taxes for Inflation.* Washington, D.C.: American Enterprise Institute, 1975.

Morgan, David R. *Overtaxation by Inflation.* London: Institute of Economic Affairs, 1977.

Organization for Economic Cooperation and Development (OECD). *The Adjustment of Personal Income Tax Systems for Inflation.* Paris: OECD, 1976.

Prest, Alan. "Inflation and the Public Finances." *Three Banks Review* no. 97 (Mar. 1973): 3–29.

Ruppe, Hans George. "General Report on Inflation and Taxation." In

Cahiers de droit fiscal international, International Fiscal Association, 31st Congress, Vienna 1977, *62*:90–121.

Tanzi, Vito. "Inflation and the Indexation of Personal Income Taxes in Theory and in Practice." *Banca Nazionale del Lavoro Quarterly Review* no. 118 (Sept. 1976): 241–71.

2

Inflation and the real progression of the rates: problems and solutions

In this chapter, we assume that the only inflation-induced distortion in the personal income tax system is caused by the progressivity. In particular, we assume that (1) either there is no capital income problem, or (2) that capital incomes have already been adjusted. We also ignore the issue of collection lags. In this way we can focus on one basic aspect of the problem: the fact that inflation pushes taxpayers into brackets levied with higher tax rates even when their real income has not changed.

Effects of inflation on personal income tax liability

In most countries, personal incomes above certain exempted levels are taxed with progressive statutory rates. These rates apply to income brackets specified in money terms in the tax legislation. Personal exemptions, as well as some of the deductions or tax credits, are also fixed in current values. Such a legal structure for the personal income tax guarantees that, in the absence of evasion, higher taxable incomes will be subjected to higher average tax rates.[1] This feature has generally been considered desirable from both an equity and a stabilization point of view: because it promotes the objective of income redistribution and conforms to the principle of ability to pay; and because the progressivity of the income tax generally increases its built-in flexibility and this increase is supposed to moderate cyclical fluctuations.

In an inflationary situation, however, the above-mentioned characteristics of the income tax may, and often do, create difficulties, because the growth in the money incomes for most taxpayers will necessarily exceed any growth in real income. It may even happen, as it did in recent years in several countries where the Phillips relationship broke down, that while money incomes are rising, real income may actually be falling. Still, the unadjusted tax system will not differentiate real from purely inflationary increases; the average tax rate for most taxpayers is, thus, likely to grow and to exceed, in relation to real incomes, the levels contemplated when the tax structure was established. Some taxpayers, who because of their low incomes in relation to the exemptions and deductions to which they were entitled had previously been exempted from paying any taxes, may now become taxable. Others who were already taxed may become subject to higher average (and often also marginal) tax rates. If the inflationary pressures continue, and if the government does not react in some way to correct this situation, the increase in money incomes may in time cause increases in tax revenues that are not desirable from an equity, resource allocation, or stabilization point of view.

If the growth in real income is ignored, and if there is no substantial change in the pretax distribution of income, the increase in the ratio of personal income tax revenue to some concept of gross income (i.e., adjusted gross income or personal income or national income) will depend on the rate of inflation and the legal structure of the tax.[2]

As far as the structure of the tax is concerned, the level of the exemptions or allowances and their relation to the per capita income of the country is particularly important. If these exemptions are several times the per capita income of the country, as is true in some developing countries, then even with two-digit rates of inflation many taxpayers are still exempt from the tax for a long time. If, on the other hand, these exemptions are low in relation to the per capita income of the country, as is generally true in most industrialized countries,[3] then they will quickly lose their importance and even relatively poor individuals will experience substantial increases in income tax burdens. In such a case, not only the tax burden but also the number of taxpayers will increase, thus creating problems for the tax administration.

In addition to the exemptions, the rate structure and the width of the income brackets to which the rates are applied are also important, because inflation, besides shrinking the real size of the exemptions, will also lead to a shrinkage of the real size of the brackets. Consequently, the wider the income brackets, the longer it will take for a given rate of inflation to push a taxpayer into a higher income bracket, where he will face a higher marginal tax rate.[4] And, obviously, the steeper the increase in the rates, the more responsive will the revenues be to inflationary increases in current incomes.

In most countries where income above the exemptions is levied at progressive tax rates that increase up to a given statutory maximum, the average tax rate for a taxpayer will be zero when his income is lower than the exemptions, and, once part of the income becomes taxable, will not increase at a constant rate but will follow the form of an

S, or logistic, curve, rising at an increasing rate at first and then, eventually, slowing down to approach a maximum near the highest marginal tax rate.[5] This pattern is particularly important for wage and/or incomes policy. For taxpayers in some income ranges, the inflation-induced increase in the average tax rate will be particularly high. If these particular taxpayers happen to be unionized, they are likely to react to that increase by asking for a wage settlement aimed at maintaining (or, depending on their expectations, at increasing) their real disposable income. This issue is discussed in some detail in a later chapter. At this point, attention needs to be focused on the fact that the rate structure, and the way in which it relates to the wage structure, can contribute to what has been called a wage-push inflation. The increase in the average tax rate at any level of income will depend on the relationship between the marginal and the average tax rates, which in turn depends on the effective progressivity of the income tax structure.

The pattern described in the preceding paragraph characterizes most income taxes around the world. If the income tax were truly proportional – that is, if there were no progressive rates and no exemptions, or if the exemptions were a fixed *proportion* of income – the average tax rate would not be affected by inflation.

Given the rate of inflation, the rate of growth in real income, and the legal income tax structure, the increase over a given period of time in the average tax paid by an individual that can be attributed to inflation will depend on the initial position of the taxpayer in the income distribution – that is, on the level of his income (and on the particular status of the taxpayer; i.e., marital status, number of children, etc.) which will determine the exemptions and deductions to which he is entitled.

Empirical studies for Australia,[6] Canada,[7] the United Kingdom,[8] the United States,[9] and Italy[10] have shown that:

1. The interaction of inflation and the structure of the personal income tax has had the effect of generally increasing the average tax burden at all levels of taxable income.

2. Different classes of taxpayers have experienced different increases in average tax rates. Lower-income taxpayers and those with more dependents have generally experienced the largest *percentage* increases in average tax rates. The main reason for these results is the shrinkage of the real value of the exemptions, although the rate structures have also played a considerable role.

3. Discretionary tax changes have not fully removed the effects of inflation.

The second conclusion must be interpreted with caution, inasmuch as a controversial and important point of interpretation arises. The problem is that the impact of inflation on taxpayers' liabilities can be measured in at least two different and often contrasting ways: one can either concentrate on the inflation-induced *percentage* increases in the average tax rates (this is the interpretation implied above); or one can concentrate on the percentage *points* – that is, the absolute – increases in those rates. The first way has attracted more attention, but it is the second way that is more significant in regard to the effects on disposable incomes and after-tax income distribution. When the emphasis is on the reductions in disposable incomes rather than on percentage changes in average tax rates, the empirical studies mentioned above show that these reductions are often greater for higher incomes than for lower ones. But there is less uniformity than implied by the above conclusions.[11]

Description of analytical adjustment schemes

Countries may wish to correct for changes in the average tax rates induced by inflation. If inflation is considered a passing phenomenon, they would probably opt for discretionary ad hoc adjustments. However, if rising prices are considered to be a more permanent problem, they might in some cases choose adjustment mechanisms of a more permanent nature. They would want to do this in the hope of immunizing the effective structure of the personal income tax from the effects of inflation. This second route has been taken by several countries.

The schemes actually used for these permanent adjustments do not always use indexes reflecting just the rate of inflation. In many of the countries using indexation, the indexes reflect not only the rate of price increases but also changes in other factors, of which the most important is probably productivity.[12] Even when the countries wish to make adjustments only for inflation and not for productivity changes, they still have to decide whether to adjust the personal income tax structure to reflect the full rate of inflation or only part of it. Thus, an element of discretion is often introduced in what is normally thought of as a completely automatic rule. As we see in Chapter 3, of the countries that now index their personal income taxes:

1. Some have a rule that allows for *full* adjustment for inflation on an *annual* basis (e.g., Canada).

2. Others make *annual* adjustments, but only for part of the inflationary change (e.g., the Netherlands).

3. Still others adjust the tax structure only when the rate of inflation, *in a particular year,* has exceeded a stated level – say, 5 percent (e.g.,

France). Thus, in this particular alternative, a creeping inflation will not lead to any automatic change in the nominal tax structure, regardless of the cumulative change in the average price level.[13]

4. Finally, the rule may be such that the adjustment mechanism will become effective only when the cumulative increase in the price index from a reference year has reached a certain level (e.g., Luxembourg).

It is obvious that only the first of these alternatives, if properly applied, would maintain unchanged the real effective structure of the tax. However, when the rate of inflation becomes particularly high, the difference between the first of these alternatives and the third and fourth disappears.

Before examining the countries' experiences, we shall describe briefly some of the basic schemes of indexation for inflation that have been suggested in the literature.[14] An ideal adjustment scheme for inflation should (1) be simple; (2) maintain the initial distribution of the personal income tax burden among real income levels, regardless of the source of income and of the particular family situation;[15] and (3) prevent a purely nominal increase in income from generating a real increase in the revenue from the personal income tax. Four different adjustment schemes have been proposed in the literature to correct for the impact of inflation on personal income tax liabilities. These are briefly outlined below.

The first of these would involve the equiproportional lowering of the statutory tax rates to eliminate the increase in revenue due to inflation. This adjustment might be successful in preventing the growth in the aggregate personal tax ratio, but it certainly would not prevent the unintended redistribution of tax burden among different income levels. Furthermore, the direction of these redistributional changes would most likely not be the one desired by most governments. For example, the income of a relatively poor family that because of the increase due to inflation becomes subject to personal income taxation for the first time would still be taxable, even if the statutory tax rates were reduced. On the other hand, those with the highest incomes would benefit from progressively lower marginal tax rates. Although rate reductions have been put into effect in several countries in inflationary periods, no country appears to have introduced an "indexation rule" based on this method.[16]

The second scheme would exempt from the taxable income of an individual the increase in adjusted gross income that can be attributed to inflation. Thus, for example, cost-of-living adjustments in wages and salaries would automatically be tax exempt. In general the individual would be allowed an "inflation deduction" that would depend on the rate of inflation. This inflation deduction would be calculated by multiplying the adjusted gross income of the taxpayer in the previous year by the rate of inflation for the taxable year.[17] The trouble with this scheme is that apart from any real growth, the taxable portion of income would remain constant not in real but in nominal terms. Consequently, the real value of the tax payment, and thus the average tax rate, would fall as long as the rate of inflation continues to be positive. This is clearly an overadjustment. Furthermore, its equity implications are not obvious.

Israel is the only country that, up to 1975, adopted an adjustment mechanism somewhat resembling the scheme just described. It was not an *automatic* indexation, however, because it only provided that the cost-of-living adjustment component of wages and salaries could be exempted from personal taxation *at the discretion* of the Minister of Finance. Until March 1964, the cost of living allowance was completely exempted. Since then there were limitations to the part exempted.[18]

The third scheme would deflate adjusted gross income to a base year; then taxable income in base year prices would be calculated and the resulting tax liability would be multiplied by the ratio of the price index of the taxable year to the price index of the base year. The operation of deflating gross income to the base year and then of inflating the tax liability to the current year gives this scheme an apparent complexity that has so far prevented its adoption in any country.[19] However, one of the Swiss cantons, Basel-Land, does follow this approach and uses the cost-of-living index for January 1953 as the base.

The last, and most important, adjustment scheme introduces price escalators into the income tax structure so that, over a period of time, the progressive income tax rates, in the absence of any discretionary changes, would apply to constant *real* incomes rather than to constant *nominal* incomes. To achieve this result, the limits of the taxable income brackets and the exemptions and deductions expressed in fixed monetary values would be increased on an annual basis at a rate equal to the rate of inflation. This scheme has received the greatest attention and support and, to varying degrees, has been introduced in a number of countries, including most recently Canada, in 1974, and Australia, in 1976.[20]

At this juncture, we must point out that if inflation is accompanied by real growth in per capita income, neither the aggregate personal tax ratio to GNP, nor the initial distribution of the tax burden, would remain unchanged unless the adjustment is made with a kind of super-index that takes into account not only the change in the price index but also the change in real per capita income. Indexing only for inflation is tantamount to accepting the conclusion that the rise in the ratio of personal income taxes to national income and the inevitable redistribution of the income tax incidence are acceptable when caused by real growth but are not acceptable when caused by inflation. Some countries, including Iceland, and, since September 1974, Denmark have not accepted this conclusion and have subsequently "super-indexed" their income tax structure.[21]

Special problems with adjustment schemes

To achieve the proper brackets and exemptions indexation, any adjustment scheme must solve some difficult problems.[22] The most important among these are: which of the various indexes of price changes to use for escalating the nominal income tax structure; and how to reduce the lag between the current rate of inflation and the rate used for indexation.

The choice of the index

The choice of the index depends to a large extent on the objective to be achieved through indexation.[23] That the choice of a proper index is fundamental to the success of indexation is rather obvious and needs no elaboration. As is well known, all indexes of price changes suffer from sampling and reporting errors and in some countries they may also suffer from political manipulations. Since the main objective of indexation seems to be the prevention of price-induced increases in the real tax burdens of taxpayers, the most used of the indexes has been the consumer, or retail, price index, because this is supposed to reflect the change in the purchasing power of the money incomes of the taxpayers. Besides the problems mentioned above, three issues have been raised with respect to this index. These relate to (1) the representativity of the index for taxpayers at different income levels; (2) the impact of changes in indirect taxes; and (3) the impact of changes in the international terms of trade.

Representativity of index. Several studies for different countries have shown that the basket of goods included in that index may not be and, in many cases almost certainly is not, representative of the expenditure pattern of the whole population. For example, price changes may be more favorable to taxpayers with higher incomes than to those with lower incomes when food prices increase at a faster rate than prices of other products.[24]

The countries that have indexed their taxes have made no attempt at generating indexes that would be applied to different income classes.

However, at least one country, the Netherlands, has constructed a special index – the total population index – that is more general than the consumer price index, and that is supposed to reflect better the expenditure of the whole population and not just that of a particular subgroup of it. In the particular case of the Netherlands, because of lower increases in food prices in recent years, the annual rate of increase of this total population index has been slightly lower than that of the consumer price index.

Whenever relative prices are changing, as well as absolute prices, which is often the case, the use of a single index for adjusting all the brackets and the exemptions will *not* leave unchanged the distribution of the real tax burden. The reason for this is obviously that taxpayers with different incomes will experience different losses in the real value of their incomes. In such a situation, either the adjustment could be made with multiple indexes – each relevant to taxpayers at particular income levels – or alternatively, the single-index adjustment could be accompanied by a discretionary change of the nominal tax structure. It is obvious that the information requirements for these adjustments are such that neither of these alternatives will leave all taxpayers with exactly the same preinflation real tax burden.

Changes in indirect taxes. The issue is whether the index should or should not reflect the effects on prices of changes in indirect taxes and, less importantly, in subsidies which may be viewed as negative indirect taxes. Simply stated, if indirect taxes are raised (lowered), should this be allowed to lead to an adjustment in the nominal tax structure and thus to an automatic decrease (increase) in income tax liability? The standard theoretical position on this issue has been that if the additional revenues from the indirect taxes are reflected in higher governmental spending, which presumably increases the welfare of the taxpayers, then the index should not reflect the change in indirect taxes. In other words, it should be corrected for these changes. Other observers, however, have pointed out that taxpayers generally do not see the connection between higher taxes and higher benefits from public spending (assuming that such a connection exists), so they may view in the same fashion an increase in the consumer price index regardless of whether it is due to an increase in taxes or to other factors.[25] If this second position is the valid one, then no adjustment in the index ought to be made.

This discussion may give the impression that the issue is just a theoretical one, without any practical significance. This, however, is not so. In the Netherlands, which now adjusts the index for changes in

indirect taxes and subsidies, the differences between corrected and un-
corrected total population index have been significant for particular
years. For example, in 1972, without the correction for the change in
indirect taxes and subsidies, the total population index changed by 8.0;
with the correction it only changed by 5.7. In 1973 the difference was
somewhat smaller: 8.1 and 7.8, respectively. In pursuance of the Act
on the construction of a wage-regulating price index, Denmark has also
generated an index whereby "taxes and duties are, to the extent possible, deducted from the prices collected, whereas subsidies provided in
order to achieve a general price reduction are added to the prices."[26]
For 1973, the increase in the CPI of this country was 14.4 (January
1973–January 1974), whereas the increase in the wage-regulating price
index was 12.9. For January 1974–January 1975, the corresponding increases were 13.5 and 14.4. The consumer price index used by Australia for indexing the personal income tax is also adjusted to remove
the price effect of discretionary changes in indirect taxes. The consumer price index that will be used for indexing the brackets of the
Swedish income tax, starting in 1979, will also remove the effects of
changes in the value-added tax.

In contrast with the Netherlands, Denmark, and Australia, Canada
has opted for the unadjusted consumer price index on the ground that
in a federal country, where various local governments have the power
to change the sales taxes just for a part of the country, it would be very
difficult and perhaps inequitable to make adjustments for changes in
taxes.

Changes in terms of trade. Suppose that the prices of the products that a country imports increase more than the prices of exports,
with a consequent deterioration in the country's terms of trade. Depending on the relative share of imports in national income, the consumer price index will go up accordingly. The question that arises is:
Should the adjustment in the brackets and in the exemptions reflect
fully this increase? If it does, the disposable income of taxpayers would
remain unchanged in real terms whereas real national income has fallen. It would make sense in such a situation to let disposable incomes
fall, so that at least part of the real reduction in nominal income that has
taken place is reflected in a reduction in real after-tax income for the
taxpayers. But this means that the consumer price index used to adjust
the exemptions and the brackets should be corrected for changes in the
terms of trade. In the case described above (a worsening of the terms of
trade), the adjustment in the price index would be downward, so that
taxpayers' real liabilities would go up.[27] *Mutatis mutandis,* an im-

provement in the terms of trade could lead to an upward adjustment in the price index and a consequent reduction in real tax liabilities.

In addition to the consumer (or retail) price index that has been discussed in this chapter, other indexes – reflecting changes in nominal income or in average earnings – have been used in a few countries. These indexes are related to a form of indexation that transcends the issue of inflation. Chapter 9 deals in some detail with these superindexes and with the rationale for using them.

The problem of lags

There are two types of lags that are relevant to the discussion of adjustment of taxation for inflation: One is the lag between the current rate of inflation and the rate reflected in the adjustment scheme; the other is the lag between the earning of income and the collection of taxes. The first of these, which is the relevant one from the point of view of bracket indexation, can be long and can create difficulties, especially when the rate of inflation is high and changing. As an example, consider Canada. When indexation was started on January 1, 1974, it was decided that, given the time needed to prepare the income tax forms, the latest month for which price increases could be observed was September 1973. It was further decided that, since the increase in the CPI between September 1972 and September 1973 would be sensitive to the behavior of prices in those particular terminal months, the index to be used in 1974 would reflect the *average* increase for the twelve-month period ending September 30, 1973 over the twelve-month period ending September 30, 1972. This same lag applies to future years. For the Netherlands, the lag is even longer, inasmuch as the index for a given year reflects the change in prices for the twelve-month period ending in July of the previous year, over the twelve-month period ending July of the year before that. For Australia, the lag is similar to that of Canada. Substantial lags exist in all the other countries that index their tax systems. When the rate of inflation is stable, these lags may not create serious difficulties; however, whenever the rate of inflation accelerates or decelerates, the index being used for making the adjustment in a given year will no longer be adequate, so that the ratio of tax payment to current income will change, causing difficulties for stabilization policy and bringing about distortions in the distribution of the tax payments. Some of these issues are discussed in later chapters.

3

Inflation and the real progression of the rates: countries' experiences

In this chapter, I outline the practical experiences of several countries in trying to maintain a constant real progression of the rates through the indexation of exemptions and brackets.[1] The countries are classified into four groups on the basis of the type of adjustment made. For the first group, the connection between the adjustment made and the rate of inflation is *direct* and *complete,* apart from discrepancies introduced by some of the special problems mentioned in Chapter 2. For the second group, the connection is still direct, but it is no longer complete. For the third group, the connection between inflation and the adjustment made is somewhat more tenuous, because substantial discretionary elements enter into the adjustment mechanisms. Finally, for the fourth group, although one can still talk about *inflationary* adjustments, and inflationary changes remain the most important factor, other elements enter the picture, so that one is hesitant to continue referring to these adjustments as indexation *for inflation.*

Countries with full, annual, automatic inflationary adjustments
The laws which describe the adjustment mechanisms are not always easy to interpret, but it appears that Canada, Australia, and Argentina are the only countries that qualify for this category. Up to 1974, Uruguay also belonged to this group. In these countries, the exemptions and deductions in fixed amounts, as well as the brackets, are fully, annually, and automatically increased to reflect changes in the consumer price index. This is undoubtedly the purest form of automatic adjustment for inflation.

Canada
The Canadian scheme, proposed on February 14, 1973 by the then Minister of Finance, went into effect on January 1, 1974 with a 6.6 percent inflation-induced escalation of the whole nominal structure of

the personal income tax. For 1975, the increase in exemption levels and in bracket limits due to indexation was 10.1 percent. For 1976, 1977, and 1978 it was 11.3, 8.6, and 7.2 percent, respectively. Beginning with 1976, the indexed personal exemptions and deductions are rounded to the nearest ten dollars.

Tables 1 and 2 are largely self-explanatory. They show the impact that indexation has had on the Canadian nominal income tax structure between 1974 and 1978. Table 3 shows, for typical taxpayers, the tax reductions resulting from indexation in 1974 and 1975. As it was not easy to judge the impact of inflation on tax incidence by income groups,[2] it is equally difficult to judge that of indexation. Table 3 shows that the *absolute* amounts of tax reductions increase with the level of income. Furthermore, these reductions become progressively larger between 1974 and 1975. This is shown by columns (5) and (6) in the table. On the other hand, the percentage reductions in tax liabilities – shown in columns (7) and (8) – are much greater for smaller incomes than for larger ones. Finally, the relationship of the tax reduction to before-tax incomes – see columns (9) and (10) – is similar at most income levels.

The revenue "losses" to the government due to indexation were estimated at about Can$400 million in 1974, Can$750 million in 1975, and Can$2 billion in 1976.[3] Also, the number of taxpayers fell from 8.9 million in 1974 to 8.5 million in 1975, largely as a result of the raising of the basic exemptions. This reduction in taxpayers is assumed to have simplified the administration of this tax. The Canadian legislation contemplates the escalation of the tax structure when prices rise but not the deescalation when prices fall. The escalation of the nominal structure is done using a consumer price index not adjusted for changes in indirect taxes or for changes in terms of trade. The brackets and exemptions for the current tax year are escalated for the change in the average price index between the year that ended the previous September and the year before that. Thus, considerable differences may exist between the current rate of inflation and the one reflected in the adjustment scheme.

Australia

On May 20, 1976, the Australian Treasurer announced that as of July 1, 1976 the nominal structure of the Australian personal income tax would be automatically indexed on the basis of changes in the consumer price index. Thus, the government decided to implement the recommendation of the Mathews committee. The escalation of the structure for 1976–7 was 13 percent, which reflected the change in the

Table 1. *Canada: federal personal exemptions subject to indexing (in Canadian dollars)*

Exemption	1973	1974: inflation factor 6.6%	1975: inflation factor 10.1%	1976: inflation factor 11.3%	1977: inflation factor 8.6%	1978: inflation factor 7.2%
Single status	1,600	1,706	1,878	2,091	2,270	2,430
Married status	3,000	3,198	3,522	3,921	4,260	4,560
Aged, additional	1,000	1,066	1,174	1,307	1,420	1,520
Incapacitated, additional	1,000	1,066	1,174	1,307	1,420	1,520
Dependent child under age 16	300	320	352	392	430	460
Dependent child age 16 or older	550	586	646	719	780	840
Other dependent under age 16	300	320	352	392	430	460
Other dependent age 16 or over	550	586	646	719	780	840
Dependents' earnings not affecting taxpayer's claim:						
Wife	300	314	334	372	400	430
Dependent child under age 6	1,100	1,166	1,274	1,418	1,540	1,650
Dependent child age 16 or over	1,150	1,220	1,332	1,505	1,640	1,760
Other dependent under age 16	1,100	1,166	1,274	1,418	1,540	1,650
Other dependent age 16 or over	1,150	1,220	1,332	1,505	1,640	1,760

Source: Canadian Tax Foundation, *The National Finances* (Toronto: annual publication).

Table 2. *Canada: taxable income brackets subject to indexing and tax rates*

1973		1974: inflation factor 6.6%		1975: inflation factor 10.1%	
Taxable income bracket (Can$)	Rate (%)	Taxable income bracket (Can$)	Rate (%)	Taxable income bracket (Can$)	Rate (%)
First 500	15	First 533	12	First 587	9
501– 1,000	18	534– 1,066	18	588– 1,174	18
1,001– 2,000	19	1,067– 2,132	19	1,175– 2,348	19
2,001– 3,000	20	2,133– 3,198	20	2,349– 3,522	20
3,001– 5,000	21	3,199– 5,330	21	3,523– 5,870	21
5,001– 7,000	23	5,331– 7,462	23	5,871– 8,218	23
7,001– 9,000	25	7,463– 9,594	25	8,219–10,566	25
9,001–11,000	27	9,595–11,726	27	10,567–12,914	27
11,001–14,000	31	11,727–14,924	31	12,915–16,436	31
14,001–24,000	35	14,925–25,584	35	16,437–28,176	35
24,001–39,000	39	25,585–41,574	39	28,177–45,786	39
39,001–60,000	43	41,575–63,960	43	45,787–70,440	43
60,000+	47	63,961+	47	70,441+	47

Source: Canadian Tax Foundation, *The National Finances* (Toronto: annual publication).

average level of the CPI between March 1975–March 1976 and the March 1974–March 1975 period. The consumer price index is adjusted to remove the price effect of discretionary changes in indirect taxes but not of changes in the terms of trade.[4] The escalation of the nominal structure applies to brackets, allowances for dependents, and most but not all other deductions expressed in nominal amounts. The budget cost of the escalation of the nominal income tax structure has been estimated at $1,050 million in 1976–7. As in Canada, the brackets and exemptions will not be adjusted downward in the face of a decline in prices.

Argentina

Beginning on January 1, 1974, Argentina introduced the automatic adjustment for exemptions and deductions. This *indexation for exemptions* was intended to keep off the tax rolls those taxpayers who because of very low incomes should not be subjected to any income taxation. The indexation was based on changes in the consumer price index between January 1 and December 31 of the year preceding the tax year. Up to the end of 1976, the tax brackets had been adjusted annually on an ad hoc basis and recently the adjustments had far exceeded the rate of inflation. However, the basic income tax law (No.

1976: inflation factor 11.3%		1977: inflation factor 8.6%		1978: inflation factor 7.2%	
Taxable income bracket (Can$)	Rate (%)	Taxable income bracket (Can$)	Rate (%)	Taxable income bracket (Can$)	Rate (%)
First 654	6	First 710	6	First 761	6
655– 1,307	18	710– 1,419	16	762– 1,521	16
1,308– 2,614	19	1,420– 2,838	17	1,522– 3,042	17
2,615– 3,921	20	2,839– 4,257	18	3,043– 4,563	18
3,922– 6,535	21	4,258– 7,095	19	4,564– 7,605	19
6,536– 9,149	23	7,096– 9,933	21	7,606–10,647	21
9,150–11,763	25	9,934–12,771	23	10,648–13,689	23
11,764–14,372	27	12,772–15,609	25	13,690–16,731	25
14,378–18,298	31	15,610–19,866	28	16,732–21,294	28
18,299–31,368	35	19,867–34,056	32	21,295–36,504	32
31,369–50,973	39	34,057–55,341	36	36,505–59,319	36
50,974–78,420	43	55,342–85,140	39	59,320–91,260	39
78,421+	47	85,141+	43	91,261+	43

20,628 of December 29, 1973) was amended by Law No. 21481 of December 30, 1976, which introduced the annual automatic indexation of brackets on the basis of changes in the consumer price index between the end of the current taxable year and the end of the previous year. Thus, in the case of Argentina, the lag in the index is much shorter than for Canada and Australia. The index is not adjusted for changes in terms of trade or indirect taxes.[5]

Uruguay

The following description of the Uruguayan income tax system relates to the situation that prevailed there between 1968 and 1973. As of January 1, 1974, the government of this country decreed the "suspension" of the tax on the income of individuals, although a schedular tax on industry and trade remained in effect. Obviously, without an income tax, there is nothing to index at the moment.

The Uruguayan adjustment scheme was almost identical to the Canadian one. Here, too, the nominal income tax structure was adjusted fully, annually, and automatically for the change in the consumer price index. This mechanism had been in effect since 1968 when, on the basis of amendments made in 1967 to the income tax law (arti-

Table 3. Canada: tax reductions attributable to indexing, 1974 and 1975 (married couple under 65 with two children under 16, all income earned, standard deduction)

| | Federal and provincial tax[a] | | | Tax reductions | | | | Tax reductions as percent of income | |
| | Without indexing (Can$) | After indexing (Can$) | | Absolute (Can$) | | Relative (%) | | | |
Income (Can$) (1)	(2)	1974 (3)	1975 (4)	1974 (5)	1975 (6)	1974 (7)	1975 (8)	1974 (9)	1975 (10)
4,000	7	0	0	7	7	100	100	0.2	0.2
5,000	133	51	14	82	119	62.6	89.5	1.6	2.4
6,000	383	298	193	85	190	22.2	49.6	1.4	3.2
7,000	646	555	444	91	202	14.1	31.3	1.3	2.9
8,000	920	827	704	93	216	10.1	23.5	1.2	2.7
9,000	1,198	1,101	978	97	220	8.1	18.4	1.1	2.4
10,000	1,498	1,389	1,252	109	246	7.3	16.4	1.1	2.5
12,000	2,129	2,002	1,843	127	286	6.0	13.4	1.1	2.4
15,000	3,145	2,996	2,793	149	352	4.7	11.2	1.0	2.3
20,000	5,198	4,950	4,617	248	581	4.7	11.2	1.2	2.9
30,000	9,699	9,358	8,965	341	734	3.5	9.6	1.1	2.5
50,000	20,138	19,636	18,862	502	1,276	2.5	6.3	1.0	2.6

[a] Provincial tax used is the lowest existing provincial rate.

Source: Adapted from Table 1 of paper by J. R. Allan, D. A. Dodge and N. S. Poddar, "Indexing the Federal Income Tax: A Federal Perspective," Canadian Tax Journal, July/August 1974 and from table by Canadian Finance Department as reproduced on p. 12 of Financial Times' Tax Newsletter (London), November 1974.

cles 40 and 41 of Law 14.100), the personal exemption and dependent allowance were adjusted in line with changes in the consumer price index. Since the brackets were expressed as multiples of the personal exemption, the whole nominal structure of the tax came to be fully and directly tied to the cost-of-living index.

Countries with annual, automatic but incomplete adjustments

The only three countries that could be put in this group are Sweden, the United Kingdom, and Peru. In these countries the income tax is indexed but only in part. For example, in Sweden, the indexation of the brackets does not extend to the exemptions and deductions, whereas in the United Kingdom and in Peru the deductions are indexed but not the brackets.

Sweden

In November 1976, the government of Sweden proposed that personal income taxes be indexed for inflation. A commission was appointed to look at this issue. On October 20, 1977, a government bill (prop. 1977/78:49) was sent to Parliament and, after heated discussion, it was adopted. Indexation will influence the income tax collections starting on January 1, 1979. The brackets will be expressed in terms of a "basic unit" which for 1979 is calculated at SKr5,000. This basic unit will be changed annually to reflect movements in the consumer price index between August of the year before the taxable year and August of the year before that. The effects on the price index attributed to changes in the value-added tax will be removed. It is important to emphasize that only brackets are indexed and not the exemptions and deductions which are fixed in money amounts. Therefore, the effect of inflation on the real progression of the rates is not completely removed.

United Kingdom

Whereas Sweden has chosen to index the brackets but not the exemptions and deductions, the United Kingdom has recently opted for the opposite. Section 22(2) of the Finance Act 1977 states: "In the year 1978/79 and subsequent years the personal reliefs allowed in this section [which exclude child tax allowances] shall be changed by not less than the same percentage as the increase in the retail price index for the previous calendar year." The Chancellor decided to apply this section to the year 1977/8 by increasing the "personal reliefs" by 12 percent. The cost of such an increase for a full year was estimated at around £1,200 million. Discussion of this tax indexation in the United Kingdom has emphasized that because of Britain's constitution, any act of Parliament supersedes any previous act. Therefore, "a finance bill which set tax allowances short of full indexation would override this year's, decreeing that they should be indexed."[6]

Peru
Since 1973 (Decree No. 19.653 of 1972), Peru has adjusted personal exemptions and deductions by an index related to the annual minimum wage. Since the minimum wage is generally itself adjusted fully for changes in the consumer price index, the personal exemptions are de facto automatically escalated by the rate of inflation as measured by the CPI. Since 1973, the escalation of the exemptions has closely paralleled changes in the CPI. No automatic adjustments are made in the brackets.

Countries with automatic indexation but with discretionary elements
Alternative but equally interesting examples of what could be called a corrupt, or less direct, approach to indexation for inflation are provided by France, Luxembourg, the Netherlands, and Israel.

France
Article 3 of the "Loi des Finances" for 1968 states that the government is required to adjust the structure of the personal income tax whenever inflation in a particular year, as measured by the consumer price index, exceeds the rate of 5 percent. By implication, no adjustment is required as long as the rate of inflation remains below that threshold. Furthermore, the various brackets can be adjusted differently. Thus, for example, between 1968 and 1972, the consumer price index rose by 25.5 percent; over this period the limits in the taxable income brackets rose 31.6 percent for the smallest bracket and 20.2 percent for the highest. At the same time, the marginal rates on each bracket were lowered by five percentage points.[7] In 1973, there was no clear pattern in the adjustment. The limits for middle-level incomes were not changed, those for higher incomes were increased mildly and those for lower incomes somewhat more. In 1974 and 1975 the brackets were raised strictly in line with the rate of inflation – 12 and 10 percent, respectively. In 1976, the brackets were again raised by different proportions: 9.5 percent for the five lowest brackets, 6 percent for the next five, 3 percent for the following two, and no increase for the highest bracket. In this particular year, the rate of inflation was 9.5 percent.[8]

Furthermore, most of the deductions in fixed amounts have not been changed.

The French experience thus provides an example of indexation – if this is the correct term in this case – being used to achieve objectives – such as the redistribution of the tax burden – unrelated to what is presumed to be the main objective of indexation. The French experience is interesting also because it shows that it is not necessary to adjust the personal income tax every year but one can specify the adjustment mechanism in such a way that it will become operational only when the rate of inflation becomes significant. However, there is a price to be paid for this option, inasmuch as a creeping inflation which persisted for several years below the threshold level could seriously distort the structure of the tax without ever setting in motion the corrective mechanism. In this respect the alternative used by Luxembourg appears more attractive.

Luxembourg

Luxembourg provides another example of partial indexation. Article 3 of the 1967 Income Tax Law requires that whenever "the average consumer price index for the first six months of a year shows, in relation to the average index for the first six months of the year preceding the coming into effect of the scale, a variation of at least 5 percent" the government shall recommend a revision of the nominal tax structure in proportion to the variation of the CPI.[9] Since 1972, all the brackets have been adjusted strictly in line with the change in the price level.

The Netherlands

In contrast to France and Luxembourg, in the Netherlands the legislation concerning indexation, which was enacted in 1971, did not put any restriction in terms of the rate of inflation or the cumulative change in the price index that are necessary to set in motion the adjustment mechanism; however, it did specify that the adjustment could be limited to only 80 percent of the rise in the relevant index if, in the view of the responsible authorities, "financing difficulties" would result from full indexation.[10] This discretion was used in 1972 and 1973, when the special index for tax adjustment rose by 5.7 percent and 7.8 percent, respectively. In those two years, the nominal income tax structure was escalated by 4.56 percent and 6.24 percent, respectively. It was used again in 1975, when the escalation in the nominal tax struc-

Table 4. *The Netherlands: tax reductions attributable to indexing, 1975*

Taxable income (guilders)	Reductions in tax payments (guilders)	Reductions as percent of taxable incomes
10,000	30	0.30
15,000	30	0.20
20,000	47	0.24
30,000	80	0.27
40,000	134	0.34
80,000	249	0.31
120,000	334	0.28

Source: Adapted from Table 4 in OECD, *The Adjustment of Personal Income Tax Systems for Inflation* (Annexes 1, 3, and 4), Paris, 1975.

ture was 6.64 percent, while the increase in the special index was 8.3 percent. Furthermore, in September 1973, it was decided that the automatic inflation adjustment would not be used at all in 1974. However, as a discretionary measure, an increase of the personal allowance was accorded. A further increase of the personal allowance was announced in March 1974 to take effect from July 1974. For 1976, the adjustment for inflation was used again but was limited to 80 percent of the rise in the relevant index and only for taxable incomes subject to marginal income tax rates of 49 percent and lower. Furthermore, except for the lowest rate of 20 percent, all the rates were raised by one percentage point. In 1977 and 1978, the adjustment was also limited to 80 percent.

By limiting indexation to 80 percent of the special index, the government can continue raising more revenue than it would if full indexation were used. By the same token, this limitation assures that some of the distortions in the tax incidence due to inflation will not be avoided. For 1972 and 1973, the revenue losses to the government due to indexation were 465 million guilders and 880 million guilders, respectively, or about 2.7 percent and 4.4 percent of personal income tax revenues for those years. Obviously, these losses increase with an increase in the rate of inflation. For 1975 they were estimated to be about 1,350 million guilders.

The effect of the Dutch inflationary correction on various income groups for 1975 is shown in Table 4.

Israel

The Income Tax Law of July 1975 abolished the system of indexation that had been in existence up to that time and replaced it by one somewhat akin to the Dutch. From that time on, the nominal structure of the income tax would be linked to the consumer price index. However, whereas the escalation of the nominal values will be full and automatic for the tax credits (which in the new law have replaced some deductions) and for the remaining tax deductions, that for the tax brackets will be less than full if the Minister of Finance deems it desirable.[11] In 1976, the first year for which the adjustment was in effect, the brackets were increased by only two-thirds of the change in the consumer price index.

Countries with indexation mechanisms not directly related to inflation

Unlike the countries already discussed, Brazil, Chile, Denmark, and Iceland adjust their personal income tax structures not by direct reference to an objective indicator of change in the purchasing power of money, such as the consumer price index, but by reference to other indexes, such as earnings of industrial workers, legal minimum wages, per capita income, and so on. Thus, to varying degrees, the adjustment schemes in these countries reflect changes both in prices and in other variables such as productivity, economic conditions, or governmental willingness to adjust "minimum wages" or "basic salaries."

Brazil

The Brazilian indexation system has received considerable attention in recent years.[12] As far as taxation is concerned, it was introduced in 1961 by Law No. 3898 with the decision to express the personal exemptions and the upper limits of the taxable income brackets as multiples of the largest monthly minimum wage for the country.[13] Up to 1964, the income brackets were adjusted in line with the minimum wage, which, in turn, moved closely with the rate of inflation. However, after 1964, the new government, in its attempt to stabilize the economy, chose to increase the minimum wage by less than the rate of inflation. This would have resulted in increases in tax burdens at all income levels – a result not wanted by the government. Consequently, in November 1964, the link to the minimum wage was cut. A new law came into existence with a mechanism that combined the French approach with that of Luxembourg (Law No. 4506). Income tax brackets were to be adjusted in line with the price level any time that inflation exceeded 10 percent in a given year or 15 percent in three years. This alternative remained in effect until 1967, when new legislation gave the Minister of Finance the option of adjusting the brackets either in line with the rate of inflation or with the minimum wage.

This modification introduced a very important discretionary element in the indexation process. The available evidence indicates that the government of Brazil has taken full advantage of this discretionary power, as can be seen from Tables 5 and 6. The departure from pure indexing was particularly significant in 1973 and 1974, when the adjustment mechanism was used by the Brazilian government in its attempt to improve income distribution by redistributing the tax burden. The upper brackets were adjusted upward by 15 percent in 1973 and 12 percent in 1974, while the lower ones were adjusted upward by 26 percent and 41 percent, respectively. Also the personal exemptions were raised by more than the rate of inflation.[14] The effects of these discretionary changes can easily be seen by comparing 1972 and 1974 in Tables 5 and 6. Since 1975, all brackets have been escalated by uniform percentages, but these percentages have lagged behind the inflation rate.

We find, thus, in Brazil, as we did in France, another example of the use of indexation to achieve an objective – the redistribution of the tax burden – not immediately related to it.

One aspect worth mentioning is that taxes on wages and salaries are withheld at the source, whereas those on other incomes are paid the year after income is earned – when the price index is much higher; consequently, with high inflation, incomes other than wages and salaries benefit substantially by the delay. To equalize the burden, the nominal value of withheld taxes can now be escalated by the change in the price level, but the escalation cannot, at the moment, exceed 30 percent, which is less than the rate of inflation.

Chile

Chile's indexation of the tax system goes back to 1954, when in the face of persistently high inflation, the government decided to relate the exemptions for the schedular income taxes, which were applied with proportional rates on different types of incomes, and the brackets for the global complementary tax, which were applied with progressive rates on the total income of the taxpayer, to the minimum wage. The latter was normally, but not always, adjusted on the basis of the change in the consumer price index of the previous year. This system worked

Table 5. *Brazil: upper limits of income brackets expressed as units of monthly minimum wage*

Income brackets	Marginal tax rates (%)	1964	1965	1966	1967	1968	1969	1970	1971	1972	1973	1974
1	3	24.0	24.0	22.7	25.4	24.8	27.0	26.9	26.9	26.8	28.3	34.3
2	3	30.0	30.0	27.3	30.4	29.7	28.9	28.8	28.8	28.7	30.5	36.9
3	5	45.0	45.0	36.4	40.6	39.6	38.6	38.5	38.5	38.3	40.6	49.0
4	8	60.0	60.0	50.0	55.8	54.4	54.0	53.8	53.8	53.6	56.5	68.1
5	12	75.0	75.0	72.7	81.1	79.2	77.2	76.9	76.9	76.6	80.7	96.3
6	16	90.0	90.0	100.0	111.6	108.9	106.1	105.8	105.8	105.3	110.5	130.6
7	20	120.0	120.0	136.4	152.1	148.5	144.7	144.2	144.2	143.6	149.9	175.0
8	25	150.0	150.0	181.8	202.9	198.0	192.9	192.3	192.3	191.5	198.7	228.4
9	30	180.0	180.0	272.7	304.3	297.0	289.4	288.5	288.5	287.2	296.5	330.1
10	35	250.0	250.0	363.6	405.7	396.0	385.8	384.6	384.6	383.0	387.6	419.1
11	40	350.0	350.0	545.5	608.6	594.0	578.7	576.9	576.9	574.5	568.1	579.3
12	45	450.0	450.0	727.3	811.4	792.0	771.6	769.2	769.2	766.0	739.2	713.3
13	50	600.0	595.2	—	—	—	—	—	—	—	—	—
14	57	800.0	800.0	—	—	—	—	—	—	—	—	—
15	65	—	—	—	—	—	—	—	—	—	—	—

Note: The limits in each year are calculated on the basis of the minimum wage of the previous year.
Source: Ministério da Fazenda, Secretaria da Receita Federal, *Anuario Economico-Fiscal* (1970); Ministerio da Fazenda, Secretaria da Receita Federal, *Instruçoes para Pagamento de Imposto* (1971 a 1974). From Fernando A. Rezenda da Silva, *O Imposto Sobre a Renda e a Justiça Fiscal* (Rio de Janeiro: IPEA, 1974) p. 110.

Table 6. *Brazil: Upper limits of income brackets expressed as units of per capita income*

Income brackets	Marginal tax rates (%)	1960	1961	1962	1963	1964	1965	1966	1967	1968	1969	1970	1971	1972	1973	1974
1	0	3.8	7.5	7.1	4.5	3.8	4.1	4.0	4.1	3.8	3.9	3.7	3.4	3.2	3.2	3.6
2	3	5.7	9.3	8.9	5.6	4.8	5.2	4.8	4.9	4.6	4.2	3.9	3.7	3.4	3.4	3.8
3	5	7.6	10.9	13.4	8.4	7.1	7.7	6.4	6.6	6.1	5.6	5.2	4.9	4.5	4.5	5.1
4	8	9.5	12.5	17.8	11.2	9.6	10.3	8.8	9.0	8.4	7.8	7.3	6.9	6.3	6.3	7.1
5	12	12.6	14.0	22.3	14.0	12.0	12.9	12.8	13.2	12.2	11.2	10.4	9.8	9.0	9.0	10.0
6	16	18.9	15.6	26.8	16.8	14.3	15.5	17.6	18.1	16.8	15.4	14.3	13.5	12.4	12.4	13.6
7	20	25.2	18.7	35.7	22.4	19.1	20.7	24.0	24.7	22.9	21.0	19.6	18.4	17.0	16.8	18.2
8	25	31.5	21.8	44.6	28.0	23.9	25.8	32.0	32.9	30.5	28.0	26.1	24.6	22.6	22.3	23.7
9	30	37.8	24.9	53.5	33.7	28.7	31.0	48.0	49.3	45.8	42.0	39.1	36.8	33.9	33.2	34.3
10	35	41.1	31.1	65.4	46.7	39.8	43.0	64.1	65.8	61.1	56.0	52.2	49.1	45.2	43.4	43.6
11	40	63.0	37.4	77.3	65.4	55.8	60.2	96.1	98.6	91.6	84.0	78.3	73.7	67.9	63.7	60.2
12	45	126.0	49.8	89.2	84.1	71.7	77.5	128.1	131.5	122.2	111.9	104.4	98.2	90.5	82.8	74.2
13	50	189.1	62.3	104.1	112.2	95.6	102.5	—	—	—	—	—	—	—	—	—
14	57	—	77.9	119.0	149.6	127.4	137.7	—	—	—	—	—	—	—	—	—
15	65	—	93.4	148.7	—	—	—	—	—	—	—	—	—	—	—	—
16	—	—	140.1	178.5	—	—	—	—	—	—	—	—	—	—	—	—
17	—	—	—	237.9	—	—	—	—	—	—	—	—	—	—	—	—
18	—	—	—	—	—	—	—	—	—	—	—	—	—	—	—	—

Note: The limits in each year are calculated on the basis of the per capita income of the previous year.

Source: Ministéria da Fazenda, Secretaria da Receita Federal, *Anuario Economico-Fiscal* (1970); Ministério da Fazenda, Secretaria da Receita Federal, *Instruções para Pagamento de Imposto* (1971 a 1974). From Fernando A. Rézende da Silva, *O Imposto Sobre a Renda e a Justiça Fiscal* (Rio de Janeiro: IPEA, 1974).

Table 7. *Chile: schedule for income tax in labor income*

Taxable income (in basic tax unit)	Marginal rates (%)
Up to 2	3.5
2–5	10.0
5–10	15.0
10–15	20.0
15–20	30.0
20–40	40.0
40–80	50.0
Above 80	60.0

relatively well for many years but became inadequate after 1971 when the rate of inflation accelerated sharply. The reasons for the breakdown are the following. Only the taxes on wages and salaries and the "additional" tax – levied at 37.5 percent on nonresident individuals and foreign legal entities and at 40 percent on profits distributed abroad – were withheld at the source. For other incomes, taxes were paid in the year when the declaration of income was presented – normally the following year. The law required that the payment be adjusted by 100 percent of the increase in the consumer price index that occurred during the year covered by the declaration (and not during the year when the payment was made). In the 1972–4 period, due to the acceleration in the rate of inflation, the monetary correction lagged substantially behind the current rate of inflation and became inadequate; real revenue from incomes other than wages and salaries fell.

From the beginning of 1975 – on the basis of new legislation[15] – the link to the minimum wage for indexing the nominal structure was cut and a new system of tax payment was introduced. The nominal structure of the income tax on income from work is now escalated by a *unidad tributaria basica,* a basic tax unit that is calculated by the tax authorities every month, in part on the basis of the rate of inflation two months earlier. The new rate schedule is shown in Table 7. The basic exemption as well as other deductions are also related to this *unidad tributaria basica.* This whole structure relates to *monthly* incomes and to *monthly* basic tax units. Incomes other than wages and salaries are subjected to a global income tax, also levied with rates applicable to incomes expressed as multiples of *annual unidad tributaria basica.* No precise information is available on how these basic tax units are calculated. For incomes for which withholding at the source is not applied, a system of advance payments is followed. These advance payments are themselves indexed for the rate of inflation. There is little doubt that Chile has developed the most comprehensive system of correction of income taxes, including those on enterprises.

Denmark

A new income tax law enacted in 1969, which became effective in 1970, introduced two novelties: (1) it established four basic rates, ranging from 18 percent to 45 percent, levied on four income brackets above a basic personal exemption, and required that Parliament vote every year on whether these rates should be applied, in the coming year, at 100 percent of their basic value or by more (up to 105 percent) or less; (2) it specified that these rates (at the yearly legislated value) would be levied on income brackets that would be adjusted annually, starting in 1971, on the basis of an index (which was corrected for changes in indirect taxes) reflecting the change in the cost of living.[16] Between 1971 and 1974, the income brackets were escalated to reflect the changes in prices and the basic rates were applied at 91 percent of their basic values. In 1974 the brackets' limits were about 23 percent above the 1970 level. The basic exemption had been raised by the same proportion.

Table 8 gives some idea of the effect of indexation on taxpayers in different income classes. The table gives tax payments on the basis of 1973 and 1974 (indexed over 1973) schedules. The reductions associated with indexation range from 7.1 to 0.9 percent of tax payments. As proportions of tax payments, they are generally higher for lower income groups, but no clear pattern is found when they are related to taxable incomes. The total reduction (the "revenue loss") amounted to DKr0.8 billion, or 3.3 percent of the tax revenue in 1974.

On September 20, 1974, the Danish Parliament voted a new schedule for individual income taxes to be used in 1975.[17] It also changed the indexation scheme. The personal deduction and the brackets would now be related to changes in the index for hourly earnings of an industrial worker, which, of course, reflects price changes, union power, productivity changes, and other factors.[18] Thus, the Danish scheme is no longer an adjustment for inflation alone, as the index now used comes close to the one proposed in Chapter 9. The change was apparently motivated by the belief that indexation for price changes alone had not prevented sharp increases in tax burdens on the middle-income groups. These increases had been brought about by the interaction of economic growth and a very progressive structure. Obviously, the use

Table 8. *Denmark: tax reductions attributable to indexing, 1974*

Taxable income 1974 (DKr)	Tax payments (DKr)		Reductions due to 1974 indexing		
	With 1973 schedule	With 1974 schedule	Absolute (DKr)	Percent of 1973 tax payment	Percent of taxable income
10,000	688	639	49	7.1	0.5
20,000	2,326	2,277	49	2.1	0.2
30,000	4,444	4,242	202	4.6	0.7
40,000	7,174	6,972	202	2.8	0.5
50,000	10,751	10,339	412	3.8	0.8
60,000	14,391	13,979	412	2.9	0.7
80,000	21,671	21,259	412	1.9	0.5
100,000	29,529	28,890	639	2.2	0.6
150,000	50,004	49,365	639	1.3	0.4
200,000	70,479	69,840	639	0.9	0.3

Source: Adapted from Table 2 in OECD. *The Adjustment of Personal Income Tax Systems for Inflation* (Annexes 1, 3, and 4) (Paris, 1975).

of an index that reflects real growth in per capita income, in addition to changes in the cost of living, implies a greater reduction in tax revenue as compared to one that indexes only for inflation.

Iceland
Since 1966, Iceland has had a provision in its income tax law for the indexation of the nominal structure of the income tax. There is no official information available on this country, but it would appear that the original intention was to escalate annually the brackets, personal allowances, and certain special deductions on the basis of an index that would reflect increases in prices as well as in real incomes. In other words, the adjustment would be on the basis of an index similar to that proposed in Chapter 9. However, although that was the original intention, the income tax itself does not specify how the tax index is to be calculated; consequently, the authorities have had a lot of discretion in the determination of the index, which has thus become a flexible instrument of tax policy.

Table 9 provides year-to-year changes in the cost-of-living index, in real household income, and in the income tax index. The latter should approximate in a given year the summation of the other two indexes in the previous year. The table shows that although for several years the index does in fact approximate that sum, it does not for other years.

Table 9. *Iceland: income tax index (percentages)*

Year	Cost-of living index	Real household income	Income tax index
1965	7.1	5.5	—
1966	10.6	4.0	12.5
1967	3.7	−1.5	14.5
1968	13.0	−7.2	0
1969	21.7	−5.0	0
1970	13.2	14.4	8.5
1971	8.0	14.5	20.0
1972	10.4	12.3	a
1973	25.0	9.5	28.0
1974	42.6	9.0	a
1975	50.0	−16.5	51.0

a In 1972 and 1974 there were reforms in the income tax.
Source: National Economic Institute of Iceland.

But in most cases it does exceed the index of the cost of living, showing that in a nonautomatic fashion the authorities are still taking into account real income growth.

Switzerland

Several Swiss cantons – including Aargau, Basel-Land, Basel-Stadt, Graubünden, and Solothurn – have had for several years provisions for some automatic indexing of their income taxes. These provisions are too complex to be described briefly here.

4

Inflation and the taxation
of capital gains:
problems and solutions

Inflation and capital gains

The taxation of capital gains has always created difficulties for experts and governments. An economic definition of income of the Schanz-Haig-Simons type, which is the most accepted one for taxation, would call for the inclusion of capital gains in taxable income on an accrual basis, inasmuch as the ability to pay of the taxpayer is clearly enhanced by these gains.[1] In practice, however, various difficulties have prompted most countries to either exempt them or tax them only when they are realized. Even then, only part of the gains are generally included in taxable income; or, alternatively, they are taxed at lower rates than other incomes. In the absence of inflation, this preferential tax treatment definitely favors those who receive these gains.

When inflation is present, capital gains will be distorted and, as normally measured, will no longer conform to the Schanz-Haig-Simons definition of income. As Goode has put it, "Appreciation in the price of an asset that reflects only a general rise in prices is a fictitious gain because it gives the investor no increased command over goods and services."[2] The tax laws generally do not make a distinction between gains that reflect an actual real increased command over economic resources (real gains) and those that do not (fictitious gains). Thus, during inflationary periods, at least part of the capital gains tax will inevitably become a tax on wealth, rather than income, because it will be levied on the fictitious gains. The rate of such a wealth tax depends on the marginal tax rate and the rate of inflation.

Although it is widely recognized that inflation distorts capital gains, proposals aimed at neutralizing the effects of inflation on the taxation of capital gains have been opposed on various grounds:[3]

1. Some experts believe that capital gains have received preferential treatment because of the anticipation of inflation at the time the legislation was enacted; they argue that, if prices had been expected to re-

main stable, the taxation of capital gains would not have been as light as it is. For example, the Canadian Minister of Finance responsible for the introduction of indexation to that country, Mr. Turner, gave as one of the reasons for not adjusting capital gains for inflation the fact that "at the time of tax reform, it was decided that only one half of capital gains would be taxable, partially in recognition . . . of inflation."[4] Furthermore, it is pointed out that because capital gains are taxed only when the asset is sold (i.e., on realization) and not as they accrue, the asset holder receives an interest-free loan of the tax that he would have paid on accrual. The value of this benefit to the asset holder depends on the rate of interest.

2. Inasmuch as those who receive capital gains generally belong to higher income groups, and the inflation surtax is steeply progressive, the benefits from this type of adjustment would go to the rich, thus making the incidence of the income tax less progressive than it would be in the absence of adjustment.[5]

3. Some assets are bought with borrowed funds (e.g., a mortage on a house); thus, the asset holder gains from the erosion of the real value of his liability brought about by inflation. The benefit from this erosion is particularly significant if the loan was obtained at preinflation low rates of interest. Thus, either the effects of inflation on both assets and liabilities are taken into account or the effects on neither.

4. The adjustment of capital gains for inflation will bring about a fall in income tax revenue during an inflationary period, when orthodox Keynesian thinking requires an increase in revenue. In other words, the adjustment would reduce the stabilizing power of the tax.

5. The adjustment of capital gains for inflation will give one group of investors a protection that other groups (say those who make financial adjustments) do not have. It will thus be inequitable and will also affect the allocation of savings.[6]

The first of these arguments is not very convincing. It is true that prices have been going up in most countries since World War II, but capital gains taxation precedes that period. For example, in the United States, it was enacted in 1913 together with the "individual" income tax. Up to that time, the United States had experienced more years when prices declined than when they rose.[7] The second argument seems to be based on the assumption that inflation-induced distortions are welcome as long as they make the tax system more progressive. However, if one accepts the view that the progressivity of the system should not be the result of accidental changes but should reflect the intention of the legislators, distortions cannot be welcome regardless of whether they increase or decrease that progressivity. The third and fifth arguments are not against the adjustment of capital gains for inflation *per se* but mainly against improper or incomplete adjustments in the tax system. Proper adjustments should take into account liabilities and should be extended to financial assets.[8] Finally, the fourth argument is based on a view of the interrelationship between economic activity and inflation that may no longer reflect current reality.

Proposed solutions
Relatively few countries tax capital gains. For those that do, three adjustment mechanisms for fictitious (or illusory) capital gains have been frequently suggested and, in some cases, adopted. The first could be called the inclusion ratio; the second is the arbitrary escalation of the historical cost basis; and the third is the price-related indexation of the historical cost basis.

Inclusion ratio
This method would relate the proportion of the realized capital gain that would be taxed, or the tax payment itself, to the number of years that the asset has been held. Normally, the longer the time the asset has been held, the lower will be the proportion of the gain taxed. Of course, only by accident would this approach give the correct adjustment for inflation. In most cases, the results would not be at all consistent with the objective of avoiding the taxation of illusory gains.[9] As a simple example, one can assume that the current value of an asset has been increasing at the rate of inflation, so that there have been no real gains. Still, in this case, part of the illusory gain would be taxed. Furthermore, if the rate of inflation is stable, and if the capital gains are partly real and partly fictitious, then the proportion of the nominal capital gain that should be subjected to tax should *increase* with time rather than fall.[10] But, of course, the rate of inflation is not stable, so adjustments of this kind are bound to give wrong results.

Arbitrary escalation of cost basis
This method would increase the acquisition cost of the asset (net of depreciation) by an arbitrary percentage per year. Thus, the longer the asset is held, the higher would the cost become, given the percentage yearly increase. If the rate of inflation were stable, an escalation equal to that rate would give a correct cost basis to be used for the calculation of the capital gains. However, the rate of inflation is not stable, so that only by accident would this method provide the correct adjustment.

Indexation of historical cost basis
This method would provide the inflation adjustment gain as follows:

$$
\begin{array}{c}\text{inflation}\\\text{adjusted}\\\text{gain}\end{array} = \begin{array}{c}\text{net sales}\\\text{price}\end{array} - \left(\begin{array}{c}\text{historical}\\\text{cost}\\\text{basis}\end{array} \times \begin{array}{c}\text{inflation}\\\text{adjustment}\\\text{factor}\end{array}\right)
$$

Alternatively, the procedure could be as follows:

$$
\begin{array}{c}\text{inflation}\\\text{adjusted}\\\text{gain}\end{array} = \left(\dfrac{\begin{array}{c}\text{net sales}\\\text{price}\end{array}}{\begin{array}{c}\text{inflation}\\\text{adjustment}\\\text{factor}\end{array}} - \begin{array}{c}\text{historical}\\\text{cost basis}\end{array}\right) \times \begin{array}{c}\text{inflation}\\\text{adjustment}\\\text{factor}\end{array}
$$

These two procedures give the same result for the inflation-adjusted gain to be included in taxable income or to be taxed by a separate capital gains tax.[11] If the asset is depreciable, the historical cost basis must be net of depreciation based on historical cost. The inflation adjustment factor measures the increase in the relevant price index over the holding period. The price index to be used should be a general one rather than one related to capital assets alone. The reason for this is that only a general index would measure whether the asset holder has increased his command over goods and services. This method, if properly applied, brings about a correct adjustment of capital gains, so that fictitious gains are removed from the tax base. The method is conceptually simple, although it too is not entirely free of difficulties.

In the first place, there is the issue of choosing a proper price index. The countries that have used this method have relied on either a consumer price index or, in one case (because of the shortcomings of that index), a wholesale price index. Brinner, in his discussion of this issue, has come out flatly in favor of the consumer price index.[12] However, one must ask whether in adjusting *capital* gains, which relate almost exclusively to *capital* assets, one should use an index that reflects exclusively the prices of *consumption* goods.[13] In other words, is the proper definition of income expressed in command over, or opportunities related to, "consumption goods" or, more generally, command over "economic resources?" This last question was very much debated at the Brookings Conference on Inflation and the Income Tax. In Musgrave's view – supported by Denison, Fellner, and Blinder but opposed by Gordon and Pechman – "the choice of a base for taxation largely dictates the appropriate index to be used. If one has a consumption tax, a consumer price deflator should be used. If one feels that income is the correct tax base, then a national income deflator should be used.'[14] In Denison's view, the main question for selecting an index is "Which corresponds most closely to the definition of income that is subject to the personal and corporation income taxes?"[15] He concludes that the most appropriate index would be the implicit deflator for national income. When changes in the prices of consumption goods lag behind changes in the prices of capital goods (including land) an inflation adjustment factor based on the consumer price index will leave the asset holder in a situation wherein after paying the tax on the inflation adjusted gain, he would not be able to buy the same basket of consumption *and* capital goods, as when he bought the asset.

In the second place, there is the administrative difficulty of determining the historical cost, or the base-year value of the asset. This can become a serious problem when the asset has been acquired at various dates (such as is the case with shares or bonds), or when historical costs have been distributed over time (such as with improvements and/or extensions to buildings).

Thirdly, and perhaps of greater significance, is the fact that indexation of assets, to be equitable, must extend to monetary liabilities, inasmuch as the asset may have been bought with borrowed funds. Indexing just the assets and not also the liabilities would be particularly inequitable during periods when inflationary expectations have lagged behind actual rates. In such periods, asset holders would experience drops in the real values of their liabilities, because the interest rates that they will be paying are low in real terms, and these falls may compensate for the taxation of unadjusted capital gains.

To make this point in the sharpest fashion, let us consider some extreme examples. Assume two individuals, *A* and *B,* who buy two identical assets for $100 each. *A* finances the purchase running down his own savings; *B* finances it through the sale of a marketable perpetuity. Assume that at the time of the purchase, the price index stood at 1.0 and was expected to remain there. The rate of interest was 5 percent so that *B* has financed the purchase by committing himself to paying a perpetual income stream of $5 per year. Assume now that immediately after the purchase has taken place, prices begin to rise and a constant rate of inflation of 5 percent per year sets in. Expected price changes equal actual price changes. In such a situation, one must expect that the prevailing rate of interest will settle at around 10 percent, that is, the original real rate plus the expected rate of inflation. After ten years, when the price index has reached 1.63, the two individuals sell their identical assets for the same price of $200. In this situation, if we ignore what has happened to liabilities, the inflation adjusted gain as defined above is

$$\$200 - [100 \times 1.63] = \$37$$

and this is the same for both individuals. However, it seems obvious that *B* has gained more. In fact, he started with no equity and now he could use part of the proceeds from the sale to buy back the perpetuity, whose market value, due to the change in interest rates, has fallen to $50. Thus, in effect *B*'s capital gain, at current prices is $150– far more than *A*'s. If *B* had originally used $50 out of his own savings and had borrowed $50 from a bank to be repaid after ten years[16] his inflation adjusted gain would be

$$\$200 - [(\$50 \times 1.63) + 50] = \$68.50$$

In this last example, only the equity-financed part of the purchase price is indexed.

These are extreme cases but they help to emphasize the fact that a true assessment of gains cannot ignore the effects of inflation on monetary liabilities. On the other hand, taking these effects into account is generally very complex. Furthermore, in order to do so, a realization of these gains at the time of the sale of the asset must at times be assumed. Since the seller often does not have to realize these gains (on liabilities) at the time the asset is sold, such an implicit realization will conflict with the general principle that capital gains are only taxed on realization, rather than accrual. These complications have led some experts to suggest that only the part of the asset acquired with equity capital should be indexed. The part financed by loans should not be indexed as in the last example above.

The indexation of historical costs often reduces taxable capital gains to insignificant amounts; in fact, for some taxpayers the gains become losses. Some observers have remarked that indexation will sharply reduce revenue while increasing administrative complications. Thus, why bother to tax capital gains? In Chile, it was exactly this type of reasoning that led to the abolishment of capital gains taxation. In France, on the other hand, it was explicitly recognized that these taxes are not levied for revenue but for equity reasons.[17]

Countries' experiences

About a dozen countries have introduced adjustment mechanisms that presumably deal with the effect of inflation on capital gains. One must say "presumably" because the connection with inflation is not always explicit. A perusal of tax legislations revealed: five countries relying on the inclusion-ratio method of adjustment; four relying on some arbitrary escalation of historical costs; and seven relying on the indexation of historical costs.

Inclusion ratio

The countries in this group include Colombia, Finland, Mexico, Spain, and Sweden.

In *Colombia* capital gains from the sale of owner-occupied homes held beyond a two-year minimum holding period are reduced by 10 percent per year. In *Finland,* capital gains derived from the sale of real property held for six years are reduced by 20 percent before they are taxed. Beyond the sixth year, the gains are reduced by 20 percent for each additional year. For properties held more than ten years, no tax is paid. In *Mexico,* capital gains derived from the sale of real property held for more than six years are reduced by 10 percent per year. In *Spain,* capital gains from the sale of assets held for more than three years are reduced by 5 percent per year. In *Sweden,* the inclusion ratio applies only to capital gains derived from the sale of movable property (such as shares, bonds, etc.). Beyond a two-year minimum holding period, capital gains from movable property are reduced at the rate of 25 percent per year.

Arbitrary escalation of cost basis

Examples of this approach are provided by Belgium, Denmark, France (for "speculative" gains) and Norway. Capital gains on the sale of real property have been taxable in *Belgium* since 1966. In the calculation of the taxable gain, the asset holder is allowed to escalate the acquisition price by 5 percent per year for the holding period. In *Denmark,* the arbitrary increase in the acquisition cost is 6 percent per year. In *France,* in the calculation of capital gains from speculative activities, the acquisition price is increased by 5 percent for each year of ownership. In *Norway,* the acquisition cost for nondepreciable real property is adjusted as follows: no adjustment for the first five years of ownership; 5 percent annual escalation for the next 15 years; and 7 percent annual escalation beyond the twentieth year. However, the acquisition cost, so adjusted, cannot exceed by more than three times the original historical cost.

Indexation of historical costs

The countries that rely on this more sophisticated form of inflation adjustment of capital gains include Argentina, France, Israel, and

Sweden. Furthermore, Chile used to have such a system until it abolished the taxation of capital gains; and Ireland and Luxembourg are, at this time, considering the introduction of such a system.[18] These experiences are more interesting than the ones described above, so more detail will be provided.

Argentina. The Argentine capital gains tax *(Impuesto a las Ganancias Eventuales)* was reformed by Law No. 21284 of April 2, 1976. According to this law, capital gains above an exempted amount, that for April 1976 was fixed at Arg$150,000, are taxable at the rate of 15 percent. The cost of acquisition, as well as the exempt amount, are indexed for price changes. The table of inflation factors to be used for the adjustments is prepared by the Direccion General Impositiva (the tax collection agency) on the basis of changes in the nonagricultural wholesale price index and are updated on a quarterly basis.[19] Capital losses can be deducted from capital gains of the same year or of the following ten years. The law does not refer to any indexation for these losses carried forward. Also no reference is made to monetary liabilities.

France. Capital gains taxation was introduced in France by a law of July 19, 1976. This tax is very complex, thus only the points relevant to inflation adjustments are mentioned here. The tax treatment of capital gains depends on the type of asset and the length of time the asset was held. For the determination of the taxable base for nonspeculative gains on real estates other than the principal residence, the acquisition price is escalated by the percentage change in the consumer price index.[20] Furthermore, for each year beyond the tenth that the asset has been held, the adjusted gain is reduced by 5 percent.[21] For the determination of capital gains on *movable* capital held more than one year, the acquisition price is also indexed. If these assets have been held more than ten years, the gain is not taxable. Capital losses can be offset against gains and can be carried forward for five years, but they are not indexed. No account is taken of changes in the real value of liabilities.

Israel. Up to 1975, Israel adjusted capital gains with a system somewhat akin to the inclusion ratio. For real assets held between two and fifteen years the tax was reduced by 0.5 percent per month. Beyond fifteen years there was a further reduction of 1 percent per year. After thirty-seven years the tax liability was reduced to zero. For other assets, the yearly reduction was 5 percent. Since 1975, capital gains on assets held more than twelve months are split into an "inflationary gain" and a "real gain." The difference between the inflation-adjusted acquisition cost and the unadjusted one is the "inflationary gain." The difference between the net sales price and the inflation-adjusted acquisition cost is the "real gain." Inflationary gains are not exempt from taxation but are, instead, taxed at a much lower rate than real gains – 10 percent versus the normal rates on ordinary profits up to a limit of 50 percent. Incomes from real gains can be spread over a period of up to six years. If the asset has been held less than one year all the gain is considered real. Assets held between one and two years receive less beneficial treatment than those held more than two years. If the asset is a depreciable one, the adjusted acquisition price is net of adjusted total depreciation charges. The latter are calculated by multiplying the year charges based on historical costs by the change in the cost of living index between the middle of the period of depreciation and the date of sale of the asset. No account is taken of monetary liabilities.

Sweden. Capital gains on the sale of real property held more than two years are adjusted for changes in the consumer price index. The adjustment is made by multiplying the acquisition cost by inflation factors fixed annually by the National Tax Board. Seventy-five percent of the gains so calculated is taxed, regardless of the period of ownership.

Ireland. Assets sold on or after April 6, 1978 will benefit from an adjustment of the acquisition cost for inflation. The adjustment will come about through the indexation of the acquisition cost by the percentage change in the consumer price index between mid-February before the fiscal year in which the asset was acquired and mid-February before the fiscal year in which the asset is sold. The adjustment is limited to the determination of taxable monetary gains and cannot be used to inflate monetary losses or to convert monetary gains into deductible losses. As capital gains taxation was first introduced on April 6, 1974, the starting period for the evaluation of costs for assets owned before that date will be April 1974.

Luxembourg. In Luxembourg, too, a recent tax proposal would redefine capital gains to exclude the taxation of fictitious ones. This will be achieved by multiplying the historical cost by an inflation factor based on the change in the consumer price index over the holding period.

Chile. The method of indexing historical costs for inflation was in existence in Chile up to recently. It, however, led to the problem that after the escalation of the base many capital gains became capital losses. As a consequence of this, capital gains taxes were abolished.

Concluding comments

From this survey of inflation and the taxation of capital gains some basic conclusions follow. First, adjustments are more common than has been generally assumed. At least a dozen countries have adjustments which most likely were prompted by the existence of, or the expectation of, inflation. These adjustments are very varied and range from relatively primitive attempts at neutralizing the impact of inflation to much more sophisticated ones. The countries that have indexed the historical acquisition costs have normally done so using the consumer price index, even though this may not be the most appropriate index for that purpose. Furthermore, there has been very little discussion of what index to use. Capital losses have not been indexed, so that in those cases in which these losses could be carried forward for several years, their real value would be sharply reduced. Finally, the effect of inflation on the real value of monetary liabilities has also been ignored, so that particular individuals who bought assets with borrowed funds obtained at preinflation rates could have made rather substantial gains from the adjustment mechanism.

5

Inflation and the taxation of interest income: problems and solutions

The problems associated with the taxation of capital gains in an inflationary situation are somewhat simpler to understand than those connected with the taxation of interest income. Perhaps for this reason they have received far more attention. As recently as 1974, Roger Brinner and Alicia Munnell could write that "it is not just as necessary to adjust wages, *interest,* and dividends for inflation" as it is to adjust for the effect of inflation on capital gains.[1] As is shown in the following section, contrary to their view, when the price level is changing, the taxation of interest income does create special and serious adjustment problems.[2]

The problems

To set the problem in the proper context, let us first consider a situation in which prices are expected to remain stable and where these expectations are fully realized. Let us assume also that an individual can lend his savings at a rate of interest of 5 percent, which will be called the real rate. To simplify the presentation, we shall avoid the complications that would be introduced by considerations of term structures of the interest rate; we shall, thus, refer to one particular rate of interest. We shall also assume that the marginal income tax rate for this particular individual is 50 percent.

Given these assumptions, if an individual lends $1,000 and after one year receives $50 of interest income – in addition to the return of his principal – this income will be taxed at the marginal tax rate of 50 percent. Consequently, after paying the tax, he will be left with $25 or with a net-of-tax real rate of interest on his financial investment of 2.5 percent. In this case, when there is actual and expected price stability, the tax on interest income will never reduce that income to a negative figure unless the income tax has marginal rates of more than 100 percent.

In this situation, issues that may arise in connection with the taxation of interest incomes are: whether, with the taxation of interest income, there is double taxation of savings;[3] whether the tax on interest income will lead to some readjustment in the portfolio of the asset holder by inducing him to substitute assets with nontaxable returns, such as money,[4] for those with taxable returns, such as bonds;[5] and (3) whether his propensity to save is affected by the tax-induced reduction in the rate of return on savings.[6]

Let us now consider the effects of price changes. For any period, inflation can catch individuals by surprise or it can be, partly or totally, anticipated. If it is unanticipated, and if the individuals assume that the price increase is a temporary phenomenon not to be repeated in the future, the market rate of interest (and the interest incomes) will not change. However, if inflation is anticipated, most observers will agree that the expected price change will bring about an increase in the market rate of interest. Whether the market rate will increase by as much as, by less than, or by more than the rate of inflation depends on several practical and/or theoretical considerations. Most important among the practical factors are: (1) the existence of institutional ceilings on interest rates ("usury laws") and how operational they become, (2) inertia, and (3) divergences between inflationary expectations and actual price changes, because it is expectations that affect the interest rates. Most important among the theoretical factors are: output fluctuations, and the existence of income taxes and their level.

If inflation brought about increases in the market rate of interest that exceeded the rate of inflation, one could argue that at least from an equity point of view, no adjustment in the definition of taxable income might be needed. In such a case, an adjustment might be seen as a bonus to interest-incomes receivers, inasmuch as the bases have adjusted automatically for inflation. This case is important enough from a theoretical point of view to justify a fuller treatment in a later chapter. However, the empirical evidence available from various countries indicates that at least up to now, interest rates have not increased by more than the rate of inflation. Therefore, we shall find it convenient to analyze the taxation of interest income within the context of the prevailing theory of interest under inflationary conditions. This theory, developed several decades ago by Irving Fisher[7] has received considerable empirical support in recent studies for several countries.[8]

Fisher's theory maintains that if the rate of inflation is fully anticipated and stable – in other words, if the future price level is known – the market rate of interest will tend to approximate the sum of the real rate of interest (assumed to be unchanged) and the anticipated price change.[9] More generally, if r is the rate of interest when no price change is expected, Π is the anticipated rate of inflation, and r^m is the market rate of interest, then

$$1 + r^m = (1 + \Pi)(1 + r) \tag{1}$$

therefore

$$r^m = \Pi + r + \Pi r \tag{2}$$

The last term, Πr, can generally be ignored unless the rate of inflation is large.[10] In the numerical example, we shall ignore it and will assume that $r^m = \Pi + r$ even when the compounding is not continuous.

The acceptance of the Fisherian solution, concerning the rate of interest in an inflationary situation, is not essential to our basic argument; however, it does make its presentation much easier. Consequently, we shall proceed within the framework of Fisher's analysis. The case that we shall make for adjusting the definition of interest for tax purposes when there is inflation would be strengthened whenever the market rate increased by less than the rate of inflation.

Let us now assume that the anticipated rate of inflation, Π, is 10 percent per year. Then the rate of interest should rise to $r^m = 15$ percent. In this particular situation, and in the absence of any income tax on interest income, the individual who lends $1,000 would receive $1,150 after one year. In the absence of taxes, this individual would not be any better off or worse off than he would have been had he received back $1,050 when there was no inflation. This is so because $100 out of the $150 of interest income just compensates him for the loss caused by inflation on his original financial capital of $1,000.[11]

But let us now bring the tax on income into the picture. Assuming the marginal tax rate still to be 50 percent, the individual must pay $75 in taxes.[12] A 10 percent increase in the price level, following a period of price stability, has led to a 200 percent increase in taxable income and at least to a comparable percentage increase in tax liability. But this means that the individual has received a negative real interest rate of 2.5 percent, inasmuch as the net-of-tax return is not enough to compensate him for the erosion in the real value of his financial capital. The higher the rate of inflation, and the higher the marginal tax rate at which the income of the individual is levied, the more profound is the real loss that the creditor is likely to experience. The tax on interest income becomes, in fact, more than that; it comes to be a tax on the capital itself. More formally, let A represent the amount of the loan in the base year. Then, in the absence of inflation the tax, t, would be levied on $A(1 + r) - A$ or

$$[A(1 + r) - A]t = (Ar)t \tag{3}$$

When inflation is present the tax would be:

$$[A(1 + r + \Pi) - A]t = (Ar)t + (A\Pi)t \tag{4}$$

Since $A\Pi$ is not a genuine income but only an adjustment for inflation that is necessary to maintain constant the real value of the loan, it follows from Equation 4 that the tax on interest income, in an inflationary situation, consists of a tax on real income – $(Ar)t$ in the above equation – plus a tax on the capital itself – $(A\Pi)t$. Such a situation requires a kind of correction not provided by the general adjustment associated with the indexation of brackets and exemptions. More specifically, it requires an adjustment of the taxable base to make it conform more closely with a proper economic definition of income.

Many countries allow a deduction for interest payments made by borrowers. This tax treatment of interest payments greatly increases the advantage that debtors receive from inflation. This advantage depends not only on the rate of inflation but also on the debtor's marginal tax rate.

In the Fisherian situation described above, a *new* borrower who agrees to pay the inflation-adjusted rate of interest receives no benefit from inflation if his marginal income tax rate is zero but receives increasingly important benefits as his marginal tax rate rises.[13] Thus, given a stable rate of inflation of 10 percent, the individual who borrowed $1,000 at a market rate of interest of 15 percent would pay a *real* rate of interest of 5 percent if his marginal tax rate were zero, but he would pay a real rate of interest of zero if his marginal tax rate were 33.3 percent, and a negative rate of 2.5 if his marginal tax rate were 50 percent. Since wealthier individuals pay higher marginal tax rates, the equity implications of such treatment are rather obvious. A borrower's position will become more attractive with an increase in the rate of inflation and the marginal tax rate.

Proposed solutions

In the example used in the previous section to illustrate the distortion in the taxation of interest income when inflation is present, the loan was for one year, its nominal value was assumed to be fixed, and the market rate of interest exceeded the rate of inflation. For loans of this type, and with a nominal rate of interest exceeding the rate of inflation, the solution is quite simple and follows closely the guidelines suggested by a proper definition of income. It can be stated in two alternative ways, although the result is the same.

Adjustment of interest

In the first alternative, one would determine at the end of the period, the inflationary component of interest income received by multiplying the principal A by the rate of inflation (Π). This inflationary component, $A\Pi$, would then be subtracted from the nominal interest income, Ar^m. Thus the (taxable) real component is:

$$Ar^m - A\Pi = A(r_m - \Pi) \tag{5}$$

In these calculations, Π refers to the *actual* rate of inflation for the taxable year. Furthermore, it would not matter whether the rate of inflation had been totally, or only partly, reflected in the nominal rate of interest. Applying this formula to the example in the previous section ($A = 1.00$; $r^m = 0.15$; $\Pi = 0.10$) would give a taxable interest of $50.

An adjustment along these lines has been suggested in the Meade report for types of assets, such as saving and time deposits, where the average balance held by an individual in a financial institution may change frequently due to additions or withdrawals through the year.[14] The report proposes that total interest income received by a given account in one year be multiplied by the difference between the nominal rate of interest and the rate of inflation. The result would then be divided by the nominal rate of interest. The nominal rate may, in this case, have to be an average for the year if it has not remained constant. Thus, if Ar^m is total interest income received (on an average balance equal to A, and an average nominal interest rate equal to r^m) and Π is the rate of inflation over the period, the formula proposed for taxable income is:

$$\frac{Ar^m (r^m - \Pi)}{r^m}$$

This formula gives the same result as Equation 5, as can be seen by taking $Ar^m = \$150$; $(r^m - \Pi) = 0.05$ and $r^m = 0.15$. Taxable interest income is then equal to $50, which is the same figure found above.[15] This first alternative solution is also implicitly adopted in the version of indexed loans that has been used in Colombia since 1972.[16] For such loans, the market rate of interest, r^m, is explicitly made up of two components: an agreed upon real rate, which supposedly reflects the one that would prevail in the absence of inflation, and a monetary correction Π to compensate the lender for the inflation-caused erosion in the real value of the principal over the period of the loan. The monetary correction is not known ex ante, so it must be calculated ex post. In terms of Equation 5, the product of the monetary correction, Π, and the principal, A, would indicate the nontaxable portion of interest-income received. Legally, this portion could either be exempted from taxation (as it seems to be in Colombia) or it could simply not be considered an income at all (as is the case in Chile).[17]

Adjustment of principal

The second alternative would be identical to the indexation of historical cost basis used in connection with capital gains. From the total end-of-period receipts of the lender – consisting of return of principal plus interest payment – a deduction consisting of the original loan indexed by the change in the price index over the period would be allowed. The difference would be the taxable portion of interest income. Using the same symbols as previously taxable interest income would be:

$$(A + Ar^m) - A(1 + \Pi) = Ar^m - A\Pi \tag{6}$$

Equation 6 gives exactly the same result as Equation 5. This solution has been implicitly adopted in the version of indexed loans used in Brazil. In this version, it is stipulated that the borrower will pay periodically a given interest on the original loan and, at maturity, would return to the lender an amount equal to the original loan escalated by any price change over the period. Only the periodic interest payment is taxed.[18] Thus, on a $1,000 loan, the lender might get $50 a year in interest and, at maturity, he would get back the $1,000 escalated by the change in the price index over the period of the loan. Only the $50 would be taxed.

Perhaps it ought to be pointed out that if the rate of inflation is high and the period of the loan is long, the impact of inflation on the taxable portion of interest is no longer negligible. In terms of Equation 2 (this chapter) this means that the term Πr can no longer be ignored. For example, if the lender keeps receiving $50 a year, on the original loan of $1,000, over several years during which the inflation rate is, say, 20 percent per year, the real value of the $50 will be progressively and considerably reduced. Thus, even if at maturity the lender received back the original $1,000 escalated for the change in the price index over the period of the loan, he would still have suffered a loss. Consequently, proper indexation of loans would require that: (1) either the $50 itself be adjusted on a yearly basis (or more often if necessary) in line with the rate of inflation, while at maturity the principal is repaid adjusted for the price change over the whole period, or (2) the principal itself be adjusted each year (or more often if necessary) and the agreed interest rate – 5 percent in our example – be applied against the monetary value of the principal for that year. In both situations, the agreed upon rate of interest would determine the taxable portion of interest income.

So far it has been assumed that (1) the market value of interest exceeds the rate of inflation, and (2) the monetary value of the loan (or more generally of the liability) remains unchanged except for agreed upon adjustments between borrowers and lenders in indexed loans. However, the market rate of interest may, at times, fall below the rate of inflation; and the liability may be marketable, so that at any moment of time its market value may differ from its redemption value. This is obviously the case with bonds. In attempting to find solutions in both of these situations, one is reminded of a maxim attributed to Lord Keynes, which states that it is far better to be approximately right than to be precisely wrong. One can be precisely wrong when he ignores the effects of inflation on the taxation of interest income because of those difficulties. But one will be only approximately right for most of the proposed solutions.

In a way, both of these difficulties become significant because inflation adjustments may be necessary even when a proper economic definition of economic income is not the guiding principle for taxation. And in many countries, this economic definition is clearly not the guiding principle. The basic link here is whether the market values of assets and liabilities should be taken into account when making adjustments for inflation in relation to the taxation of interest income. In theory, as required by a proper definition of income, they should be. In practice, however, countries often do not recognize capital gains as incomes and ignore capital losses; and when they do recognize them, they do it only when they are realized rather than as they accrue.

When capital gains (and losses) are ignored by the tax legislation of a country, it would seem to follow that only interest payments are relevant. In this case, a country that wished to provide some adjustment for inflation to interest incomes could follow the first method of adjustment described in this section. In other words, it would ignore any differences between market values and redemption values of the liabilities and tax only real interest income. In cases when real interest income becomes negative (i.e., when the rate of inflation exceeds the nominal rate of interest) taxable interest income would be reduced to zero. A variant of this method has been recently recommended for the Netherlands, a country that does not tax capital gains, by H. J. Hofstra. He would vary the proportion of interest received that would not be regarded as income on the basis of the inflation rate.[19] The adjustments that he proposes are shown in Table 10.

Table 10. *Inflation rate and taxable proportion of interest income*

Inflation rate (%)	Proportion of interest not regarded as income
1	Nil
2	1/5
3–4	1/3
5	2/5
6–8	1/2
9–11	3/5
12–15	2/3
Over 15	3/4

When capital gains are taxed and capital losses are taken into account, changes in the price of marketable liabilities as well as negative real rates of interest must be taken into account. As to the negative rates, if the application of the first adjustment scheme suggested in this section left a taxpayer with negative (taxable) real component, he could be allowed to use it as a deduction against other current or future incomes.[20] As to the changes in the market values of the liabilities, the relevant distinction is between capital gains taxed on accrual and those taxed on realization.

Assume that, expecting price stability, an individual buys a twenty-year $1,000 bond, paying an interest rate of 5 percent per year. The individual holds the bond for two years before selling it. During these two years the annual inflation rate is 10 percent. The market rate of interest rises enough in the first year to reduce the market value of the bond to $800. At the end of the second year that value is still $800.[21]

In such a situation, if a country taxes capital gains strictly on accrual, the individual would report the following incomes for the two years:

First year $[\$800 + \$50] - [\$1,000 (1.10)] = -\$250$
Second year $[\$800 + \$50] - [\$800 (1.10)] = -\$30$

In other words he would report losses of $250 and $30, respectively, which he would use as deductions against other incomes.

If the country taxes capital gains strictly on realization, the individual would report the following incomes, respectively:

First year $50
Second year $[\$800 + \$50] - [\$1,000 (1.21)] = -\$360$

Thus, the individual would report a positive income of $50 the first year and a net loss (to be deducted against other incomes) of $360 in the second year.

However, a country may wish to provide partial accrual somewhat along the line of the first adjustment system described in this section. In this case, the first year's taxable income is equal to the interest payment minus the inflation-induced erosion in the real value of the loan. Taxable income for the second year is equal to total receipts minus the historical cost indexed for the price change in the second year. Thus:

First year $50 − $100 = −$50
Second year [$50 + $800] − [$1,000 (1.1)] = − $250

The adjustment mechanisms outlined above have been described considering the effects of inflation on the lender. However, in countries where interest payments are deductible expenses for income tax purposes, the borrower benefits from inflation because when he repays the loans, fixed in monetary terms, he pays with depreciated money. Therefore, it should be obvious that while the lender must adjust downward for tax purposes the interest income that he receives, the borrower must adjust upward the interest that he pays. Thus, *mutatis mutandis,* the adjustment schemes that have been described must apply in reverse to borrowers. For example, looking at Equation 5 (this chapter), it had been suggested that $A\Pi$ – that is, the increase in the nominal value of the principal necessary to maintain its real value unchanged – ought to be exempted from income taxation so that the only income on which the lender would pay a tax would be $A(r^m - \Pi)$. Similarly, the borrower would be allowed a deduction only for $A(r^m - \Pi)$ and not for $A\Pi$, because the latter is actually a repayment of capital.

Countries' practices

Several countries have attempted to take into account the impact of inflation on taxable interest income. Many of these have done so through the practice of indexed loans; others have allowed a more direct adjustment of interest income proceeds. Generally, these countries have ignored the connection between changes in the rate of interest and changes in the real value of the liability. In other words, although the adjustments have attempted to remove the inflationary part of interest payments and deductions, they have not attempted to relate interest incomes to capital gains as required by a proper economic definition of income.

Argentina. Article 20 of the Income Tax Law No. 20628 of

December 29, 1973, modified by Law No. 21481 of December 30, 1976, deals with interest incomes in Argentina. The Interest incomes received from savings accounts and certificates of deposits in banking institutions have been exempted from taxation on the ground that these interest payments at best just compensate the lender for inflation-induced erosion in the capital. On the other hand, loans among individuals are taxed without any adjustments for inflation. However, if the contract between lender and borrower *explicitly* includes an indexation clause, the indexed part of total interest payment is not taxed. The normal form of indexation is to agree on a real rate payable on a principal that is adjusted in line with changes in the consumer price index published by the National Tax Bureau on the basis of information provided by the National Statistical Office. In recent years, part of the fiscal deficit has been financed with indexed loans. It is interesting to note that whereas for indexed loans the escalation of the principal is tax free, for nonindexed loans all the interest payments are taxable. Obviously, this brings a tremendous distortion in the allocation of capital and savings and raises a serious issue of equity. In the case of Argentina, these distortions have in recent years been minimized by the widespread evasion of taxes on interest income. The authorities have been aware of the inequity of taxing interest incomes when the real rate is sharply negative and the inflation rate is very high. Interest income as a tax base has been relatively insignificant.

Austria. The information available for Austria is limited. Apparently this country allows loan contracts with indexation clauses. The indexed portion of interest payments is not considered an income and consequently is not taxed.

Belgium. In Belgium, there is no explicit inflation adjustment for interest incomes subject to tax. However, in recognition of the fact that savings deposits suffer an erosion in their real value due to changes in prices, the law has allowed that a specific amount of interest incomes received from these deposits be exempt from taxation. This amount has been adjusted from time to time in a discretionary fashion.

Brazil. In Brazil, loan agreements can either be indexed or nonindexed. For indexed instruments, mainly savings account and government bonds, the value of the principal is adjusted every quarter and a constant rate of interest is paid on that adjusted value. The adjustment or "monetary correction" that is made on the basis of the changes in wholesale prices is not taxed. For nonindexed instruments, however, which include Treasury bills, commercial papers, some certificates of deposits, and so on, there is no adjustment for inflation and the full interest income is taxed. However, interest income received from these instruments, as well as from the taxable portion of the indexed instruments, is taxed with schedular rates that are lower than the normal income rates.

Canada. Canada has not paid any attention to the impact of inflation on interest income in spite of the fact that it has introduced bracket indexation. However, in recognition of the fact that inflation does affect interest income, beginning in 1974 – the same year that bracket indexation was introduced – the first $1,000 of interest income received by individuals from Canadian sources has been exempted.

Colombia. As described in the text, Colombia has had indexed loans for several years. For these, the monetary correction has been exempt from taxation. In recent years, however, ceilings have been imposed on that monetary correction, thus breaking the direct link with inflation. For nonindexed loans, all interest income is taxable.

Chile. In Chile, indexed loans have also been used. The principal has been escalated in line with an index reflecting price changes. This monetary correction is not considered an income and, consequently, is not taxed. Only the agreed part of the fixed interest rate levied on the indexed base is subject to taxation.

Denmark. There are no legal provisions explicitly related to the indexation of loans in Denmark. In recent years, however, several contracts have included an indexation clause. Individuals who have received interest payments in connection with these contracts have not reported as income the part related to the escalation of the principal. The tax authorities have, reportedly, not challenged this practice.

Israel. In Israel, various types of financial instruments, such as government bonds, deposits in savings institutions, and so on, carry an indexation clause. However, the escalation of the principal is limited to somewhat less than 100 percent of the increase in prices. The monetary correction is not taxed. Nonindexed interest payments, however, are fully taxed. The less than full indexation of the principal is justified on the ground that taxing fully nonindexed loans and excluding fully the monetary correction for the indexed ones brings about inequities in the tax treatment of interest incomes.

Germany. In Germany, there is no adjustment of the interest payment for inflation. However, the Income Tax Reform Act which became effective on January 1, 1975 exempted the first DM300 (or DM600 in the case of married couples) of interest received, mainly in recognition of the inflation-induced erosion in the real value of the principal.

United Kingdom. The British Government, in June 1975, introduced a limited scheme that would allow pensioners to save in a manner that would protect their savings from inflation. There is a limit of £500 per person. This saving is indexed in line with changes in the Retail Price Index. This "monetary correction" is tax free. At the end of five years, an additional tax-free bonus of 4 percent of the purchase price is also received. There is, in addition, an index-linked save-as-you-earn scheme limited to £20 per month over five years. For this, too, the monetary correction is tax free.[22]

Conclusion

This chapter has dealt with the problem that arises when interest income is taxed in an inflationary situation. The chapter has reviewed several possible adjustment schemes for solving this problem. It has also briefly described the implicit adjustment mechanism related to the existence of indexed loans. The problems which arise with indexed loans are essentially problems of equity when part of financial savings are indexed and part are not. In this particular case, the nonindexed loans will be discriminated against, and this will lead inevitably to a reallocation of savings toward the channels receiving preferential treatment.

6

Inflation and the taxation
of business incomes

In addition to incomes from wages and salaries, capital gains, and interest, some individuals receive dividends, rents, and profits from unincorporated business enterprises and partnerships. These other incomes are also distorted by inflation and require corrections that extend beyond that provided by *bracket indexation*. Although much of the discussion in this chapter is of some relevance to corporate profits and, consequently, to dividends, as our subject is *personal* income taxation, the problems as well as the solutions typical to corporations are not dealt with in detail.[1]

By and large, business accounting relies on historical data. If prices never changed, historical data would provide accurate information for the preparation of balance sheets and income statements of business enterprises. However, in the real world, some prices are changing at all times and these changes may be either around a relatively stable average or, as it has been more often the case in the period since the end of World War II, around an average that has itself been moving in an upward direction. When prices are changing, and these changes are not taken into account, the balance sheets and the income statements of enterprises will be distorted, and this will affect their tax liabilities, as their measure of taxable profits will be distorted.

The balance sheet will be distorted because the value of assets (land, buildings, machines, etc.) will be kept at the original, and largely outdated, acquisition prices. The income statement will be distorted because costs and revenues are likely to have occurred at different dates and will thus be reflected in monetary units of different real value. These distortions are particularly relevant in the valuations of inventories and in the determination of depreciation charges. For both of these, but to a much greater extent for depreciation, the time lag between the acquisition of the inputs (capital equipments, raw materials, intermediate products, etc.) and the sale of the output may be long and may thus reflect very different price levels. And, of course, to the extent that enterprises realize capital gains, these will also be distorted. Adjusting business income for these inflation-induced distortions is no easy matter.

For lack of any specific and consistent evidence to the contrary, in the discussion concerning rents and incomes from other business activities, gross receipts will be assumed to move broadly in line with inflation, although, of course, they may be greatly affected by the business cycle. The basic issue, then, is whether the various items that make up the "cost of doing business," and which thus determine taxable income, also keep up with changes in the purchasing power of money. As will be shown, many of these items do not adjust automatically for inflation.

It is normally assumed that generally, though perhaps not always smoothly, outlays such as wages and salaries, compensation of executives, rents, property taxes, advertising and marketing expenses, repairs and other similar deductions do adjust for general price changes. It is also recognized that particular problems arise with respect to the deductions for the cost of material inputs – inventory valuations – and for depreciation charges. On the other hand, the impact of inflation on monetary liabilities is often ignored, although that impact can be considerable.

Some of the basic theoretical issues related to the taxation of business incomes received by individuals can be discussed in a simplified manner in connection with rental incomes. Rents provide a convenient example of a link between depreciation charges and monetary liabilities. Thus, we discuss adjustments for depreciation when the assets are acquired with equity and when assets are acquired with debt financing. Subsequently, we discuss the issue of inventory valuations and finally conclude with a brief discussion of adjustments for larger enterprises.

Inflation and rental incomes
All-equity case

We start our discussion of depreciation under inflationary conditions when there is no debt involved. We shall assume that an individual uses his own savings to purchase a house for $100,000. He rents it for $8,000 a year. As allowed by the tax laws, he depreciates the house over, say, a forty-year period, using a straight-line method of depreciation accounting. Thus, he can claim a yearly depreciation allowance of $2,500. He pays property taxes of $1,000 per year, which he claims as an expense against gross rental income. Therefore, his taxable rental income will be:

$8,000 − [$2,500 + $1,000] = $4,500

Suppose now that in the second year prices increase by 10 percent. The rent, as well as the property tax, adjusts in line with inflation but not depreciation, as this is based on the historical (unadjusted) purchase price of the house. Thus, in the second year taxable rental income will be:

$8,800 − [$2,500 + $1,100] = $5,200

If prices continue rising at the same rate, in the third year it will be:

$9,680 − [$2,500 + $1,210] = $5,970

The 10 percent inflation rate has brought about increases in taxable rental income of 15.55 percent and 14.81 percent in the first and second year of inflation. Thus, taxable rental income has been overstated and the individual is not recovering his real capital through the depreciation charges; therefore, the tax that he pays becomes partly a capital tax. With any positive rate of inflation, a yearly stream of $2,500 discounted to the present, using the assumed constant rate of inflation Π as the discount factor, will generate a present value less than the historical cost of the investment,[2] or

$$\sum_{i=0}^{40} \frac{\$2,500}{(1 + \Pi)^i} < \$100,000$$

Alternatively, one can emphasize the fact that yearly charges of $2,500, compounded at the rate of inflation, will not generate at the end of the period enough funds to repurchase an identical house, or

$$\sum_{i=0}^{40} \$2,500 \, (1 + \Pi)^i < \$100,000 \, (1 + \Pi)^{40}$$

For this particular situation – the all-equity case – the solution is simple and unequivocal. The yearly depreciation charges need to be adjusted – that is, indexed – in line with the rate of inflation. In our example, if depreciation were indexed, taxable rental income for the second and third year would be:

$8,800 − [$2,500 (1.10) + $1,100] = $4,950

and

$9,680 − [$2,500 (1.21) + $1,210] = $5,445

With the indexation of the depreciation charges, taxable rental income will increase by the same percentage as the price index and the depreciation charge for any one year will always be 1/40th of the value of the asset in that particular year. Consequently, the present value of this stream discounted using the rate of inflation as the discounting factor will be equal to the historical cost, or

$$\sum_{i=0}^{40} \frac{\$2,500 \, (1 + \Pi)^i}{(1 + \Pi)^i} = \$100,000$$

And, if one wishes to emphasize the terminal value of these charges:

$$\sum_{i=0}^{40} \$2.500 \, (1 + \Pi)^i \, (1 + \Pi)^{40-i} = \$100,000 \, (1 + \Pi)^{40}$$

All-liability case

Suppose now that the individual has not used his own savings to purchase the house but, rather, has borrowed the full amount – $100,000 – at the preinflation rate of 5 percent for forty years. The individual agrees to pay each year $2,500 on the principal plus the interest on the balance due. This is, of course, not the usual format for mortgage loans but it helps to emphasize the basic point being made. All the other conditions remain the same as previously and interest payments are deductible expenses.

In this situation, and without any inflation adjustments, the taxable rental income for the first three years will be, respectively:

$8,000 − [$2,500 + $1,000 + $5,000] = −$500
$8,800 − [$2,500 + $1,100 + $4,875] = $325
$9,680 − [$2,500 + $1,210 + $4,750] = $1,220

With inflation adjustment for depreciation, these taxable incomes would be, respectively:

$8,000 − [$2,500 + $1,000 + $5,000] = $500
$8,800 − [$2,750 + $1,100 + $4,875] = $75
$9,680 − [$3,025 + $1,210 + $4,750] = $695

But is indexation of the depreciation allowances justified in this case when debt has been used for purchasing the asset that is being depreciated? The above calculation has, in fact, ignored the effect of inflation on the real value of the liability, although that liability must have been reduced by the erosion of the real value of the monetary unit. How can this effect be taken account of? There are several alternatives.

First, it can be assumed that in each of these years the borrower has realized a gain equal to the product of the inflation rate and the outstanding monetary value of the liability.[3] Under this assumed realization the taxable rental income for the second and third year would be:

$$\$8,800 - [\$2,750 + \$1,100 + \$4,875 - \$9,750] = \$9,825$$
$$\$9,680 - [\$3,025 + \$1,210 + \$4,750 - \$9,500] = \$10,195$$

Presumably, while the borrower reports these monetary gains as income, the lender would claim deductions equivalent to $9,750 and $9,500 for the two years. Although from a theoretical point of view this is perhaps the best solution, it faces some practical and/or legal problems. The major problem is that it converts for tax purposes an as-yet-unrealized gain into a realized one. However, at least as a possibility, it must be recognized that an increase in the price level this year might be followed by a fall in later years. Thus, if a full realization of gains is assumed in years when there is inflation, a full realization of losses must also be assumed in years when there is deflation. Furthermore, since most countries that tax capital gains do so only when these gains are realized and tax only a portion of those gains, this alternative would be opposed on legal grounds in most countries.[4]

An alternative that would rely on strict realization of gains from liabilities would require that the actual yearly repayment of the debt ($2,500 in our example) be indexed for inflation and the monetary correction be reported as income.[5] The objective of this adjustment would be to calculate the taxable rental income (or profit) under the assumption that the repayment of the principal remains unchanged in real terms, vis-à-vis what it would be without inflation. If, in our example, this adjustment is combined with the indexation of the depreciation charges, we would get the following taxable rental incomes for the second year and third year.

$$\$8,800 - [\$2,750 + \$1,100 + \$4,875 - \$250] = \$325$$
$$\$9,680 - [\$3,025 + \$1,210 + \$4,750 - \$525] = \$1,220$$

Thus, *in this particular example,* the indexation of assets as well as liabilities gives exactly the same taxable rental income as had been obtained without any indexation. Of course, this is largely the result of our choice of payments streams and of depreciation charges.[6] If these streams changed, the perfect equivalence found above, between gains from indexing depreciation and losses from indexing liabilities, would disappear.

The same solutions discussed above can be applied with obvious modifications when the assets have been financed partly with equity capital and partly with debt. The realization that depreciation allowances based on historical costs become inadequate during inflation, coupled with the fact that it is difficult to take proper account of monetary gains, has led some experts to propose that only the self-financed proportion of costs ought to be adjusted for inflation. For example, after pointing out that "the inflationary gains made on borrowed funds are reflected in the inflationary rise in value of such business assets as have been acquired using the borrowed funds"[7] the Hofstra report goes on to propose that "the revaluation of business assets is thus limited to those which the firm has acquired using its own capital."[8]

In the previous discussion, it has been assumed that the depreciation that is allowed under the tax laws in the absence of inflation would reflect closely the true economic depreciation. The issue gets more complicated when the depreciation allowed for tax purposes would exceed, in the absence of inflation, the true economic depreciation – that is, the rate at which the asset is actually used up. In such a case, some writers have argued that there would be less justification for correcting for inflation, particularly when the reason for allowing this excessive rate of depreciation was in fact the anticipation of inflation.

Inflation and inventory profits

The preceding section has been related to one particular type of business income – that derived from rental activities. For rental incomes, the issue of inventory accounting during inflation is generally not relevant. But for other types of business activity, it can be very important. Businesses buy material inputs, process them, and sell products that incorporate them. Between the purchase of the inputs and the sale of the output there may be a considerable lag. If there is inflation, the dollar used to buy the inputs would be more valuable in terms of general purchasing power than the dollar received from the sale of the output. If inputs are measured at historical costs and outputs at current costs, inventory profits (or "stock appreciation") would result. These inventory profits would then result in a higher income tax liability. However, these profits are not genuine but illusory, because they result from the fact that inputs and outputs are evaluated at prices that are strictly comparable but which tend to understate real costs.

The problem of inventory profits is particularly significant under the traditional first-in, first-out (FIFO) accounting method, because this method assumes that the goods sold during the year have used the earliest-purchased, and thus lowest-priced, inputs.[9] This inflation-induced distortion can be dealt with in various ways ranging from arbitrary adjustments to inflation-indexing. An example of an arbitrary adjustment is the one introduced in the United Kingdom in 1974, which allowed enterprises to revalue (for taxation purposes) opening inventories by 10 percent of the profits computed under normal FIFO method. In some other countries, the government has allowed in particular years arbitrary increases in the value of inventories. It is very unlikely that these adjustments would provide a precise correction for inventory profits.[10]

Unlike the FIFO method, the last-in, first-out (LIFO) method assumes that the inputs used are those most recently purchased; therefore, it leads to profits that are much less sensitive to inflation than is the case with FIFO. Many countries do not permit use of LIFO. In the United States, where LIFO is permitted and companies are allowed to change accounting method only once, few enterprises used LIFO up to 1973. However, the high rate of inflation experienced since 1974 has prompted many companies to make the shift in order to reduce their tax liabilities.[11]

LIFO introduces an adjustment that is not strictly in line with general price-level indexing. In fact, it amounts to indexation using the specific price indexes of the particular inputs being used. If the prices of these inputs are increasing faster than the general price index, the net worth of a company could increase without leading to additional taxes. In fact, under LIFO accounting method, as long as inventory holdings (in physical terms) do not fall, gains due to price changes are assumed not to be realized and, not being realized, are not taxable. As one expert has put it: "LIFO theory . . . comes very near to the idea that if you have the same number of tons of raw material at the beginning and the end then you haven't made any profit – that number rather than worth is the basis of wealth."[12] This statement may be acceptable to accountants, but it is doubtful that many economists would find tons rather than worth "the basis of wealth." Economists would generally agree with George Terborgh that: "In principle, the inflation adjustment should reflect what has happend, not to specific prices, but *to the dollar itself,* in terms of its general purchasing power over finished goods and services." He goes on to state that he "agree[s] wholly with the decision of the Financial Accounting Standards Board to employ a single general index for all adjustment."[13] This would point at the use of a FIFO method with the valuation adjusted in line with a general index.

Inflation and current cost accounting

In our discussion of depreciation charges under "Inflation and rental income," the method used for adjusting for inflation was the indexation of historical costs by some general price index. In the discussion of inventories, on the other hand, in addition to the method of indexing inventories for charges in a *general* price index, LIFO was also mentioned as an alternative. If inventories are not depleted, LIFO amounts to an indexation using a *specific* price index, namely, that of the goods in stocks. Thus, strictly speaking, LIFO is not consistent with an adjustment based on general price changes.

A lot of controversy has centered around whether historic cost accounts should be adjusted by reference to a general price index to reflect their "current purchasing power" (CPP), or whether they should reflect current cost accounting (CCA) or "value to the business," as suggested by the Sandilands report. A full discussion of this issue is beyond the scope of this study, but a few comments cannot be avoided. From a taxation point of view, a practical advantage of CPP accounting over CCA is simply that the values that are derived with the former often have far more objectivity than those derived with the latter.[14] Since historical costs are generally known, once the general price index has been chosen, there cannot be any conflict about the resulting adjusted values. Thus, the scope for litigation is narrow. This, however, is not likely to be the case with current cost accounting. "Value to business" can be a rather ambiguous concept, which may reflect: (1) a net realizable value (i.e., the "disposal value" of the asset); (2) the contribution of the asset to future earnings (i.e., the discounted present value); or (3) the replacement cost of the asset (or the current acquisition price).[15] The Sandilands report suggests that in most cases, the current acquisition price of the asset, which should be the most easily determinable of the three, will reflect the "value to business." However, in a world of rapid technological developments, it is not always clear what "replacing" an asset means, as the replacement would often have technical characteristics different from those of the asset being replaced. It is easy to anticipate frequent litigations between tax authorities and lawyers and accountants representing the business sector over whether an asset has been "replaced" by an identical one.

Regardless of whether current cost accounting generates accounts which provide better signals for managers and investors for their investment decisions, adjustments by use of a general index (CPP) are better when the issue is one of recovery of invested capital, as it should be when tax liabilities are being determined. Do the depreciation charges allow the investors to recover their capital in real terms? This is the basic question answered by CPP but not by CCA. Furthermore, if one argues for the use of *specific* indexes in an inflationary situation, he should also be prepared to argue for this type of accounting in periods of price stability. Even when the general price index remains unchanged, the prices of specific commodities or particular groups of inputs vary according to different trends. Inflation may accentuate these divergent trends but does not create them. However, without inflation, there could not be *general* price level accounting.

For the reasons we have mentioned, we shall accept the conclusion that *for purposes of determination of tax liability,* it is much simpler and possibly more justifiable to use a general price index, rather than specific indexes, for making inflation adjustments.

Practical experiences and conclusions

Once it is agreed that inflation adjustments for business enterprises are needed there remain the issues of how comprehensive these adjustments should be and which index, or indexes, of price change should be used. In this case, recourse to an economic definition of income as a reference point is not very helpful because of the complexity of the problem. One could, for example, define the income of a business enterprise "as that amount which, if there were no additional investment or withdrawals by the stockholders during the period, could be distributed by the enterprise to its stockholders, while the amount of stockholders' equity at the end of the period, was unchanged from the beginning of the period."[16] But what is an *unchanged* stockholders' equity? Is it unchanged vis-à-vis its future earning power (its operating capacity) or unchanged in the sense of having, at the end of the period, the same amount of (real) general purchasing power?

As to the comprehensiveness of the adjustments for business incomes, they could be limited to depreciation and inventories; or they could extend to nondepreciable assets, such as land, and even take into account monetary liabilities. In terms of actual countries' experiences, the practice has been to start with limited and specific adjustments (most often for depreciation or inventories) and, if inflation remained severe, to proceed to more comprehensive adjustments, as in Brazil and Chile, where all historical figures in both balance sheets and income statements are adjusted in line with a general price index.

Over the years, many countries have felt the need to make adjustments for the distortive impact of inflation on the taxable profits of enterprises. There have been basically three approaches: (1) simple ad hoc adjustments of depreciation allowances; (2) one-time or successive revaluations of nonmonetary business assets, including nondepreciable ones; and (3) comprehensive adjustment schemes of a permanent nature.[17]

Several countries have authorized the adjustment of depreciation allowances in situations where prices had changed to such an extent as to make this adjustment almost inevitable. This has been particularly true in the wake of substantial currency devaluations, which sharply increased the replacement cost of capital assets that were imported. At times, the adjustment has reflected the extent of the devaluation. At other times, it has reflected the change in some relevant price index. The main objective of this approach has been to adjust taxable income, so that the enterprises would generate enough funds to replace the depreciated capital assets. The countries that have pursued this road include Argentina, Austria, Colombia, and Israel.

Revaluation of nonmonetary business assets has been quite frequently used in European, Asian, and Latin American countries. In Europe, these adjustments became inevitable at the end of World War II, when financial statements based on historical costs became hopelessly distorted; these adjustments were necessary if the enterprises were to generate the needed funds. France, Italy, Belgium, Germany, the Netherlands, and some other countries followed this approach. The objective was basically the stimulation of investment, and the revaluation was often optional. The range of nonmonetary assets which could be revalued varied from country to country, with Germany providing the most comprehensive scheme. Several countries, recognizing that inflation would be advantageous to firms that financed the purchase of assets with loans, limited the degree to which those firms could revalue their assets. In all of these cases, it was thought that the inflationary period had been an exceptional one that required a once-for-all correction.

Although, in many cases, the underlying objective of this adjustment had been to revalue in accordance with current replacement costs, the difficulty of finding indexes which could be applied to specific assets led many countries to use aggregate price coefficients. But some countries – Belgium, the Netherlands, and Germany – did base the adjustment on estimated replacement costs. Indonesia, Japan, and Korea are among the Asian countries that have at times revalued business assets. Here again the adjustments have been optional in some cases and compulsory in others. And in all cases, they have come in the wake of serious inflationary pressures. At least eight Latin American countries have, since 1942, adopted revaluation schemes. In general, the Latin American pattern has been somewhat different from that followed by European and Asian countries owing to the more chronic nature of inflation in this continent and to frequent currency devaluations. Generally, the countries have started by correcting the depreciation basis, perhaps to adjust it for recent devaluations. They have then proceeded to other adjustments for particular items. Finally, more comprehensive systems have been developed, which take into account assets as well as liabilities.

These comprehensive systems require, for tax purposes, the yearly adjustment of all items in the balance sheets of enterprises in line with general indexes of price change. Thus, all assets – including nondepreciable ones – as well as liabilities are adjusted. The objective is to measure real changes in the net worth of the enterprises. These systems have found their fullest expression in Brazil and Chile.[18] Argentina has also been considering the introduction of a similar system. The Chilean scheme, which was adopted in 1959, relies on the consumer price index to make the adjustments in the various items to determine the yearly change in net worth. The Brazilian scheme is based on the wholesale price index.

It is not clear what kind of lesson one can draw from the experiences of these countries. One thing is certain: Inflation does distort seriously the accounting of business enterprises, so that with the passing of time and the continuation of inflation, historical values depart more and more from current values. This inevitably brings distortions and generates "profits" which may not be income at all. In these circumstances, periodic corrections seem to be in order, but they must be based on the assumptions that enterprises lose as well as gain from inflation. The experience with continuous adjustment schemes is too limited to give us any directives.

7

Inflation, lags in collection, and the real value of income tax revenue

The literature dealing with the impact of inflation on taxation has been biased by the recent experiences of the industrialized countries. For these countries, inflation has generally been associated with increases in the real value of income tax revenues, so that many authors have been led to believe that the main inflation-induced problems are the prevention of this supposedly unwanted, or at least unlegislated, increase in revenue and the neutralization of the inevitable effects on the redistribution of the tax burden among income groups. However, the increase in real revenue is likely to occur mainly when (1) the lags in the collection of income taxes are short, and (2) these taxes are elastic. However, while these characteristics seem to prevail in many industrialized countries, they are not common to all countries.

When one deals with countries with income taxes collected with somewhat longer lags and with elasticities not much greater, or even less, than unity, the consequences of inflation can be very different, especially when the rate of inflation becomes high. Unfortunately, these alternative situations are not products of an economist's imagination but, on the contrary, have either existed or continue to exist in many developing countries and perhaps even in some industrialized countries. For these countries, the problem has not been an *increase,* but rather an inflation-induced *fall,* in real income tax revenue. In many cases, this fall has itself become a contributing factor in the inflationary process when the affected governments have financed the fiscal deficits through the printing of new money.

There has been hardly any analysis of what happens to real tax revenue when the tax systems are not elastic, the lags in tax collection are not short, and the rate of inflation becomes high. The main objective of this chapter is to show that when the rate of inflation becomes high, the inevitable lags in the collection of income taxes become very important and, unless compensated by high elasticities, may often lead to a decrease in real revenue.

Theoretical analysis
Taxable events and de jure elasticity

We shall call a *taxable event* one that creates a legal financial liability on the part of a taxpayer toward the state. For example, the earning of income may create an obligation on the part of the income earner to pay an income tax. Let us assume that an individual earns Y dollars, and that this income is subject to a proportional income tax levied at the rate of α. However, while this liability has been created at the moment the taxable event has occurred (i.e., at the moment when income has been earned) the government will receive the payment only at a later time. The taxpayer himself or, alternatively, the employer, who may have withheld the tax, will transfer the tax money after some delay.

These lags introduce complications in the proper definition of tax elasticity and even that of the average tax rate. In a theoretical world in which payments are made at the same time that the taxable event occurred, there would be a clearly definable elasticity of the tax payment with respect to income, that would not be affected by any lag in the payment. As national income changed, depending on the legal characteristics of the tax, the percentage change in the tax collection would be more than, or less than, or equal to, the percentage change in national income. This theoretical, or de jure, elasticity would consequently be equal to, or more or less than, unity. In this lagless world, if the elasticity of the income tax were greater than unity, inflation would, *ceteris paribus,* bring about a real increase in tax payment, so that the ratio of taxes to national income would in fact rise.[1]

An alternative way of looking at this theoretical, or de jure, elasticity is to relate the tax collection, *at a given time,* to the income at the time when the event that created the legal liability occurred (in other words to its legal base). In this case, if the earning of an income Y_0 – where 0 indicates the period when the taxable event occurred – creates a tax liability equal to αY_0, which because of a lag in collection, is paid, say, two periods later, when normal income has risen to Y_2, we could calculate the elasticity (or even the average tax rate) by relating the tax payment αY_0 to the original Y_0 rather than to the present higher income, Y_2, as is generally done. However, the elasticity – or even the average tax rate – so calculated would be different from the effective one normally estimated statistically – which relates revenue received in a given period to income of the same period and thus ignores the legal connection defined above.[2] In conclusion, whenever nominal income is growing and there are lags in tax collection, both the elasticity of the tax and the average tax rate will be different if estimated with respect to current income and not with respect to the income prevailing at the time of the taxable event. This difference can become substantial whenever there is considerable inflation associated with sizable lags. The nature of these lags will be discussed later. For the time being, it is sufficient to assume that these lags exist and that somehow they can be measured.

Inflation, lags, and real tax revenue

The impact of different lags and rates of inflation on the real value of one dollar of tax revenue can be estimated by solving the equation:

$$R = \frac{1}{(1 + p)^n} \tag{1}$$

where R is the real value of a dollar of tax revenue collected today but measured in prices of the period when the taxable event occurred; p is the *monthly* rate of inflation, and n is the size of the lag also expressed in months.

Table 11 has been calculated by solving the above equation in relation to various rates of inflation and lags. The table assumes that income taxes are collected, successively, with lags which may be zero, one month, two months, three months . . . up to twelve months. Surely, these alternatives embrace the realities of the tax systems of most countries, although particular income taxes may be, and are at times, collected with even longer lags. These lags are shown horizontally at the top of the table. Vertically, on the left, the table indicates selected monthly rates of inflation. Again, it starts with the assumption of a zero inflation rate per month, then it considers 1 percent per month, 2 percent, 3 percent, and then, selectively, rates all the way up to 50 percent per month. All of these rates have been experienced by some countries, at least for some months, in recent years. The alternative lags and rates of inflation provide a matrix which is likely to include the experience of most countries.

If the price elasticity of the income tax system of a country were one, as it would be with proportional income taxes or with progressive taxes indexed for inflation, the table could also be used to raise questions about the effect of inflation on total income tax revenue. In other words, it would allow us to answer the following question: Assuming that income taxes in a given country are collected with an average lag of x months, and that the country is experiencing a monthly rate of inflation of y, what will be the impact on the real value of its income tax revenue?[3] Each row in the table will then tell us what happens to the real value of the income tax revenue when, given a certain rate of inflation, the length of the lag changes from zero to twelve months. Thus,

Table 11. *Impact of lags in tax payments and of rates of inflation on the real value of tax revenue*

Monthly rates of inflation (%)	Lags in payment of taxes (monthly)												
	0	1	2	3	4	5	6	7	8	9	10	11	12
0	1.00	1.00	1.00	1.00	1.00	1.00	1.00	1.00	1.00	1.00	1.00	1.00	1.00
1	1.00	0.99	0.98	0.97	0.96	0.95	0.94	0.93	0.92	0.91	0.90	0.90	0.89
2	1.00	0.98	0.96	0.94	0.92	0.91	0.89	0.87	0.85	0.84	0.82	0.80	0.79
3	1.00	0.97	0.94	0.91	0.89	0.86	0.84	0.81	0.79	0.77	0.74	0.72	0.70
4	1.00	0.96	0.92	0.89	0.85	0.82	0.79	0.76	0.73	0.70	0.68	0.65	0.63
5	1.00	0.95	0.91	0.86	0.82	0.78	0.75	0.71	0.68	0.65	0.61	0.58	0.56
6	1.00	0.94	0.89	0.84	0.79	0.75	0.70	0.67	0.63	0.59	0.56	0.53	0.50
7	1.00	0.93	0.87	0.82	0.76	0.71	0.67	0.62	0.58	0.54	0.51	0.48	0.44
8	1.00	0.93	0.86	0.79	0.74	0.68	0.63	0.58	0.54	0.50	0.46	0.43	0.40
9	1.00	0.92	0.84	0.77	0.71	0.65	0.60	0.55	0.50	0.46	0.42	0.39	0.36
10	1.00	0.91	0.83	0.75	0.68	0.62	0.56	0.51	0.47	0.42	0.39	0.35	0.32
20	1.00	0.83	0.69	0.58	0.48	0.40	0.33	0.28	0.23	0.19	0.16	0.13	0.11
30	1.00	0.77	0.59	0.46	0.35	0.27	0.21	0.16	0.12	0.09	0.07	0.06	0.04
40	1.00	0.71	0.51	0.36	0.26	0.19	0.13	0.09	0.07	0.05	0.03	0.02	0.02
50	1.00	0.67	0.44	0.30	0.20	0.13	0.09	0.06	0.04	0.03	0.02	0.01	0.01

for example, if the monthly rate of inflation were 10 percent, and the country collected its taxes with zero lag, it would not experience any fall in the real value of its revenue; however, if it collected its taxes with one month lag, it would experience a 9 percent fall; if it collected its taxes with a lag of five months, it would experience a 38 percent fall, and so on. The higher the monthly rate of inflation, and the longer the lag in payment, the greater will be the reduction in the real value of taxes that a country will experience. This is seen clearly in the table by moving down the rows and reading from left to right.

Alternatively, the columns in the table show what happens when, given a certain average lag in collection, the rate of inflation is assumed to become progressively higher. Thus, for example, a country that had an average lag of four months would lose 4 percent of the real value of its tax revenue if, after a period of stability, it entered an inflationary period in which prices increased at the rate of 1 percent per month; it would lose 18 percent if the rate of inflation rose to 5 percent per month, and 32 percent if it rose to 10 percent. If the rate of inflation should become extremely high, say, 50 percent per month, the real value of taxes would be reduced to 20 percent of what they would be in the absence of inflation. If the rate of inflation is zero, there is no fall in the real value of taxes, inasmuch as the value of the dollar collected would remain unchanged over time.[4] Alternatively, if the lag should be zero, then there would be no decrease in the real value of the tax revenue regardless of the rate of inflation.[5]

Table 11 measures the *percentage* falls in income tax revenue associated with various inflation rates and collection lags. How important this fall is in terms of total revenue depends also on what the ratio of income taxes to national income would be at a zero rate of inflation. The higher that ratio, the greater the *absolute* revenue loss. Assume, as an example, that at zero inflation, income tax revenue would be 2 percent of national income. A 3 percent monthly rate of inflation combined with a seven-month collection lag would reduce real revenue by about 20 percent or by 0.4 percent of national income. However, if at zero inflation, the ratio of income tax revenue to national income had been 10 percent, the inflation-induced fall would have been 2 percent of national income.

In summary the main conclusions so far are: First, given the rate of inflation, *and assuming that the price elasticity of the income tax system is one,* the longer the lag in the collection of taxes, the greater will be, *ceteris paribus,* the net inflation-induced real reduction in the tax revenues that the government receives. Second, given the lag in the collection of taxes, the higher the rate of inflation, the lower, *ceteris paribus,* will be the real value of the tax revenue. Thirdly, the more important is the income tax in the revenue system of a country, the greater will be the absolute revenue loss. Finally, the table shows also the percentage gains in revenue that are possible to a country from the reduction of the lags in payments.

Inflation, lags, and tax incidence by type and level of income

The analysis outlined in the previous section can be used, with some modifications, to assess the effects of inflation and collection lags on individuals in different income groups. In many countries, income taxes from wages and salaries are withheld at the source and are thus paid with hardly any delay. On the other hand, taxes on capital incomes are often paid with delays of many months. When there is inflation, this differential lag may give the receivers of capital incomes considerable advantages, because when they eventually meet their tax obligations, they do so with inflated dollars. The result is a distortion of the income tax incidence that would have prevailed if there had been price stability.[6] Furthermore, since the receivers of capital incomes are more likely to belong to higher income groups,[7] the distortions may not be considered equitable.

In order to assess these effects let: p and Π denote the rate of inflation on a monthly and on an annual basis, respectively; n denote the collection lag expressed in number of months; and T_0 and T_Π denote the average tax rates, for individuals or for income classes, when the annual rate of inflation is zero and Π, respectively. These average tax rates are the tax payments made in a given period, divided by the incomes of the same period.

Equation 1 can be rewritten as:

$$T_\Pi = \frac{T_0}{(1 + p)^n} = \frac{T_0}{(1 + \Pi)^{n/12}} \tag{2}$$

Solving this equation for alternative values of T_0, n, and Π, one can derive estimates for T_Π. Table 12 gives the results when Equation 2 is solved for $T_0 = 0.10; 0.20; 0.30; 0.40$; $n = 2; 4; 6; 8$ months; and Π ranging from 5 percent per year to 500 percent per year. Let us analyze this table.

Assume, first, that in the absence of inflation, two individuals, A and B, would both have identical incomes and pay income taxes equal to 40 percent of their incomes (last four columns in Table 12). Assume, however, that for individual A the collection lag is only two months (i.e., $n = 2$), whereas for B it is eight months (i.e., $n = 8$). Going down the $n = 2$ and the $n = 8$ columns, for $T_0 = 0.4$, it can be seen from the table how inflation would change their average tax rates. At an inflation rate of 20

Table 12. Inflation and average tax rates (ratios to taxpayer's incomes)

Π	$T_0 = 0.1$				$T_0 = 0.2$				$T_0 = 0.3$				$T_0 = 0.4$			
	$n=2$	$n=4$	$n=6$	$n=8$	$n=2$	$n=4$	$n=6$	$n=8$	$n=2$	$n=4$	$n=6$	$n=8$	$n=2$	$n=4$	$n=6$	$n=8$
0.050	0.099	0.098	0.098	0.097	0.198	0.197	0.195	0.194	0.298	0.295	0.293	0.290	0.397	0.394	0.390	0.387
0.100	0.098	0.097	0.095	0.094	0.197	0.194	0.191	0.188	0.295	0.291	0.286	0.282	0.394	0.387	0.381	0.375
0.150	0.098	0.095	0.093	0.091	0.195	0.191	0.187	0.182	0.293	0.286	0.280	0.273	0.391	0.382	0.373	0.364
0.200	0.097	0.094	0.091	0.089	0.194	0.188	0.183	0.177	0.291	0.282	0.274	0.266	0.388	0.376	0.365	0.354
0.250	0.096	0.093	0.089	0.086	0.193	0.186	0.179	0.172	0.289	0.278	0.268	0.259	0.385	0.371	0.358	0.345
0.300	0.096	0.092	0.088	0.084	0.191	0.183	0.175	0.168	0.287	0.275	0.263	0.252	0.383	0.367	0.351	0.336
0.350	0.095	0.090	0.086	0.082	0.190	0.181	0.172	0.164	0.285	0.271	0.258	0.246	0.380	0.362	0.344	0.327
0.400	0.095	0.089	0.085	0.080	0.189	0.179	0.169	0.160	0.284	0.268	0.254	0.240	0.378	0.358	0.338	0.320
0.450	0.094	0.088	0.083	0.078	0.188	0.177	0.166	0.156	0.282	0.265	0.249	0.234	0.376	0.353	0.332	0.312
0.500	0.093	0.087	0.082	0.076	0.187	0.175	0.163	0.153	0.280	0.262	0.245	0.229	0.374	0.349	0.327	0.305
0.600	0.092	0.085	0.079	0.073	0.185	0.171	0.158	0.146	0.277	0.256	0.237	0.219	0.370	0.342	0.316	0.292
0.700	0.092	0.084	0.077	0.070	0.183	0.168	0.153	0.140	0.275	0.251	0.230	0.211	0.366	0.335	0.307	0.281
0.800	0.091	0.082	0.075	0.068	0.181	0.164	0.149	0.135	0.272	0.247	0.224	0.203	0.363	0.329	0.298	0.270
0.900	0.090	0.081	0.073	0.065	0.180	0.161	0.145	0.130	0.270	0.242	0.218	0.196	0.359	0.323	0.290	0.261
1.000	0.089	0.079	0.071	0.063	0.178	0.159	0.141	0.126	0.267	0.238	0.212	0.189	0.356	0.317	0.283	0.252
1.200	0.088	0.077	0.067	0.059	0.175	0.154	0.135	0.118	0.263	0.231	0.202	0.177	0.351	0.308	0.270	0.236
1.400	0.086	0.075	0.065	0.056	0.173	0.149	0.129	0.112	0.259	0.224	0.194	0.167	0.346	0.299	0.258	0.223
1.600	0.085	0.073	0.062	0.053	0.171	0.145	0.124	0.106	0.256	0.218	0.186	0.159	0.341	0.291	0.248	0.212
1.800	0.084	0.071	0.060	0.050	0.168	0.142	0.120	0.101	0.253	0.213	0.179	0.151	0.337	0.284	0.239	0.201
2.000	0.083	0.069	0.058	0.048	0.167	0.139	0.115	0.096	0.250	0.208	0.173	0.144	0.333	0.277	0.231	0.192
2.500	0.081	0.066	0.053	0.043	0.162	0.132	0.107	0.087	0.243	0.198	0.160	0.130	0.325	0.263	0.214	0.174
3.000	0.079	0.063	0.050	0.040	0.159	0.126	0.100	0.079	0.238	0.189	0.150	0.119	0.317	0.252	0.200	0.159
3.500	0.078	0.061	0.047	0.037	0.156	0.121	0.094	0.073	0.233	0.182	0.141	0.110	0.311	0.242	0.189	0.147
4.000	0.076	0.058	0.045	0.034	0.153	0.117	0.089	0.068	0.229	0.175	0.134	0.103	0.306	0.234	0.179	0.137
4.500	0.075	0.057	0.043	0.032	0.151	0.113	0.085	0.064	0.226	0.170	0.128	0.096	0.301	0.227	0.171	0.128
5.000	0.074	0.055	0.041	0.030	0.148	0.110	0.082	0.061	0.223	0.165	0.122	0.091	0.297	0.220	0.163	0.121

Note: Π = inflation rate; T_0 = ratio of tax payments to taxpayers' incomes at zero inflation rate; n = average collection lag in number of months.

percent, the average tax rates would become 38.8 and 35.4 percent, respectively. At 50 percent inflation, the tax rates would become 37.4 and 30.5 percent. Obviously, the individual who pays with the longer lag benefits much more from inflation; furthermore, the differential increases with an increase in Π.

For the two taxpayers, let us now assume not only different lags but also different incomes. Assume that A receives a low enough income, so that if there were no inflation, the average tax rate for him would be only 10 percent. B, on the other hand, receives a much higher income, so that his average tax rate would be 40 percent. A's income is mostly from wages and salaries, and B's is mostly from capital sources. Therefore, it is assumed that A pays with a two-month average lag, whereas B pays with an eight-month lag.[8] In this case, an annual inflation rate of 20 percent would reduce A's average tax rate from 10 to 9.7 percent but would reduce B's from 40 to 35.4 percent. An inflation rate of 50 percent would reduce A's tax rate to 9.3 percent and B's to 30.5 percent. Thus, the benefits that taxpayers derive from delays in tax payments depend not only on the rate of inflation but also on their income level. As wage earners normally have lower incomes (and thus lower effective tax rates) and shorter lags, their average tax rates are reduced much less than those of taxpayers receiving capital income.

Inflation, lags, and income tax revenue when the elasticity is not one

An assumption used above was that of a unitary de jure elasticity of the income tax system. This implies that inflation per se, in the absence of any other factors, would not generate any *real* increase or fall in revenues. The assumption of unitary elasticity for the income tax system may be realistic for some developing countries. However, if personal income taxes are progressive and are collected with a short lag, then, as the current literature on the impact of inflation on taxes has emphasized, the inflationary conditions would bring about, *ceteris paribus*, an increase in the real value of revenues by shrinking the real size of the exemptions and of the brackets and possibly by distorting the tax bases.[9] Thus, if taxes are collected with a lag, the gain coming from the above-mentioned progressivity (and possibly from distortions in components of incomes other than wages) would have to be balanced against the losses emphasized in the table. Whether revenues in real terms would increase or decrease over a given period for the country as a whole, and for particular taxpayers, would depend on the interrelationship between the elasticity, the rate of inflation, and the lag in collection.

Given the existence of a lag, and given an elasticity that exceeds unity, a *steady* increase in the general price level (that followed a period of price stability) will at first lead to the same fall in real revenue as shown in the table; then, as the average price level becomes progressively higher, and as the increase in the price level is accompanied by a greater than proportional increase in nominal tax revenue, real tax revenue (and thus the share of revenue in the income of the current period) will start increasing and will continue increasing as long as the price level keeps rising. In time, the initial loss in revenue will be made up, and if inflation continues, real revenue will rise. The shorter the lag in collection, and the higher the elasticity, the more quickly will the real level of tax revenue regain and exceed the preinflationary level. The relationships between real revenue and the rate of inflation, the level of prices, the elasticity of the tax, and the size of the lag are analyzed mathematically in the Appendix.

The lag in the collection of a given tax – that is, the lapse of time between the taxable event and the tax collection connected with that event – is made up of two parts which could be called, respectively, the *legal* lag and the *delinquency* lag. The first is the government-sanctioned delay in payment which carries no penalty. For example, a self-employed individual is normally required to pay his income tax some time after the earning of the income. The delinquency lag exists when the payment is made after the time it falls due. In most cases, the legal lag is the most important, although, under particular circumstances, the delinquency lag can become very significant.

Concluding remarks

The foregoing analysis indicates that countries which face highly inflationary pressures, or which are likely to face them at some stage, should pay much more attention to the impact that lags in the payment of income taxes may have on real revenue. No country, of course, can collect income taxes without any delay. However, for most countries, the necessary delay – that is, the legal lag – in tax collection can be substantially reduced, while the government still recognizes the fact that taxpayers require time to gather all the information needed to calculate the tax payments and to make them.

Policy should be aimed at trying to reduce the legal lag to some "optimal" level and the delinquency lag to zero.[10] This delinquency lag can be eliminated by stiff penalties applied on top of tax payments that have been adjusted for the change in the price level that has occurred during the delay.[11] Stiff penalties alone are not sufficient, as seen in a number of countries, because what appears to be a stiff penalty when the rate of inflation is low may become insignificant when the rate of inflation becomes very high.

The analysis in this chapter is of considerable relevance to the literature that deals with inflationary finance, or what is alternatively called the inflation tax.[12] This tax results when a government deficit is financed through money creation, which, by increasing the money supply and subsequently the price level, reduces the real value of the monetary unit. This reduction can be seen, as Friedman and Bailey showed many years ago, as a kind of tax on those holding money. Under simplifying assumptions, the inflation tax is equal to the tax base (the real cash balance) times the rate of inflation. This literature has always assumed that deficit financing will not have any effect on real tax revenue. However, as seen in this chapter, this assumption is hardly tenable, so that a proper analysis of inflationary finance (or of the inflation tax) can only be conducted within a general equilibrium model that takes into account the effects of inflationary finance on the real value of normal tax revenue.[13]

Appendix: relationship between lag, elasticity and inflation

Let Y_0 = real income in period zero

T_t = amount of tax in period t

m = periods of inflation (say number of months) since period zero

p = rate of inflation over m

n = collection lag as defined in this chapter

ϵ = price elasticity of income tax

Assume an income tax function of the type,

$$T = f(Y) = tY^\epsilon \tag{3}$$

where $\epsilon = 1$ for a proportional tax

$\epsilon > 1$ for a progressive tax

After m periods at a rate of inflation equal to p, nominal income will become $Y_0 e^{pm}$. Substituting this value for Y in Equation 3 and considering that today's nominal tax payments are based on the nominal income of n periods ago we can rewrite the tax function as:

$$T_t = f[Y_0 e^{p(m-n)}] = t[Y_0 e^{p(m-n)}]^\epsilon \tag{4}$$

The real tax payment (i.e., at prices of period zero) will be:

$$\frac{T_t}{e^{pm}} = \frac{t[Y_0 e^{p(m-n)}]^\epsilon}{e^{pm}} = t Y_0 e^{(m\epsilon - m - n\epsilon)} \tag{5}$$

Whether the taxpayer's real tax payment in period t is greater or smaller than in period zero depends on whether $(m\epsilon - m - n\epsilon) \gtrless 0$.

For a proportional tax $\epsilon = 1$. Therefore $(m\epsilon - m - n\epsilon) = -n < 0$. This is the case analyzed in detail in this chapter. In this case, only the lag effect is present, so that the taxpayer's real tax bill will fall. The extent of the fall will, of course, depend on the rate of inflation, p, and on the collection lag, n. These are the results shown in Table 12.

For a progressive tax $\epsilon > 1$. Assume now that $m = n$. Then $(m\epsilon - m - n\epsilon) = -m$. In this case, again, the real tax bill will be reduced by the lag. And the same will be the case if $m < n$. However, assume that $m > n$, while $\epsilon > 1$; then, whether the value of $(m\epsilon - m - n\epsilon) \gtrless 0$ depends on the relative values of m, n, and ϵ. For example, assume that $m = 6$, $n = 4$, and $\epsilon = 1.5$. Then $(m\epsilon - m - n\epsilon) = -3$. Thus, the real tax bill will still be reduced by the lag. However, assume that $m = 6$, $n = 2$, and $\epsilon = 2$. Then $(m\epsilon - m - n\epsilon) = 2$. In this case, the tax payment will increase in real terms. Obviously, given the rate of inflation, p, the shorter the lag with respect to the periods of inflation since period zero, and the higher the elasticity of the tax system, the more likely it is that real tax revenue will increase. If we set $m\epsilon - m - n\epsilon = 0$ and solve for m, it can be seen that to get an increasing tax payment in real terms with a given rate of inflation it is necessary that $m > n\epsilon/(\epsilon - 1)$.

BIBLIOGRAPHY

Aghevli, Bijan B., and Khan, Moshin S. "Inflationary Finance and the Dynamics of Inflation: Indonesia, 1951–72." *American Economic Review* 67 (June 1977): 390–403.

Hirao, Teruo, and Aguirre, Carlos A. "Maintaining the Level of Income Tax Collection Under Inflationary Conditions." IMF *Staff Papers 17* (July 1970): 277–325.

Olivera, Julio H. G. "Money, Prices and Fiscal Lags: A Note on the Dynamics of Inflation." Banca Nazionale del Lavoro *Quarterly Review 82* (Sept. 1967): 258–67.

Salama, Elías. "Estimaciones Econometricas de los Rezagos Fiscales." *Ensayos Económicos* of the Central Bank of Argentina 2 (June 1977): 25–40.

Tanzi, Vito. "Inflation, Lags in Collection and the Real Value of Tax Revenue." *IMF Staff Papers 24* (Mar. 1977); 154–67.

Tanzi, Vito. "Inflation, Real Tax Revenue, and the Case for Inflationary Finance: Theory with an Application to Argentina." IMF *Staff Papers 25* no. 3 (Sept. 1978): 417–51.

8

Sensitivity of personal income tax yield to income changes: theory and measurement

So far, this book has focused on the relationship between price level changes and the income tax. The impact of changes in real incomes have thus been ignored. However, the interplay of the progressivity of the tax with growth in real income can have effects that a country may wish to avoid. For example, adjustments for changes due to inflation alone may still leave a country with a growing ratio of revenue from income tax to personal (or national) income which can create a fiscal drag that might hinder the growth of the economy. This chapter and the next deal with some of the issues created by growth in real income. At this point, it is perhaps worthwhile to emphasize the basic difference between growth-related and inflation-related distortions. Unlike inflation-related distortions, those due to growth result exclusively from the progressivity of the tax. There is thus no problem of capital-income distortions. If the tax were truly proportional, no growth-related problem would exist.

In this chapter, the determinants of the sensitivity of the yield of the personal income tax will first be analyzed. Then a method for measuring that sensitivity will be described and applied to United States data.

The analysis of the sensitivity of the individual income tax to changes in national income has been a subject that for many years has attracted considerable attention. For a time, this attention was directed toward the contribution that this sensitivity made to stabilization. Then, however, the emphasis changed. With growth supplanting stabilization as the overriding objective of economic policy, it became more relevant to find out to what extent the tax interfered with the growth of the economy. Its elasticity, which, hitherto, had been considered a "blessing," came to be regarded as a "drag." It became obvious that under normal circumstances, a substantial rate of growth for the economy would require periodic income tax reductions unless some reforms were enacted in the tax legislation that automatically introduced the necessary adjustments. Thus, for example, Japan found it necessary to cut taxes almost every year to prevent the income tax from becoming a drag; Germany had to do the same during the period of maximum growth; and as was discussed in Chapter 3, many countries have found it necessary to index their income tax in order to reduce its elasticity especially with respect to price changes.

Determinants of the elasticity of the personal income tax yield

Let us define the elasticity of the income tax with respect to some measure of national income as:

$$E_T = \frac{\Delta T/T_0}{\Delta Y/Y_0} = \frac{\Delta T/\Delta Y}{T_0/Y_0}$$

where T_0 indicates the initial level of personal income tax yield and Y_0 indicates the initial level of national income at current prices. This elasticity gives the ratio of the relative change in tax yield to the relative change in national income (or some other aggregate measure of output). The value of E_T depends on two basic factors: (1) the progressivity of the statutory rates which implies that $(\Delta T/\Delta Y) > (T_0/Y_0)$ so that $(T_1/Y_1) > (T_0/Y_0)$ and (2) the ratio of the tax base (the actual taxable income) to national income.

When national income at current prices increases – regardless of whether the increase is real or due to inflation – the yield of the personal income tax increases for two reasons: first, because of the increase in taxable income; second, because of the progressivity of the statutory rates. This progressivity implies that additional shares of income enter the first income bracket from the zero rate bracket (i.e., the exemption) and part of the already taxed income hits higher marginal rates.

Consequently, the E_T can be decomposed in two parts: the first measures relative changes in the base, B, with respect to relative changes in national income, Y. The second depends specifically on changes in nominal per capita income and on the progressivity of the statutory rates. The first depends largely on changes in total income and on the institutional relationship between B and Y.[1] The elasticity of the tax base, B, with respect to changes in income, Y, can be expressed by

$$E_b = \frac{\Delta B/B_0}{\Delta Y/Y_0}$$

In this case, it is assumed that B *includes* the basic exemption. In other words, we assume that the base B is not personal taxable income net of basic exemptions, that is, $\sum_{i=1}^{n} (Y_i - R^0)$, but it is $\sum_{i=1}^{n} Y_i$, where Y_i represents the income of an individual i, that the law prescribes to be subjected to the tax, and r_0 represents the size of the basic exemption.[2] If it is assumed that the relationship between the tax base, so defined, and national income remains the same, then $B = K \cdot Y$, where K is a constant, regardless of the level of per capita income. Therefore, whether the increase in income is "extensive" (i.e., the increase in national income is not accompanied by an increase in per capita income), or "intensive" (i.e., per capita income increases), makes no difference to E_b.[3]

Considering now the second effect on E_T, given a progressive tax structure, the ratio of the personal income tax yield, T, to the tax base, B, will increase as *nominal* per capita income increases. Indicating this ratio by $t = (T/B)$, if the tax were truly proportional (and thus no basic exemption were allowed), the ratio T/B would remain constant when income changed; in such case $\Delta t = t_1 - t_0$ would be zero. But if the rates are progressive, or if a basic exemption is allowed (i.e., if the marginal rate is zero on the first portion of income), a change in per capita income, regardless of whether it is real or purely nominal, will give a positive value to Δt since t would increase with the increase in per capita income. This is shown graphically in Figure 1.

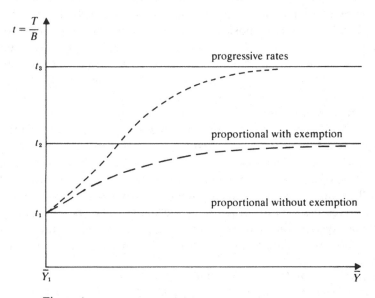

Figure 1

In Figure 1, the origin of the axes is set at a value of per capita income, $\overline{Y}_1$, equal to that which prevailed at the time the present tax law was enacted and at a value of $t = 0$. Assume that the value of t in the first year in which the law is in effect is t_1. If the tax is truly proportional (i.e., without exemption), the value of t will remain constant so that $dt/d\overline{Y}$ will be zero. If the system has just one marginal rate applied on incomes above a basic exemption, t will approach asymptotically the value of this rate; that is $\lim_{\overline{Y} \to \infty} t = t_2$; in this case, the smaller is the exemption relatively to per capita income, and the faster is the (real or nominal) increase in per capita income, the faster will be the speed at which t approaches t_2. The second derivative of $dt/d\overline{Y}$ will be negative all the way.

If the tax system is of a progressive nature, with a maximum marginal rate equal to t_3, then, as growth or inflation brings about an increase in average income $\overline{Y}$, the actual value of t will also continuously increase. The value of t will also approach a limit that is $\lim_{\overline{Y} \to \infty} t = t_3$. The speed at which such a limit would be approached, in the absence of any change in tax legislation, depends on three main factors: First, it depends on the ratio between the income at which the highest marginal rate becomes effective and the per capita income of the country;[4] second, it depends on the height of the intermediate rates and the ratio of the level of income at which they become effective to the per capita income of the country;[5] third, it depends on the annual rate of increase in per capita national income *at current prices*. The second derivative of $dt/d\overline{Y}$ will probably be positive at first; then, it will reach a point of inflection at which the rate of change of $dt/d\overline{Y}$ will be greatest; after that it will become negative and the asymptotic movement of t toward its limit t_3 will begin. The exact point at which the point of inflection is reached, if that point does exist, will depend on the rate structure.

Keeping in mind that it has been assumed that the ratio of the base to national income, B/Y, is constant, we can express the elasticity of the average tax rate; $t = (T/B)$, with respect to changes in the base B as $E_t = (\Delta t/t_0)/(\Delta B/B_0)$. The value of E_t will be zero for the first case above (proportional tax without exemption, because in such a case $\Delta t = 0$) but will acquire a positive value in the other two cases. Of course, the more progressive the rate structure is, the higher will E_t be. For a progressive tax system, the value of E_t will change over time, inasmuch as it depends not only on the rate structure but also on the level of per capita income.

Expressing now E_T in terms of E_t and E_b one gets[6] $E_T = [1 + E_t (B_1/B_0)] E_b$, but if $E_t = 0$, then $E_T = E_b$ and if $E_b = 1$, given that $E_t = 0$, E_T will also have unitary value. Therefore, if the relation between the tax base and national income remains constant,[7] $E_b = 1$, in order to make $E_T = 1$, it is necessary that E_t be zero. How can this be accomplished automatically if the income tax is progressive? A proposal which would achieve this objective is described in the next chapter.

Measurement of the sensitivity of the personal income tax: synopsis of methods

The direct measurement of the sensitivity of the personal income tax – that is, the one that would be obtained from time-series observations of the relevant variables – has always presented considerable difficulties, or has at times not been possible at all, because changes in the legal structure of this tax have been too frequent to provide enough historical observations – related to the same legal structure – to allow the determination of statistically significant coefficients. This was particularly true in the United States in the period preceding 1954, when the rates were frequently changed; it has also been true for the post-1963 period, when several important changes have taken place involving rates, personal exemptions, deductions, and other features. The period between 1954 and 1963 was, on the other hand, a rather unusual one, inasmuch as it witnessed almost no significant statutory changes in the tax.

The studies that have measured this sensitivity from historical data have followed basically two alternative routes: Either they have confined their analysis to those particular periods when there were no changes in the statutory laws,[8] or they have attempted to take account of the effects of statutory changes on the relevant historical series – revenue from the tax, taxable income, and so forth – through direct adjustments of the series[9] or through the introduction of dummy variables in the regression equations.[10] It is obvious that as the frequency and importance of statutory changes increase, so do the problems and/or the difficulties of using historical data. It is for this reason that the alternative of using cross-section data is certainly "worthy of . . . consideration"[11] and at times may be the only one feasible.

There are now at least three alternative approaches to the measurement of the sensitivity of the income tax by way of cross-section data for a country such as the United States.

The first, which seems to have been originally developed by Mishan and Dicks-Mireaux,[12] and which was subsequently applied by Blackburn,[13] calculates, for a given year, the mean tax liability, t, and the mean adjusted gross income (AGI), y, for each of the income classes reported by the Internal Revenue Service's *Statistics of Income*.[14] Once these means have been derived, an equation of the type $t = ay^b$ is fitted to the data. This exponential equation can be transformed into a logarithmic one. Regressing the logarithms of mean tax liability against the logarithms of mean adjusted gross income – that is, $\log t = a + b \log y$ – one can find directly the elasticity of the tax with respect to AGI. This is simply the b in the equation.[15]

The basic assumption underlying this approach is that the relationship between the mean tax liability and mean AGI that prevails *for each income class* is essentially the same as the relationship that would prevail for the country as a whole at that level of AGI; any divergence is attributed to error terms with an expected mean value of zero.[16] Since factors such as particular incomes (e.g., capital gains), particular deductions (e.g., interest payments), and particular family situations (number of children, family status, etc.) are likely to differ substantially *and systematically* among income classes,[17] the results obtained from the application of this method are open to legitimate questions.

A second approach has recently been followed by Pechman,[18] who has estimated the sensitivity of the tax by the use of a somewhat more complex and much more resource-demanding method. This method calculates the relationships between tax and income from a random, stratified sample of actual federal individual income tax returns filed for a particular year – the Internal Revenue Service tax file. This tax file contains more than 90,000 returns, although Pechman's estimates are based on a subsample of 10,000 returns. This is surely a very interesting, but also very costly, method that is available only to a few people.

A third method that also relies on cross-section data is the one proposed here. Unlike Pechman's, this approach uses data easily available to everybody and has also the not unimportant advantage of being very simple. Furthermore, it gives results that are practically identical to those obtained by other researchers, who have used alternative and somewhat more complex approaches. This method is particularly useful when or/and where, because of frequent changes in income tax legislation, data on the relevant variables are not available for a relatively long period of time. However, it requires the availability of data collected on a regional basis. These data are available in many other countries.[19]

The method suggested has the advantage of providing not only estimates for the elasticity and flexibility of the income tax but also estimates of the elasticity of the tax base and elasticity of the rate structure. This latter distinction can be important for policy reasons.

To analyze statistically the relationship between changes in income tax revenues and changes in income, one must have either an actual or a simulated time series of the relevant variables. This series is generally available for only a few years and for modest changes in income, so the effect of large variations cannot be analyzed. This is the main reason why cross-section approaches are important. The method suggested here is based on the hypothesis that one can simulate a time series of the personal income tax yield, taxable income, and adjusted gross income from data for the same variables at the state level or provincial level.

In the United States, per capita adjusted gross income ranges widely between high-income and low-income states: rich states have per capita incomes at least three times larger than the poorest states. Since each state is subjected to the same prevailing federal income tax legislation, the substantial range of per capita income covered by the states provides a way to analyze the sensitivity of the individual income tax of the United States over an equivalent range. More specifically, it is assumed that the relationship between per capita income tax and per capita adjusted gross income for the fifty states, in a given year, is equivalent to that which one would obtain if he had available historical data for the United States for a period of fifty years, during which the nominal tax structure remained unchanged but per capita adjusted gross income increased, say, from $2,000 in the first year to $6,000 in the last, covering the income range of the fifty states. Thus, each state is assumed to be equivalent to an observation for the United States at a specific time and thus at a given level of income.

With increases in per capita income, the structure of the United States economy changes and these structural changes have independent effects on the relationship between tax and income. For example, if the level of per capita income for the United States increased from $2,000 to $6,000, one would normally expect some changes in its income distribution, its industrial composition of output, and so forth.

Thus, the validity of the method suggested would be enhanced if the structural changes which accompanied an increase in per capita income corresponded to the structural characteristics shown by each state at its present income level. Or, putting it differently, the method implies that a state with a given per capita income equal to, say, Y_0, should have, on the average, the same characteristics as the United States economy at an equivalent per capita income. It would take a great amount of statistical work to prove definitely the validity of this assumption. The empirical evidence that is available in published sources gives it at least a qualitative support. In fact, the changes in income distribution, and in the industrial composition of output, that have accompanied the growth of the United States economy are in the same direction as those noted when one moves from the poorer to the richer states.[20] In the last analysis, reasonable results can be assumed to be a proof that the assumption is not too farfetched.

Let: T_i stand for federal individual income tax revenue that the federal government has collected from each individual in a given state in a particular year and TI_i for per capita taxable income for the same state; Y_i for per capita adjusted gross income, and $i = 1 \ldots 50$ for the index of the state.

Using these data we can find estimates for the three relationships:

$$T_i = f_i (Y_i) \tag{1}$$
$$T_i = f_2 (TI_i) \tag{2}$$
$$TI_i = f_3 (Y_i) \tag{3}$$

Thus, the data make possible an estimate of the relationship between revenues *(T)* and adjusted gross income *(Y)*, that between tax revenue *(T)* and taxable income *(TI)*, and that between taxable income *(TI)* and adjusted gross income *(Y)*.

Empirical results for the United States

The results obtained when the method described in the previous section for measuring the sensitivity of the personal income tax with respect to changes in current income is applied to U.S. data are outlined in Tables 14 and 15. Table 13, on the other hand, gives some relevant statistical information on the U.S. income tax for the 1963–76 period. This table will be useful in the discussion of the results obtained. A look at Table 14 indicates that the elasticity of the tax with respect to adjusted gross income hovered around 1.4 for the 1963–71 period; rose sharply to about 1.5 in 1972; and, fell considerably in 1974, to rise again to close to 1.5 in 1976. These changes reflect to a large extent reforms on the structure of this tax which were introduced in this period. Table 15 provides an estimate of the built-in flexibility of this tax also with respect to adjusted gross income. As one would expect from the knowledge of the elasticity of this tax, the built-in flexibility is considerably higher than the average tax rate. Furthermore, this flexibility increases sharply in the last two years of the series. Discussion of built-in flexibility will be left until the next chapter. For the rest of this section we wish to analyze briefly the statistical result in Table 14 in relation to the historical series shown in Table 13.

The results in Table 14 appear to be somewhat inconsistent with those of Table 13. For example, the ratio of tax revenue to adjusted gross income in 1963 was about 13 percent and the elasticity was about 1.4. From the knowledge of the growth of that adjusted gross income at

Table 13. *United States: statistics on individual income tax, 1963–76*

Year	Billions of dollars				Ratio					
	T	TI	AGI	GNP	TI/AGI	TI/GNP	AGI/GNP	T/TI	T/AGI	T/GNP
1963	48.2	209.1	368.8	590.5	0.567	0.354	0.624	0.231	0.131	0.0816
1964	47.2	229.8	396.7	632.4	0.579	0.363	0.627	0.205	0.119	0.0746
1965	49.5	255.1	429.2	684.9	0.594	0.372	0.627	0.194	0.115	0.0723
1966	56.1	286.3	468.5	749.9	0.611	0.382	0.625	0.196	0.120	0.0748
1967	62.9	315.1	504.8	793.9	0.624	0.397	0.636	0.200	0.125	0.0793
1968	76.6	352.1	554.4	864.2	0.635	0.407	0.642	0.218	0.138	0.0886
1969	86.6	388.1	603.6	930.3	0.643	0.417	0.649	0.223	0.143	0.0930
1970	83.9	399.9	631.7	977.1	0.633	0.409	0.646	0.210	0.133	0.0859
1971	85.4	412.4	673.6	1,054.9	0.612	0.391	0.639	0.207	0.127	0.0810
1972	93.6	445.6	746.0	1,158.0	0.597	0.385	0.644	0.210	0.125	0.0808
1973	107.9	510.6	827.1	1,306.6	0.617	0.391	0.633	0.211	0.131	0.0826
1974	123.6	572.4	906.1	1,413.2	0.632	0.405	0.641	0.216	0.136	0.0875
1975	124.6	595.6	948.1	1,528.8	0.628	0.390	0.620	0.209	0.131	0.0815
1976	140.9	674.4	1,053.6	1,706.5	0.640	0.395	0.617	0.209	0.134	0.0830

Note: T = income tax; TI = taxable income; AGI = adjusted gross income; GNP = gross national product.
Sources: International Revenue Service, *Statistics of Income; Individual Income Tax Returns* (Washington, annual); Council of Economic Advisers, *Economic Report of the President* (Washington, February annual).

Table 14. *United States: elasticity of tax revenue with respect to adjusted gross income, 1963 and 1966–76*

1963	Ln T = -4.842 (0.255)	+ 1.368 (0.034)	Ln AGI	R^2 = 0.970
1966	Ln T = -5.397 (0.348)	+ 1.418 (0.045)	Ln AGI	R^2 = 0.952
1967	Ln T = -5.295 (0.279)	+ 1.407 (0.036)	Ln AGI	R^2 = 0.969
1968	Ln T = -5.343 (0.291)	+ 1.422 (0.037)	Ln AGI	R^2 = 0.968
1969	Ln T = -5.343 (0.303)	+ 1.425 (0.038)	Ln AGI	R^2 = 0.966
1970	Ln T = -5.095 (0.267)	+ 1.381 (0.034)	Ln AGI	R^2 = 0.972
1971	Ln T = -5.372 (0.305)	+ 1.408 (0.038)	Ln AGI	R^2 = 0.966
1972	Ln T = -6.000 (0.402)	+ 1.478 (0.049)	Ln AGI	R^2 = 0.947
1973	Ln T = -4.642 (0.336)	+ 1.318 (0.041)	Ln AGI	R^2 = 0.954
1974	Ln T = -4.225 (0.385)	+ 1.270 (0.046)	Ln AGI	R^2 = 0.938
1975	Ln T = -5.149 (0.336)	+ 1.375 (0.040)	Ln AGI	R^2 = 0.959
1976	Ln T = -5.962 (0.351)	+ 1.464 (0.042)	Ln AGI	R^2 = 0.961

current prices between 1963 and 1976, and of the elasticity in 1963, it can be calculated that the ratio of the tax to adjusted gross income should have grown to more than 16 percent by 1976, or by about 3 percentage points. However, that ratio remained almost unchanged over the period. This was due to various tax reductions introduced in the United States during 1963–76. Of these, major ones were the Revenue Act of 1964, the Tax Reform Act of 1969, the Revenue Act of 1971, and the Tax Reduction Act of 1975. These tax reductions succeeded in maintaining constant the average tax rate.[21] However, they could not reduce, at any one moment of time, either the size of the elasticity or the size of the built-in flexibility. From the point of view of stabilization, this dichotomy is important and will be discussed later.

Table 15. *United States: flexibility of tax revenue with respect to adjusted gross income, 1963 and 1969–76*

1963	$T = -88.7$	$+ 0.176$ AGI	$R^2 = 0.954$
	(10.18)	(0.006)	
1969	$T = -166.1$	$+ 0.200$ AGI	$R^2 = 0.960$
	(16.55)	(0.006)	
1970	$T = -144.4$	$+ 0.179$ AGI	$R^2 = 0.964$
	(14.54)	(0.005)	
1971	$T = -155.4$	$+ 0.175$ AGI	$R^2 = 0.962$
	(15.52)	(0.005)	
1972	$T = -193.7$	$+ 0.179$ AGI	$R^2 = 0.946$
	(20.70)	(0.006)	
1973	$T = -163.8$	$+ 0.177$ AGI	$R^2 = 0.951$
	(21.52)	(0.006)	
1974	$T = -160.4$	$+ 0.179$ AGI	$R^2 = 0.939$
	(26.77)	(0.006)	
1975	$T = -263.2$	$+ 0.196$ AGI	$R^2 = 0.963$
	(23.69)	(0.005)	
1976	$T = -357.6$	$+ 0.207$ AGI	$R^2 = 0.965$
	(27.15)	(0.006)	

Table 16. *All returns: wages and salaries as proportions of adjusted gross income by income bracket for the United States, 1972–76 (percentages)*

Size of AGI (U.S.$)	1972	1973	1974	1975	1976
Less than 5,000	87.97	89.50	92.12	94.76	94.83
5,000–10,000	88.38	86.95	85.86	84.72	83.72
10,000–15,000	91.44	90.83	90.86	89.77	88.17
15,000–20,000	90.13	90.49	90.76	90.67	90.20
20,000–25,000	85.38	86.63	87.69	89.56	90.01
25,000–30,000	77.77	80.14	82.59	86.14	86.37
30,000–50,000	62.57	64.16	69.03	73.96	77.48
50,000–100,000	47.20	49.04	52.53	55.63	57.86
100,000–200,000	36.90	38.59	42.55	47.96	50.62
200,000–500,000	23.97	25.56	29.37	33.98	37.92
500,000–1,000,000	14.34	13.64	17.85	19.79	22.62
More than 1,000,000	6.21	7.21	9.98	10.04	11.35
Total	83.46	83.08	83.41	83.88	83.27

Source: U.S. Internal Revenue Service, *Statistics of Income, Individual Income Tax Returns* (Washington, D.C.: annual).

There are two other points which should be made at this stage. First, tax revenue responds in the same way to changes in current income, regardless of whether they reflect real growth or are purely inflationary, as long as there is no substantial redistribution of taxable income. Over the 1963–76 period, inflationary changes were far more important than changes due to real growth. Nevertheless, real growth alone, in the absence of any tax reform, would have increased the average tax rate by about one percentage point. Inasmuch as the ratio of the tax to adjusted gross income remained, in fact, almost constant, this means that the discretionary tax reductions introduced by the legislature had the overall effect of neutralizing not only price changes but also real income changes. In the next chapter, we discuss an indexation mechanism which would automatically achieve the same result.

Secondly, in spite of very considerable inflation, especially in the second half of the period, there was less change in the composition of the adjusted gross income than one would have anticipated. The distortion in the tax bases that one would have anticipated from that inflation is not evident from the data. This may have been in part the result of the combination of inflation with a sharp recession that may have affected nonwage incomes more than wage incomes. Table 13 indicates that the share of adjusted gross income in gross national product hardly changed over the period. On the other hand, Table 16 indicates that the share of wages and salaries in adjusted gross income also remained almost constant between 1972 and 1976, which was the period when inflation was most acute. Strangely enough, Table 16 indicates that the only groups for which the share of wages and salaries in adjusted gross income fell were those with incomes between $5,000 and $15,000. If inflation alone had played the determining role one would have expected, that incomes other than wages and salaries would have become much more important, especially for higher income group.

9

Indexing the personal income tax for inflation and real growth

Real growth and fiscal drag

Given the statutory structure of the personal income tax of a country, the average tax rate (i.e., the ratio of total income tax revenue to gross income) will increase whenever the country's income at current prices rises. It will not matter whether the increase in income is due to price changes, to real growth, or to both. The percentage increase in the average tax rate over a given period of time will depend on the rate of growth of current income and on the elasticity of the tax. The absolute increase, however, will depend also on the tax rate itself. The higher the tax rate at a given moment, the greater the absolute increase in the rate brought about by a given percentage change in income (given the elasticity).

The automatic increase in revenue brought about by increases in current income is often referred to as "fiscal drag" or "fiscal dividend." The fiscal drag can be labeled an inflationary (or monetary) fiscal drag or a real fiscal drag, depending on whether it is brought about by income changes that reflect inflation or real growth. Indexation for price changes, as discussed in Chapters 2 and 3, will remove the inflationary fiscal drag but not the real fiscal drag. Therefore, if real growth is fast, the elasticity of the tax is high, and the average tax rate is substantial, the absolute increase in the tax rate brought about by real fiscal drag can be significant.[1]

The increase in tax revenue brought about by real fiscal drag may or may not be welcome. Countries that would find it difficult, for political or administrative reasons, to raise income tax revenue, but that would like to do so, might welcome such a characteristic of the tax.[2] On the other hand, there are various reasons why such an autonomous increase in the average tax rate might not be desirable.

The first of these reasons, which a few years ago received a lot of attention in the United States, is perhaps not as important during these inflationary times. However, since times may change, it may still be worthwhile to discuss it. It is related to the concept of "full employ-ment budget surplus."[3] This surplus purports to analyze the "fiscal drag" which may result from the change in gross national saving rela-tive to the change in gross national product, when the latter is moving toward its full employment level. This concept has been extensively discussed in the literature, so an analysis of it is not necessary here. It is sufficient to point out that whenever in the process of growth in general, or in the upswing of a business cycle, tax revenue exceeds government expenditure, the public sector will, in fact, be generating saving which may slow down the growth process, or the upswing, un-less private demand is high enough to compensate for it. However, in order to evaluate the degree to which fiscal policy, per se, helps or hinders the movement toward full employment, it is necessary to evaluate the budget surplus or deficit that would occur at a full-employment level of income.

Whenever an economy is subjected to substantial and persistent economic fluctuations, it is likely that the change in public expenditure will come to be related to the long-run growth of GNP; if the elasticity of government expenditure with respect to GNP were unity, GNP would be growing faster than public expenditure in the upswing of a cycle. Because, owing to its elasticity, tax revenue will be increasing faster than GNP, the possibility that a fiscal drag will develop is clearly there.

The excess of the increase in public revenue over the increase in public expenditure is not exclusively a function of the progressivity of the personal income tax. In theory, at least, such an excess could materialize even if this tax were regressive, or more accurately, if it had an elasticity of less than unity with respect to gross national prod-uct. This could occur if the elasticity of government expenditure, with respect to GNP, were smaller than the elasticity of tax revenue, also with respect to GNP. However, if this tax is income elastic and if the upswing is prolonged, the ratio of the tax yield to both personal income and GNP is likely to increase. This will lead to the possibility that the full-employment budget will show a surplus which would increase the difficulty of attaining full employment. As Weckstein put it: "If the proportion of GNP taxed away is correct at the time of passage of the tax law, it is not likely to be correct after a few years have passed."[4]

The second reason why many countries may not want, or perhaps should not want, an automatic increase in the average personal income tax rate has to do with the meaning, or the objective, of tax legislation. Let us consider an historical example from the United States. In 1954, new and comprehensive income tax legislation was enacted. That legislation supposedly reflected the attitude of Congress, which, in a democratic society, is supposed to reflect that of the citizenry, as to the desirable distribution of the income tax burden among families, as well as to the desirable average tax burden. It seems reasonable to assume that Congress expected such a distribution of the tax burden, as well as such an average tax burden, to remain unchanged until a new structural reform was felt to be necessary because (1) new social needs required a greater, or smaller, transfer of income from the private to the public sector, (2) the distribution of the burden (the progressivity of the tax) no longer reflected the attitude of the citizens toward equity, (3) because of a combination of (1) and (2), or (4) for short-run, or stabilization, reasons. It would be absurd to assume that legislators, at the time of the enactment of the new legislation, intentionally legislated these future changes in the level and in the distribution of the tax burden, as these future changes could not have been foreseen at the time.

Congress's expectations were not fulfilled. The revenue from the personal income tax rose much faster than personal income. As a percentage of personal income it increased from 9.27 in 1955 to 10.25 in 1963. This increase would have been much greater if, over the period, the country had had a higher rate of growth, or a higher rate of inflation, or if full employment had prevailed in 1963 as it did in 1955.[5] Furthermore, and perhaps more important, there was a substantial and unintended or, at least in a true sense, unlegislated redistribution of the tax burden among the taxpayers.[6] (See Appendix.) Furthermore, the redistributional impact was not exactly in what one could assume to be a desirable direction. Large families were, for the most part, affected more than small families, due to the decreasing importance of the unchanged (in nominal terms) personal exemptions. In other words, the effect in 1963 of the 1954 legislation was quite different from that intended by Congress when the law was enacted. If one should consider the 1965–69 period, characterized by relatively minor legislative changes and by a faster rate of inflation, the conclusions would be similar.

This propensity on the part of personal income tax revenue to increase faster over time, relative to personal income or GNP, was first felt in a particularly strong fashion by two countries that experienced unusually high rates of growth: Japan and West Germany. For both of these countries, the major factor in the increase in income tax revenue was real growth rather than inflation. The Japanese reaction to these automatic and unlegislated tax increases was an annual change in nominal tax rates and/or schedules. This "tax-cut policy" resulted in very substantial yearly reductions in personal income taxes from what they would have been in the absence of these changes. These cuts resulted from yearly increases in the size of the exemptions and deductions and some decreases in the rate structure.[7]

The West German reaction was, at least until 1958, equally dynamic and resulted also in almost yearly reductions in rates and increases in the size of the exemptions.[8] These changes succeeded in keeping in abeyance the increase in the average tax rate. For a few years after 1958, however, a slowdown in that fiscal dynamism resulted in a soaring of the average tax rate.[9]

Annual, or at least frequent, discretionary changes in tax laws can prevent the average tax rate from increasing, but they are time consuming and tedious and one would hope that the legislators would occupy themselves with more important matters.[10] However, such changes are necessary as long as the elasticity of the tax system with respect to nominal income is greater than one, and as long as the resulting increase in the tax rate is not desired. In the case of the personal income tax, the elasticity which is generally much higher than one is to a large extent a direct consequence of the tax progressivity. As was shown in the section on determinants of elasticity in Chapter 8, a strictly proportional personal income tax (i.e., proportional rate without a zero-tax-rate bracket), associated with a substantially constant relation of the base of the income tax to GNP, would be expected to have, in the absence of substantial redistribution of income, a long-run elasticity of close to one. But the progressivity of the personal income tax is an important policy instrument that most countries would not wish to give up just to reduce the elasticity to unity. Besides, given the same tax yield, a progressive income tax will have a greater built-in flexibility (defined as $\Delta T/\Delta GNP$) than a strictly proportional income tax. And such a greater flexibility might still be considered by some governments a desirable feature for reducing the intensity of recessions, in spite of recent doubts raised about it.[11]

In this chapter, we wish to raise the issue of whether it would be possible to have a progressive personal income tax that (1) maintained, with the passing of time, and in the absence of a change in income distribution, the redistributive characteristics intended at the time of legislation; (2) provided some built-in flexibility against downturns in the business cycle; but, at the same time, (3) did not contribute to an undue increase in the full employment surplus; and (4) achieved these objectives automatically, that is, without the discretion of the authority. Given the way in which tax legislation is now presented in most countries, some of the above objectives could be satisfied only by means of frequent changes in tax legislation, with all the disadvantages that this course of action entails.

The proposal

The situation can be remedied by a simple change in tax legislation. Assume that the legislators have agreed, at a given moment of time, on the share of GNP that would be desirable to collect by means of the personal income tax. Assume further that they have agreed on the way in which the burden of the tax should be distributed among the income groups: in other words, they have agreed on the size of the exemption as well as on the width of each of the income brackets to which a certain tax rate applies. Assume further that they do not want the progressivity of the tax to change over time but want it to remain unchanged until a further "structural" change is desired. This implies that income groups receiving a given proportion of total personal income will continue paying the same proportion of total tax receipts regardless of what happens to their absolute income.[12]

Given the above conditions, a simple conversion will achieve the purpose. The conversion will consist in relating the exemption and the income brackets to which the marginal tax rates apply to the per capita income of the country for a given year that stands in a well-defined relation to the taxable year. The most convenient "reference year" might be the latest one for which final official estimates of per capita national income (or GNP) are available.

Let us assume that it has been decided to use as a reference the per capita income of the year which precedes the legislation. Then, if in such a year per capita income were $\bar{Y} = \$3,000$, and if the legislated personal exemption were, say, $r_0 = \$600$, a simple conversion would make the exemption $r_0 = (1/5)\bar{Y}$; then, when per capita income increased, the size of the exemption could be made to increase automatically with it. In other words, the $\bar{Y}$ in consideration would always be that of the year which precedes the payment of the tax (assuming that it is already available, or that of the year before), and the exemption would always be equal to the same *proportion* of that income.

Equally, if the width of the first bracket were, say, \$2,000, and the tax rate on that income bracket were 20 percent, then the conversion would give $0.20 [(2/3)\bar{Y}]$, in which the 2/3 refers to the ratio of the income bracket's width in the reference year to the average income of that same year (\$3,000). With the passing of time, replacing $\bar{Y}$ with the relevant and presumably growing income would assure that the ratio of the first income bracket's width to per capita income remained the same. Thus, if $\bar{Y}$ should become \$6,000, the first bracket would become $^2/_3 \times \$6,000$, that is, equal to $\$4,000$; the marginal tax rate of 0.20 would apply to this figure of $\$4,000$.

Generalizing, assume that the conversion for the base year (in our case the year before the one in which the legislation was enacted) gave the following simplified progression:

Size of exemption $\qquad r_0 = \frac{1}{5}\overline{Y}_1$

Size of first backet $\qquad r_1 = (1\ \overline{Y}_1)$

Size of second bracket $\quad r_2 = (3\ \overline{Y}_1 - 1\ \overline{Y}_1)$

Size of third bracket $\qquad r_3 = (5\ \overline{Y}_1 - 3\ \overline{Y}_1)$

Size of fourth bracket $\quad r_4 = (10\ \overline{Y}_1 - 5\ \overline{Y}_1)$

Size of fifth bracket $\qquad r_5 = (20\ \overline{Y}_1 - 10\ \overline{Y}_1)$

Size of sixth bracket $\qquad r_6 = (\text{over}\ 20\ \overline{Y}_1)$

Assume that the marginal tax rates that apply to the income tax brackets were: 0 for the exemption, a_1 for r_1, a_2 for r_2, and so on. Then replacing the first-year value of $\overline{Y}$ with the actual value of $\overline{Y}$ in each successive year would give us the width of the various income brackets, r_0, r_1, r_2, . . . to which the marginal tax rates, $0, a_1, a_2, \ldots, a_n$ are to be applied. In other words, each value of $\overline{Y}$ would generate a set of values for the r_s, so that one could say that: $r_i = f(\overline{Y})$.

A simpler way of expressing the relation is by saying that in any year t the size of each r will be equal to the corresponding one in the base year times the ratio $\overline{Y}_t/\overline{Y}_1$.

In this way the exemption as well as the size of the various income brackets to which the marginal rates apply would automatically be changed to take care of the growth (real or purely nominal) in the income of the country. Once agreed about which $\overline{Y}$ to take, the figure for it could be published by the appropriate agency of the country and would be used by the tax authorities for preparing tax tables.[13]

In Figure 2, if one should put on the horizontal axis the ratio of the actual income of people to the per capita income of the same year, and on the vertical axis the frequency of those incomes, the distribution obtained remains the same over time as long as there is no redistribution of income. In other words, the curve does not shift to the right with time as it would if the incomes of people were not weighted by per capita income.[14]

With the tax system now prevailing in most countries, the income brackets to which the exemption and the various rates apply remain the

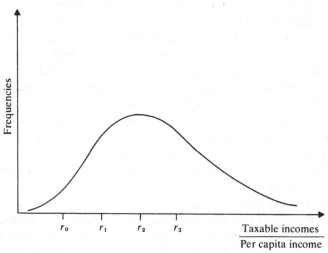

Figure 2

same over time while the whole curve shifts to the right; consequently, the proportion of total income which is taxed by the higher marginal tax rates increases. But if the incomes of people, as well as the income brackets to which the tax rates apply, were weighted by the per capita income of the year, then the relation between the incomes of the individuals and the income tax brackets would remain the same. Or, looking at the curve, the area under the curve between, say, r_1 and r_2, would remain the same even when the per capita income increased.

Characteristics of proposal

What would be some of the characteristics of such a system?

1. In the first place, it would not require continuous legislative changes as is necessary with the present system in growing countries or in those experiencing inflation. Therefore, it would permit an automatic adjustment in the personal income tax.

2. It would still help to dampen fluctuations without dampening growth. However, if in any year $\bar{Y}$ should actually decrease, the offsetting effect on the drop of income would be greater than at present, since the $\bar{Y}$ which would be used for calculating the size of the exemption and of the width of the income tax brackets would be that of the previous year. However, the use of the recession $\bar{Y}$, by making smaller the size of the exemption and income brackets, would raise the revenues from the tax in the upswings and thus might make that upswing more difficult. A simple solution to this problem would be, in such a

case, to ignore the recession $\bar{Y}$. In other words, whenever $\bar{Y}_t < \bar{Y}_{t-1}$, it should be ignored, and the $\bar{Y}$ of the previous year considered.

3. It would always reflect the legislative branch's attitude toward the "proper" tax progressivity, as expressed by the original tax law.

4. It would limit the need for tax reforms to purely structural changes as, for example, desired increases or reductions of the level of taxation or changes in the progressivity of the personal income tax.

5. If the income distribution that prevails in a country does not change to any important extent, the revenues from the tax as a percentage of GNP would remain basically the same.

6. It would prevent a purely inflationary increase in income from becoming a net burden.

Before closing this section, it might be mentioned that the indexation for price change and real growth can be done either by using a measure of per capita nominal income or, alternatively, some measure of per capita real earnings. Of the two countries that today follow an indexation scheme somehow related to that suggested in this chapter, Iceland uses per capita nominal income, while Denmark uses an index for hourly earnings of industrial workers. The alternative of using average earnings has been discussed in both the Meade report and the Mathews report.[15] The Meade report has favored average earnings, pointing out that "if unemployment rises and total output is reduced, the value of output per head of the population will fall even if the value of output per person employed remains unchanged."[16] Therefore, to avoid a perverse destabilizing effect, an index of average earnings of persons in employment is preferable. The major problem with using an index of average earnings is that these earnings can be totally out of line with what is happening throughout the economy. For example, in Italy in recent years, a peculiar indexation mechanism for wages has led to sharply increasing real wages even when the economy was in recession. Furthermore, since the measure of per capita income used is always a lagged one, and a fall in income can be ignored as suggested above, the Meade report criticism of per capita income is not damaging.

Concluding remarks

The proposal for a superindexation scheme contained in this chapter was first made in 1966 at a time when indexing was not a popular subject.[17] In recent years, because of the persistence of inflationary pressures, indexing has become a much discussed subject. However, most observers still believe that only inflation creates distortions in the personal income tax. This, however, as shown in this chapter, is not correct. But an important distinction does exist between the effects of inflation and those of growth. Whereas inflation creates distortions in the rate structure *as well as in the bases,* real economic growth creates distortions only with respect to the former. The problems of capital incomes do not exist when inflation is absent. Thus, the equity issues are less serious. The stability issues, however, are still quite serious. As Thomas F. Dernburg has recently argued:

> A personal income tax that is compatible with a productivity-based (fixed shares) incomes policy implies that incremental aggregate income, whether real or nominal, should be taxed at the same rate as the average rate on preceding income. Indexing [for inflation alone] only ensures that incremental nominal income due to price inflation is taxed at the previous average income; it does not, however, eliminate the potentially disruptive effect on the incomes agreement of the high marginal rates on real incomes.[18]

It was, in fact, this kind of argument that, in 1974, induced Danish policymakers to shift from indexation based on price changes alone to one based on productivity changes. The former type of adjustment had not prevented sharp increases in tax burdens on the middle-income groups. Dernburg goes on to support the superindexation scheme proposed in this chapter. He argues that such a scheme would help to stabilize the economy since it "keeps the aggregate tax rate constant, and fixes the government's share of the national income and it, therefore, entirely offsets fiscal drag."[19]

Appendix: effect of growth and inflation on incidence of U.S. income tax, 1954–63

John D. Dittrick[20] has calculated how typical U.S. taxpayers would have been affected if, over relevant periods, the U.S. individual income tax had been indexed according to the increase in nominal per capita income as proposed in this chapter. Over the 1954–63 period, which is the period used as an example in this chapter, nominal per capita income increased by 37 percent. Therefore, Dittrick increased personal exemptions and brackets limits by this percentage and thus derived a new tax table.[21] He then used this tax table to calculate the 1963 tax payments related to specific levels of incomes and family situations. Finally, he compared the tax payments so obtained with the ones calculated on the basis of the actual tax table that was applied in that year, which was – it will be recalled – that enacted by the 1954 law. The results are shown in Table 17. In practically all cases, the tax pay-

Table 17. *Differences in average and effective tax rates, 1963*

Income (U.S.$)	Average tax rates[a] for exemptions:			Effective tax rates[b] for exemptions:		
	2	4	6	2	4	6
4,000	0.0	0.0	0.0	− 10.8	− 40.6	0.0
6,000	0.0	0.0	0.0	− 6.3	− 16.1	− 40.7
10,000	− 1.1	− 1.6	− 2.5	− 2.6	− 7.1	− 13.5
14,000	− 3.2	− 4.2	− 3.9	− 4.2	− 7.5	− 10.1
20,000	− 5.7	− 5.5	− 6.0	− 6.2	− 7.6	− 9.7
30,000	− 8.0	− 8.1	− 8.2	− 8.4	− 9.3	− 10.3
40,000	− 8.9	− 9.1	− 9.4	− 9.2	− 10.0	− 11.0
100,000	− 6.7	− 6.8	− 7.0	− 6.8	− 7.2	− 7.6

[a] Tax liability divided by taxable income.
[b] Tax liability divided by gross income.

ments would have been somewhat lower with the indexed system. Clearly large families would have benefited much more than small ones. And equally clearly for given "relative" income levels, the tax burdens in 1963 were very different from those enacted in 1954. It would be hard to maintain that the changes were anticipated by the legislators that in 1954 enacted the new tax law.

10

Inflation, income taxes, and the equilibrium rate of interest: theory

The inflationary conditions that have prevailed in the industrialized countries in recent years have made investigators aware of the likely relationship between the rate of inflation and the nominal rate of interest. Of the various theories that may bear on this relationship, Fisher's[1] is the one that has attracted most attention. The Fisherian relationship has been analyzed in several recent studies, some of which have subjected it to empirical tests.[2]

In most of these studies, Fisher's theory has been taken at its face value: In testing its empirical validity, researchers have generally ignored important economic and institutional changes since Fisher first proposed his theory. In particular, up to 1975, no attention had been paid to the existence and importance of income taxes, and to the effects that these may have on Fisher's theoretical conclusions, which were formulated and proposed in the United States at a time when the country did not have an income tax.[3]

In a discussion of the interrelationship between income taxes and interest rates under inflationary conditions, one can either pursue an ex post analysis emphasizing the inequities and/or distortions associated with taxing the whole nominal income from interest, instead of its real component; or pursue an ex ante, or equilibrium, analysis by discussing the possibility that the existence of income taxes should lead, in the absence of fiscal illusion, to adjustments in the nominal rate of interest. In the ex post analysis, which must inevitably be related to the particular experience of a country, it is assumed that the nominal rate of interest is not affected by income taxes. In other words, it is assumed that individuals suffer from fiscal illusions. As we shall see in this chapter, an equilibrium rate of interest requires the absence of fiscal illusions. However, interest rates are rarely in equilibrium, so that, in the last analysis, the existence or not of fiscal illusions must be established by empirical analysis.

This chapter deals with the role of personal income taxes in the determination of (equilibrium) nominal rates of interest. It is thus a theoretical chapter. The next chapter will test the theory using data from the United States.

Review of Fisher's theory

In the absence of imperfections in the capital market, the interplay of market forces, according to the now-famous theory advanced at the end of the last century by Irving Fisher, would bring about an equilibrium rate of interest that could be called a real rate. At this equilibrium rate, individuals would lend and borrow; the marginal rate of substitution (between present and future consumption) would equate the marginal rate of transformation (the slope of the production possibility curve); and both of these would equate the rate of interest. We would thus get a Pareto optimum characterized by the following:

$$MRS = MRT = 1 + r$$

For an individual, this equilibrium can easily be shown graphically for a two-period model (see Figure 3). AB represents the production possibility curve,[4] MN is the market line whose slope (equal to ON/OM) is determined by the rate of interest and I_0 is the indifference curve reflecting the individual's preference between present and future consumption. In equilibrium, the production possibility curve AB is tangent to the market line MN at point D, and the indifference curve I_0 is tangent to the market line MN at point E. At point D, $MRT = 1 + r$;

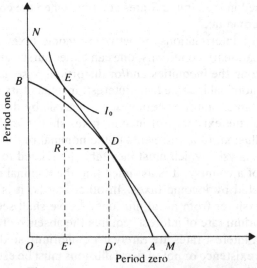

Figure 3

at point E, $MRS = 1 + r$. Since r is the same at both points we get the optimal condition $MRS = MRT = 1 + r$.

The individual that started with resources OA, would invest directly an amount $D'A$ from which he would get back $D'D$, and would lend an amount $E'D'$ from which, one period later, he would get $RD (1 + r) = ER$. In this case, the economic unit (the individual) would be a net lender. Of course, the equilibrium point E could be between D and M, in which case the individual would be a net borrower. In an economy with thousands, or millions, of economic units, there would be both net borrowers and net lenders. According to Fisher, the equilibrium real rate of interest would be the one that would clear the capital market. Through its borrowing or lending, each economic unit would contribute marginally to the determination of the equilibrium rate of interest; because of its assumed small size (in relation to the market), however, the unit would take the market rate of interest as a datum.

In the previous discussion, in which no mention was made of price changes (the implicit assumption being actual and expected price stability), real and nominal rates of interest are the same. Equally important for our later discussion is the fact that no mention was made of income taxes, which were simply assumed not to exist. Let us now introduce inflationary expectations, while still leaving income taxes out of the picture.

As argued by Fisher, and by many of his followers, if the rate of inflation is fully anticipated and stable (i.e., if the future price level is known) the equilibrium nominal rate of interest can be expected to be higher than the real rate. In the absence of money illusions, this rate can be expected to approximate the sum of the real rate and the anticipated price change. Thus, if r is the real rate of interest and Π is the anticipated rate of inflation, the nominal rate r^m would be

$$1 + r^m = (1 + r)(1 + \Pi) \tag{1}$$
$$r^m = r + \Pi + \Pi r \tag{2}$$

As the term Πr is normally ignored unless the rate of inflation is high,[5] it is assumed that

$$r^m = r + \Pi \tag{3}$$

This result is derived from the hypothesis that the real side of the economy is not affected by money; that implies the absence of money illusions, so that, the real rate of interest is assumed not to be affected. Although the mechanics by which the rate of interest changes from r to r^m is not generally described, conceivably this would be brought about by upward shifts – reflecting the expected price changes – of the production possibility curve and of the indifference curves.[6] In Figure 4, at

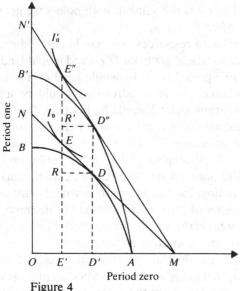

Figure 4

the equilibrium point E'' in the new inflationary situation our individual still consumes the same amount as in the noninflationary case, or OE'. Thus E'' is exactly to the north of E. He still invests directly $D'A$ and lends $D'E'$, for which activities he expects to receive, one period later, $D'D''$ and $R'E''$, respectively. The market line MN, with a slope equal to $ON/OM = 1 + r$, becomes MN', its slope equal to $ON'/OM = 1 + r + \Pi$. At this new rate of interest, it will still be true for the individual that $MRT^m = MRS^m = 1 + r^m$ where each of these incorporates the inflationary change. Once again there will be lenders and borrowers but – ignoring terms and risk structure and assuming a perfect market – they will all face the same market rate r^m. It follows that, when this rate has been established, a Pareto optimum would again be achieved, whereby the marginal rates of transformation and substitution and the rate of interest would be equal among themselves and for all economic agents.[7]

Fisher's theory with income taxes

Fisher's theory of the nominal rate of interest under inflationary situations ignored the existence of income taxes, and until recently, all those that elaborated on it, or restated it, did the same.[8] Consequently, those that have accepted this approach, have continued to assume that a stable rate of inflation would bring about an equivalent change in the nominal rate of interest, so that the real rate and the allocation of resources would not be affected.

Our objective here is to show that when income taxes are taken into account, as they should be in today's world, a nominal rate equal to the real rate plus the expected rate of inflation (i.e., the Fisherian rate) would not leave unchanged the real rate that is relevant to the lenders and would thus not be an equilibrium rate. Furthermore, the allocation of resources would, in most cases, be significantly affected. We shall argue that a higher-than-Fisherian rate would be required to leave the real rate unchanged, but that even this higher rate would not preclude various distortions in the market.

Rate effects

Let us assume that, in accordance with Fisher's theory, inflation raises the nominal rate of interest by an amount equal to the anticipated rate of price change. Let us assume that a lender loans an amount A and that income taxes are in existence, so that the interest received is taxed at a rate t, which for the time being we assume to be proportional.

In the absence of inflation, the base for the imposition of the tax would be $A(1 + r) - A$, and the tax payment would be

$$[A(1 + r) - A] \, t = (Ar)t \tag{4}$$

Since in this situation Ar would always be a *real* income, the only effect of the tax would be to reduce the real rate of interest for the individual from r to $r \, (1 - t)$, but it could never make it negative unless the tax rate t were more than 100 percent.

When inflation is present, however, the base for the tax would become $A(1 + r + \Pi) - A$, and the tax payment would thus be

$$[A(1 + r + \Pi) - A] \, t = (Ar)t + (A\Pi)t \tag{5}$$

Thus, if we assume that the actual price change is equal to the anticipated price change, the tax would levy a real income *(Ar)* and an illusory income $(A\Pi)$, which is simply a compensation for the inflationary erosion of the principal.[9] The higher the rate of inflation, Π, and the tax rate, t, the greater will be the tax on illusory income $(A\Pi)t$.[10] It will be relatively easy for $(A\Pi)t$ to exceed $Ar(1 - t)$, which is the net-of-tax real interest income. When this happens, the real rate of interest received by the lender becomes negative, and the tax on income becomes also a tax on capital. Hence, the greater the rate at which $(A\Pi)t > Ar(1 - t)$, the greater will be the negative real rate of interest that the lender receives.

It follows that, unless tax laws are rewritten to specifically exempt the illusory component of interest income $(A\Pi)$ from the base of the

Table 18. *Nominal rates of interest required to keep constant the net-of-tax real rate for a taxpayer with a 50 percent marginal tax rate (in percentages)*

Expected inflation (Π)	Gross-of-tax real rate of interest (r)	Fisher's nominal rate ($r^m = \Pi + r$)	Required rate (r^*)	Effective tax rate on real interest income[a] (z)
0	5	5	5	50
5	5	10	15	100
10	5	15	25	150
15	5	20	35	200
20	5	25	45	250
30	5	35	65	350

[a] This is the effective tax rate that results when Fisher's nominal rate is established and the whole interest income is taxes at 50 percent.

tax, the Fisherian solution (i.e., that $r^m = r + \Pi$) cannot be a theoretically valid or equilibrium one. Under the circumstances outlined above, one would expect that the rate required to compensate the lender for inflation as well as for the consequent implicit taxation of his capital, a rate that we shall call the *required rate,* would have to be somewhat higher than the Fisherian rate. Can anything be said about this rate?

Let us consider, first, a lender who in the absence of inflation would have been taxed at a proportional rate t so that his net-of-tax real rate of interest would be $r(1 - t)$. Let us also assume that if faced with an expected rate of inflation Π, the individual expects to receive a rate of interest that leaves him with the same net-of-tax real rate as he would have in the absence of inflation. In this situation the required rate, r^*, would be

$$r^* = r + \frac{\Pi}{1 - t} \tag{6}$$

If we assume that the tax rate t is 50 percent, and that the real rate of interest r is 5 percent, Table 18 shows what the required rates would be under alternative values for the rate of inflation. It also demonstrates that the differences between Fisher's nominal rates and the required rates may be quite substantial. Thus, in the absence of corrections in the income tax laws, the Fisherian nominal rate of interest r^m will no longer be sufficient to compensate the investor for the full impact of inflation. Only the required rate shown in the fourth column will leave the lender with a constant expected net-of-tax real rate of interest.[11] It should be borne in mind that although the required rates shown in

Table 18 refer to one individual, a market rate cannot make special adjustments for each individual.

Let us now turn our attention to the required rate that would apply for the whole group of lenders. If income taxes were proportional, the required rates for all lenders combined could also be obtained from Equation 6. In other words, the solution obtained for one individual would also be valid for the whole group. However, since income taxes are almost always progressive, so that different lenders, because of different levels of income, face different tax rates, it is no easy matter to estimate the aggregate required rate for millions of lenders in the economy. In the empirical tests in Chapter 11 the aggregate required rate, R^*, will be approximated by:

$$R^* = r + \frac{\Pi}{1 - T} \tag{7}$$

where r and Π have the same meanings as in Equation 6 but T is a weighted average tax rate on interest income obtained in the following way. Let Y indicate total interest income, for a given year, for all income classes combined, and yi the amount of interest income for income class i. Let $Zi = yi/Y$ be the proportion of total interest income contained in the i class, and let ti be the marginal tax rate which applies to that income class.[12] Then

$$T = \sum_{i=1}^{n} Ziti \tag{8}$$

It should be clear that the required rate so obtained would be just an approximation to the actual one, but it could be useful for empirical testing.

Welfare effects

The previous discussion has shown or implied the following points:

1. If there are no income taxes and prices are stable, the equilibrium interest rate that results from the Fisherian analysis will be associated with a Pareto optimum characterized by the condition that $MRS = MRT = 1 + r$; in this case the r (as well as the MRS and MRT) will be the same for every economic unit.

2. If prices are not stable but are expected to rise at rate Π for each time period, and if there are no income taxes, the prevailing (nominal) rate of interest would still be the same for all economic units, so that, in equilibrium, we shall still get equality between the rate of interest and the marginal rates of substitution and transformation. A Pareto optimum would still result; in this case, the nominal rate of interest r^m would exceed the real rate by the expected rate of inflation, and would

thus provide the lender with a real return equal to the real rate. Even in this case, however, one might argue that the adjustment in the nominal rate would reflect the *average* expected rate of inflation. Presumably, the inflationary expectations of different individuals are likely to differ from that average, depending on their psychological makeup (some will be pessimists, some optimists), on their confidence in the ability of the government to control inflation, or simply on the differential impact of past and present inflation on the particular basket of goods they have been buying.[13] Therefore, the nominal rate that becomes established will appear too high to some and too low to others, inasmuch as the real rate would have changed for many individuals. The resulting equilibrium is unlikely to be the same as the one that would have prevailed in the absence of inflation.

3. If we assume that there are income taxes, then the after-tax real rate, as shown above, could easily become negative and would affect the rate of saving as well as the choice between lending and holding commodities. It would, however, still be the same for all lenders as long as the income taxes are levied with proportional rates; therefore, although less saving and lending might conceivably be forthcoming, the *MRT*s and the *MRS*s for all the economic agents would be equated among themselves and with the monetary rate. It is to be expected that, in this case, the problem of different inflationary expectations among individuals might also disturb the equilibrium.

Let us now assume that, as happens in reality, taxes are not proportional but progressive, and that they do not discriminate between the real and the illusory components of interest income. In this case, the real after-tax interest rate would depend not only on the rate of inflation but also on the income level of the individuals – it would, in other words, differ among the economic agents. This implies that no rate of interest, even if adjusted for price changes or for the average tax rate, could bring about a collective equality between the marginal rates of substitution and transformation and the rate of interest. The reason for this is that while the nominal (market) rate of interest will be the same for everyone, the net-of-tax real rate for each individual will depend on the level of income.[14] Thus, the more progressive the income tax, and the more uneven the distribution of income, the greater will be the range of net-of-tax real rates of interest faced by the individuals. Because each individual will adjust his own consumption and his own real investment to the rate that is relevant to him, and since there is a range of these rates, it is evident that we cannot any longer achieve the collective equality between $1 + r$, *MRS* and *MRT*. The lack of this equality implies that distortions have now been introduced into the economy and that they are not eliminated by the adjustment in the nominal rate. No required rate is now capable of bringing about the allocation of resources that would have prevailed in the absence of income taxes. The resulting distortions may consequently bring about welfare losses that do not exist in the traditional Fisherian model.

Additional considerations

To avoid misunderstandings, it is perhaps necessary to emphasize that the theory formulated in this section is a theory of the rate of interest required to leave the individual taxpayer who lends money in the same situation as he would have been in the absence of inflation. It is *not* a theory of a long-run equilibrium rate of interest under inflationary conditions. The determination of such an equilibrium rate would require that several factors we have not considered be taken into consideration. The most important among these factors are:

Portfolio effect. Inflation, if anticipated, increases the nominal rate of interest, thus raising the opportunity cost of holding money balances. If the demand for money is interest elastic, real money balances will be reduced; therefore, a larger share of savings will be channeled into capital accumulation, leading to an increase in aggregate capital stock.[15] As a consequence of this increase, the marginal product of capital will fall. In equilibrium, the marginal product of capital must be equal to the real rate of interest; thus, the latter will also fall.

Wealth effect. Inflation reduces the real value of money balances, thus causing a fall in total real private wealth. Such a fall may stimulate more saving and thus lead to a decline in the real rate of interest.[16]

Effect on real tax revenue. As we saw in Chapter 7, inflation will almost always affect real tax revenue because of the progressivity of taxes and the collection lag. This effect may be positive or negative. Consequently, the size of the public sector deficit, which has to be financed through borrowing or money creation, will be affected.[17]

Effect of the change in the real rate of interest on supply of saving as well as on the demand for saving. The relationship between the supply of saving and the households' real disposable income may be affected by the real net return to savers as suggested in a recent study.[18] And, of course, investment is affected by the cost of capital. To the extent that inflation changes the real rate of interest, both saving and investment will be directly affected.

The relationship between the personal income tax rate and the corporate income tax rate will also be important. If the corporate rate exceeds the personal rate, and if corporations finance their investments through borrowing, then inflation will lead to an increase in the net real rate of interest received by households.[19]

Some, but not all, of these factors have been considered in a theoretical model developed by Feldstein.[20] That model assumes that the exogenous variables are: the rate of population growth, the personal income tax rate on interest income, the tax rate on the incomes of enterprises, and the rate of growth of money. Given these exogenous variables and a production function, an investment function, a liquidity preference function, and a saving function, Feldstein is able to determine the *theoretical* value of the equilibrium rate of interest. Unfortunately, his theoretical model is not amenable to an empirical test. However, it does indicate that, in the United States, where the rate for the corporate income tax (at about 50 percent) is likely to exceed the rates which apply to most of the interest income received by households, the equilibrium rate should, *ceteris paribus,* exceed our required rate.

As it is impossible to test whether, in an inflationary situation with income taxes, the rate of interest approaches some theoretically determined equilibrium level, we shall, in the next chapter, pursue the more mundane task of testing whether *grosso modo* the rate of interest has adjusted to the level that would leave individual lenders in the same situation they would have been if, *ceteris paribus,* there had been no inflation. This is the approach that has been followed in much of the empirical literature.

Conclusions and implications

The most important conclusion that follows from our discussion (ignoring the difficulties discussed above in connection with the welfare effects) is that in the absence of adjustments for the taxation of interest incomes, only the required rate of interest (which incorporates the effect of income taxes) would leave individuals in the same situation as they would have been in the absence of inflation. The unadjusted Fisherian rate – that is, the real rate plus the expected rate of inflation – would clearly not be enough to compensate the lenders. Therefore, if it were, in fact, true that the nominal rates would adjust fully for the direct effects, as well as for the tax-induced indirect effects, of inflation,[21] the rates of interest that we would observe in the real world would have to be higher than those implied by the unadjusted Fisherian model.

In such a situation we might experience a process not too dissimilar from the one described by Lundberg in connection with the effect of income taxes on wages.[22] In the attempt to preserve their real rate of returns, the savers would contribute to inflation by increasing interest rates by more than the rate of inflation. The impact of this tax push on the rate of inflation would depend on many factors, among which one must include the reaction of the consumer price index to a rise in the rate of interest.[23] Since various savers have different marginal tax rates, it is not easy to test the extent of the potential change in the rate of interest above the level indicated by the Fisherian solution. In practice and in the absence of corrections, institutional limitations may prevent the establishment of the required rate, thus leading to the excessive taxation of interest incomes.

The reactions of the economic agents to this excessive taxation of interest incomes may be several: As savers they may decrease, or increase, their savings.[24] As financial investors, they are likely to reduce the savings that they make available to others; instead, they may use these savings for the direct accumulation of real assets (such as real estate, works of art, durable goods, jewels, etc.) as has been reported in many countries under severe inflationary pressures. Or, they may bypass the financial intermediaries and invest directly in equities. This is the process of disintermediation which has also been reported to be taking place in some countries in recent years.[25] Or, they may export their savings, thus creating or aggravating balance of payments difficulties.

11

Inflation, income taxes, and interest rates: some empirical results

In the previous chapter, it was shown that in an inflationary situation, the nominal rate of interest that would leave a lender with the same preinflation real interest income, and a borrower with the same preinflation cost of borrowing, would have to be r^* where:

$$r^* = r + \frac{\Pi}{1 - t} \tag{1}$$

In this equation r is the rate that would prevail in the absence of inflation,[1] Π is the rate of inflation over the relevant period, and t is the rate at which the interest income of the individual is taxed. If this rate of interest were established, the lender who received it would be as well off or as badly off, *qua* lender, as in the noninflationary situation provided, of course, that he did not suffer from money illusions.[2] Equally the borrower who paid the required rate, r^*, would also be no better or worse off.

If income taxes were levied with proportional rates, the t in Equation 1 would be fixed so that the required rate, r^*, would be the same for every taxpayer, regardless of the level of his income. Consequently, if such a rate came to be established, the real positions of lenders and borrowers would not change except in relation to loans contracted in the preinflationary era and covering several years. However, in most countries, income taxes are levied with progressive, rather than proportional, rates. This means that taxpayers at different income levels are taxed at different rates. It follows that Equation 1 has to be rewritten as:

$$r^*_i = r + \frac{\Pi}{1 - t_i} \tag{2}$$

Where i now refers to the particular individual or income class. Since t_i depends on the income level, the required rate is no longer the same for all individuals. Consequently, no uniform market rate could ever adjust to leave *all* lenders and/or borrowers in the same situation as before inflation.

If the market rate of interest should adjust fully for the rate of inflation, and for some *average* tax rate, it would still be too high for some taxpayers and too low for others, depending on the income tax rates that were levied on them. More specifically, the higher the income of individuals, and consequently their marginal tax rate, the higher must be the rate of interest that as *lenders* they would have to receive – or, as *borrowers* they would have to pay – in order to remain in the pre-inflation real situation. However, ignoring risk and other factors which may influence individual loans, the interest rates that come to be established in the market are uniform for all taxpayers, so that some taxpayers are bound to gain, or lose, more than others.

This chapter has two objectives. First, an attempt is made to get empirical estimates about gains and/or losses by income classes associated with the recent inflation in the United States and the taxation of interest income. This analysis will be conducted in relation to income classes in the *U.S. Statistics of Income* of the Internal Revenue Service, using information for 1972–76, the latest years for which the needed data are available. During these years, the rate of inflation fluctuated sharply, so these years lend themselves well to the kind of analysis that we wish to pursue. Even though the United States is used as an example, the theory and the procedure are obviously applicable elsewhere, provided, of course, that the required data are available.

Second, also using data from the United States, which is the country with, perhaps, the most developed and competitive financial market, we wish to test whether with inflation and income taxes the market rate of interest approaches the required rate. As shown above, the required rate would vary for different income classes; however, ignoring risk and term structure, there can only be one market rate. In our empirical tests we shall relate the actual market rate to an average required rate, using the procedure described in Chapter 10 in the section on rate effects.

Equation 1 (p. 118) shows the rate that would leave an individual in the same situation that would have prevailed in the absence of inflation. In that equation, the Π refers to the *actual* rate of inflation over the relevant period. However, in any moment in time, the decisions on the part of lenders and borrowers on whether and how much to lend or borrow are affected not by the actual rate of inflation but by the *expected* rate. Therefore, while the analysis about the impact of inflation on different income classes must be conducted using actual rates of inflation, that about the impact of inflation and taxes on the market rate of interest must be conducted using expected rates of inflation. Of course, whenever the actual rate of inflation differs from the expected rate, the ex post required rate will differ from the ex ante rate.

Gains and losses by income classes, 1972-76
Determination of required rates

The consumer price index rose by 3.3 percent in 1972, by 6.2 percent in 1973, by 11.0 percent in 1974, by 9.8 in 1975, and by 5.8 in 1976. If interest income were *not* taxed, these percentage changes— which correspond to the Π in the two equations above – would give the rate of interest that would leave the lenders with *zero* real interest income. In other words, if the rate of interest were exactly equal to the rate of inflation, the interest received by a lender would just be sufficient to compensate him for the inflation-induced losses in the real value of the financial assets that he had loaned. And, similarly, the interest that a borrower would pay would just balance for him the decline in the real value of his liability. However, interest income *is* taxed and at rates that, *ceteris paribus*, vary with the level of income of the taxpayers. Also, interest payments are deducted as costs from gross income in the determination of taxable income. Thus, the value of these deductions (in terms of the reduction they bring in tax liability) are closely and directly related to the income of the taxpayer.

Table 19 shows for 1972–76 the effective average tax rates – that is, the ratios of tax liabilities to adjusted gross incomes (AGIs) – for the twenty-four income classes reported in the *Statistics of Income*. These average tax rates range from very low figures to about 50 percent for very high incomes. When these rates are combined with the rate of inflation for each year in the expression $\Pi/(1-t_i)$ (where $i = 1 \ldots 24$ refers to particular income classes), one gets the rates of interest that each class should have received in order to end up with *zero* real income from interest. Anything above these rates, which are shown in Table 20, would leave the lenders with positive real interest income and anything below would leave them with negative real income. *Mutatis mutandis*, borrowers who, given their income level, paid the rates indicated in Table 20 would de facto be paying a zero real interest rate on the borrowed capital. If they paid more, they would be incurring positive real costs of borrowing, while they would be getting net subsidies if they paid less.

Tax incidence

In 1972, the $\Pi/(1-t_i)$ ratio calculated as described above ranged from 3.4 percent for taxpayers with AGIs less than $1,000 to 6.1 for those with incomes above $1 million. In 1973, the $\Pi/(1-t_i)$ ratio ranged from 6.3 to 11.7; in 1974, it ranged from 11.5 to 21.7; in 1975 and 1976, the range narrowed again. It follows that in order to receive a zero real income from a loan, a taxpayer in the lowest income class

Table 19. *Ratios of tax payments to adjusted gross incomes, 1972–6 (in percent)*

AGI ($1,000)	1972 (1)	1973 (2)	1974 (3)	1975 (4)	1976 (5)
Under 1	1.8	1.8	4.5	—	—
1–2	3.5	4.1	3.3	3.8	4.8
2–3	2.6	2.6	2.5	1.4	1.1
3–4	4.9	5.1	5.1	3.7	3.3
4–5	6.4	6.6	6.7	5.6	5.4
5–6	7.5	7.5	7.8	6.9	6.4
6–7	8.3	8.4	8.6	7.4	6.7
7–8	8.9	9.2	9.3	8.0	7.5
8–9	9.4	9.8	10.0	8.9	8.3
9–10	9.6	10.0	10.3	9.3	8.8
10–11	10.1	10.4	10.6	9.9	9.3
11–12	10.3	10.5	10.7	10.2	9.8
12–13	10.6	10.9	11.1	10.5	10.0
13–14	11.0	11.2	11.4	10.7	10.5
14–15	11.4	11.5	11.7	11.0	10.8
15–20	12.5	12.6	12.7	11.9	11.6
20–25	14.4	14.3	14.5	13.8	13.4
25–30	16.0	16.0	15.9	15.3	15.1
30–50	19.1	19.0	18.9	18.3	18.3
50–100	26.8	26.4	26.5	26.1	26.2
100–200	34.6	34.4	34.9	34.7	35.3
200–500	40.8	40.6	41.5	41.2	42.5
500–1,000	45.4	45.7	45.6	45.1	47.5
Above 1,000	45.7	46.8	49.2	48.1	51.2

Source: U.S. Internal Revenue Service, *Statistics of Income: Individual Income Tax Returns,* 1972–76 (Washington, D.C.).

should have received rates of interest of 3.4 percent in 1972, 6.3 percent in 1973, and 11.5 percent in 1974, 10.2 percent in 1975, and 6.09 percent in 1976. And a taxpayer that belonged to the highest income class should have received rates of 6.1 percent, 11.7 percent, 21.7 percent, 18.8 percent, and 11.9 percent for these years. These rates would have left the borrowers with zero net interest costs.[3]

How do these estimated rates relate to actual rates? This is not an easy question to answer, as there is not one but a whole spectrum of rates available. Table 21 shows bond yields and interest rates on selected financial assets for 1972–6. In 1976, the rates shown ranged from 4 percent to over 7 percent; in 1973, they ranged from 5 percent to 8 percent; in 1974 from 6 percent to about 10 percent, and in 1975–6

Table 20. *Interest rates required to provide lenders with zero real interest incomes, 1972–6[a] (in percent)*

AGI ($1,000)	1972 (1)	1973 (2)	1974 (3)	1975 (4)	1976 (5)
Under 1	3.36	6.31	11.52	—	—
1–2	4.42	6.47	11.38	10.19	6.09
2–3	3.39	6.37	11.28	9.94	5.86
3–4	3.47	6.53	11.59	10.18	6.00
4–5	3.53	6.64	11.79	10.36	6.13
5–6	3.57	6.70	11.93	10.52	6.20
6–7	3.60	6.77	12.04	10.58	6.22
7–8	3.62	6.83	12.13	10.65	6.27
8–9	3.64	6.83	12.22	10.76	6.32
9–10	3.65	6.89	12.26	10.80	6.36
10–11	3.67	6.92	12.30	10.88	6.39
11–12	3.68	6.93	12.32	10.91	6.43
12–13	3.69	6.96	12.37	10.95	6.44
13–14	3.71	6.98	12.42	10.97	6.48
14–15	3.73	7.01	12.46	11.01	6.50
15–20	3.77	7.09	12.60	11.12	6.56
20–25	3.86	7.23	12.87	11.37	6.70
25–30	3.93	7.38	13.08	11.57	6.83
30–50	4.08	7.65	13.56	12.00	7.10
50–100	4.51	8.42	14.97	13.26	7.86
100–200	5.05	9.45	16.90	15.01	8.96
200–500	5.57	10.44	18.80	16.67	10.09
500–1,000	6.04	11.61	20.22	17.85	11.05
Above 1,000	6.08	11.65	21.65	18.88	11.89

[a] The percentages in the table are obtained from the expression $\Pi/(1 - t_i)$. Π was 3.3 in 1972, 6.2 in 1973, 11.0 in 1974, 9.8 in 1975, and 5.8 in 1976.
Source: Table 19 and, for the rates of inflation, *Economic Report of The President* (Washington, D.C., January 1978).

they ranged from about 5 to 9 percent. Relating these rates to those required for a zero real interest income (i.e., those in Table 20), it can be seen that, while in 1972 most of the taxpayers would have been able to receive positive interest incomes on new loans; in 1973, this became difficult for taxpayers with high incomes and especially for those with incomes above $50,000; and in 1974–5 it became very difficult (and perhaps impossible) for practically everyone. In 1974, the rate of interest should have ranged from over 11 percent for low-income groups to over 21 percent for very high-income groups in order to leave them with a positive interest income. By 1974, the income tax had obviously

Table 21. *Interest rates and bond yields, 1972–6 (in percent per annum)*

	U.S. government securities			Corporate bonds (Moody's Aaa)	High-grade municipal bonds[c] (Standard and Poor's)	Prime commercial paper, four to six months	FHA New home mortgage yields
Year	Three-month treasury bills[a]	Three-to five-year issues[b]	Longer-term bonds				
1972	4.071	5.85	5.63	7.21	5.27	4.69	7.53
1973	7.041	6.92	6.30	7.44	5.18	8.15	8.08
1974	7.886	7.81	6.99	8.57	6.09	9.87	8.92
1975	5.838	7.55	6.98	8.33	6.89	6.33	9.01
1976	4.989	6.94	6.78	8.43	6.49	5.35	8.99

[a] Rate on new issues within period.
[b] Selected note and bond issues.
[c] These are tax exempt.
Source: Economic Report of the President (Washington, January 1978), p. 332.

become a capital tax for all lenders and particularly for those with high incomes.

The conclusions reached in the previous paragraph relate to *lenders* and should be reversed when borrowers are considered. Consequently, while in 1972 most of the borrowers paying the going rates of interest had positive real costs of borrowing (as the interest rates that they paid exceeded the required rates shown in Table 20), by 1974 most borrowers were receiving, as *borrowers,* net capital subsidies.

Taxpayers may be lenders or borrowers or both at the same time. Within each income class, borrowers or lenders may predominate. Therefore, whether an income class gains or loses from the tax treatment of the lending and borrowing activities of its members in an inflationary situation depends on the net balance between borrowing and lending. As lenders, individuals receive interest payments from other individuals, banks, and other financial intermediaries, corporations, and federal and local governments, as well as from foreign sources. And as receivers of various types of loans, they also pay interest to individuals, banks, savings and loans associations, corporations, and, to a much lesser extent, to governments and foreigners. To the extent that these flows (i.e., interest paid or received by individuals) are reported and are taxable, they are reflected in data from the Internal Revenue Service, which are used to calculate Table 22.

Table 22 shows for each class, and for the five years under consideration, the net difference between the total interest income received by that class and the total interest deductions claimed by that class. These net differences indicate whether the class as a whole was a net lender or a net borrower. In 1972, all the classes with AGIs of less than $8,000 or more than $30,000 were net lenders, while those with AGIs greater than $8,000 but smaller than $30,000 were net borrowers. In 1973, the net borrowers were those with incomes above $9,000 but less than $30,000; all others were net lenders. In 1974, the net borrowers were those with incomes above $10,000 but less than $30,000; all others were net lenders. By 1976, the net borrowers were those with incomes above $13,000 but below $50,000. From these estimates one can derive the following conclusion: In 1974 and 1975, when the rate of inflation became very high, the classes that benefited most from the tax treatment of interest incomes were the middle-income classes – those with incomes above $10,000 but below $30,000. For these classes, interest deductions related to home ownership must have been particularly significant. As a consequence of the tax treatment of interest incomes and interest deductions, these groups received substantial capital subsidies which may have amounted to 4-5 percent of their net debts. The interest payments that they made were far below what would have been

Table 22. *Net differences between interest received and paid by size of adjusted gross income, 1972–76 (in millions of U.S. dollars)*

AGI ($1,000)	1972 (1)	1973 (2)	1974 (3)	1975 (4)	1976 (5)
Under 1	147.3	143.4	192.8	183.5	228.8
1–2	497.3	476.9	483.7	446.9	483.3
2–3	836.5	983.8	918.1	803.6	804.6
3–4	1,102.1	1,210.6	1,399.0	1,426.9	1,364.2
4–5	995.2	1,081.8	1,523.0	1,594.5	1,291.8
5–6	911.5	951.0	1,348.2	1,377.4	1,462.5
6–7	675.9	737.3	1,161.9	1,236.5	1,370.7
7–8	285.1	540.5	732.9	791.2	1,439.2
8–9	– 36.9	121.6	440.7	804.2	1,067.7
9–10	– 357.0	– 56.1	496.7	495.5	767.8
10–11	– 269.2	– 203.0	– 49.3	210.0	496.5
11–12	– 596.7	– 425.5	– 261.3	66.5	369.4
12–13	– 662.8	– 570.5	– 294.4	– 110.3	130.2
13–14	– 632.8	– 488.2	– 610.8	– 414.6	– 124.5
14–15	– 701.0	– 771.7	– 614.8	– 405.6	– 204.0
15–20	– 2,603.7	– 3,373.3	– 3,777.4	– 2,800.9	– 2,954.2
20–25	– 901.1	– 1,645.7	– 2,122.8	– 2,357.3	– 3,069.9
25–30	– 90.7	– 249.3	– 606.2	– 1,058.8	– 1,671.4
30–50	525.1	544.9	597.1	183.6	– 290.4
50–100	453.1	543.9	1,106.9	1,057.7	1,131.9
100–200	186.8	258.0	513.5	466.3	529.0
200–500	68.8	94.5	204.8	193.5	223.3
500–1,000	13.5	32.6	51.2	38.1	65.4
Above 1,000	10.9	24.0	32.3	54.7	68.2
	+ 6,709.1	+ 7,744.8	+ 11,202.8	+ 11,430.6	+ 13,294.5
	– 6.851.9	– 7,783.3	– 8,337.0	– 7,147.5	– 8,314.4
Total Net difference:	– 142.0	– 38.5	+ 2,865.8	+4,283.1	+4,980.1

Source: U.S. Internal Revenue Service, *Statistics of Income: Individual Income Tax Returns,* 1972–6 (Washington, D.C.)

needed to leave them with zero real cost of borrowing. As far as their lending and borrowing activities were concerned, they clearly gained from inflation. On the other hand, the other classes – the lower-income and higher-income classes – were subject to substantial capital taxes, which for the very high-income classes may have exceeded 10 percent, but which were very significant even for the low-income classes. For these, the interest incomes received were far below what was needed to compensate them for the inflation-induced erosion of their loans.[4]

Net balance vis-à-vis the government

Above we have dealt with gains and losses among income classes related to the tax treatment of interest income during an inflationary situation. We consider now some gains or losses accruing to the government, as a consequence of the tax treatment of interest income and deductions. The government gains from the taxing of interest incomes but loses from the deductions accorded to interest payments.[5] The question raised here is whether, on balance, the government was a gainer or a loser over the 1972–6 period.

The net position of the income classes vis-à-vis interest incomes (the figures in Table 22) have been multiplied by the average tax rates (shown in Table 19). If the net position of a class was that of a creditor (i.e., if interest received exceeded interest paid), then the multiplication of the net income by the effective average tax rate gave a net positive tax payment. However, if the net position was that of a debtor (interest paid exceeded interest received), the multiplication of the average tax rate by the net deduction gave an estimate of the taxes lost by the Government. The results are shown in Table 23.

In 1972, the value of the interest deductions in terms of tax reductions amounted to $816.2 million, while the value of the tax payments was $634.8 million. As a consequence, the net loss in tax revenue to the government associated with the tax treatment of interest income was $181.4 million. In 1973, the tax reduction associated with net deductions was $977.2 million while the value of tax payments was $776.1 million, so that the net loss to the government in terms of foregone tax revenue was $201.1 million. In 1974, however, there was a drastic change in the net balance. In fact, while the value of the deductions rose to $1,091.3 million, that of tax payment also rose, to $1,299.0 million; the government became a net gainer by $207.7 million. In 1975 and 1976 the government remained a net gainer by $239 and $241.3 million, respectively. Between 1973 and 1976 there was thus a net change of over $400 million in the position of the taxpayers vis-à-vis the government. Consequently, the government was definitely a winner from inflation in this context.[6]

Concluding remarks

The discussion on gains and losses by income classes has tried to show to what extent income classes have gained or lost through the tax treatment of interest incomes and payments during the inflation of 1972–6. The main beneficiaries are clearly the middle-income classes, which are more likely to have substantial deductions related to their home mortgages. It was also shown that the government was a net gainer. Thus, the tax treatment of interest income per se resulted in a

Table 23. *Net balance vis-à-vis government, 1972–6 (in millions of U.S. dollars)*

AGI ($1,000)	1972 (1)	1973 (2)	1974 (3)	1975 (4)	1976 (5)
Under 1	2.6	2.6	8.7	—	—
1–2	17.4	19.6	16.0	17.0	23.2
2–3	21.7	25.6	23.0	11.3	8.9
3–4	54.0	61.7	71.3	52.8	45.0
4–5	63.7	71.4	102.0	89.3	69.8
5–6	68.4	71.3	105.1	95.0	93.6
6–7	56.1	61.9	99.9	91.5	91.8
7–8	25.4	49.7	68.2	63.3	107.9
8–9	− 3.5	11.9	44.1	71.6	88.6
9–10	− 34.3	− 5.6	51.2	46.1	67.6
10–11	− 27.2	− 21.1	− 5.2	20.8	46.2
11–12	− 61.5	− 44.7	− 28.0	6.8	36.2
12–13	− 70.3	− 62.2	− 32.7	− 11.6	13.0
13–14	− 69.6	− 54.7	− 69.6	− 44.4	− 13.1
14–15	− 79.9	− 88.7	− 71.9	− 44.6	− 22.0
15–20	− 325.5	− 425.0	− 479.7	− 333.3	− 342.7
20–25	− 129.8	− 235.3	− 307.8	− 325.3	− 411.4
25–30	− 14.5	− 39.9	− 96.4	− 162.0	− 252.4
30–50	100.3	103.5	112.8	33.6	− 53.1
50–100	121.4	143.6	293.8	276.1	296.6
100–200	64.6	88.8	179.2	161.8	186.7
200–500	28.1	38.4	85.0	79.7	94.9
500–1,000	6.1	14.9	23.3	17.2	31.1
Above 1,000	5.0	11.2	15.9	26.3	34.9
	− 181.4	− 201.1	+ 207.7	+ 239.0	+ 241.3

Source: Derived from Tables 19 and 22.

redistribution of income in favor of the middle classes and the government. It should be emphasized that the results obtained relate to income classes rather than to individuals. Within each class, there are people who gained or lost more than the class.

The redistributional effects emphasized above would be removed, or at least reduced in intensity, if the part of interest income that was taxed and the part of interest payment that was deducted as a cost were the real one.

Income taxes and the rate of interest

For the empirical tests in this section, Equation 1 must be rewritten as:

$$r_t^* = r + \frac{\Pi_t}{1 + T_t} = r + \frac{1}{1 - T_t}\Pi_t \tag{3}$$

where r^*_t and r have the same meaning as in Equation 1 but Π_t is now not the *actual* rate of inflation over the relevant period but the period of inflation that economic agents expect at time t, the beginning of the period, to prevail over the period. T_t is the weighted average tax rate on interest income determined following the method described in Chapter 10, in the material on rate effects. This average tax rate is weighted to reflect the different importance of interest income among various income groups. Over the 1952–75 period – the period for the tests – this average tax rate ranged from a low of 25.3 percent in 1967 to a high of 34.8 percent in 1974. The mean for the 1952–75 period was 0.32.

Equation 3, this chapter, is in effect the basic Fisherian equation obtained in Chapter 10 – i.e., Equation 3 there – but in a slightly different guise. Putting $1/(1 - T_t) = b$ we can rewrite Equation 3 as

$$r_t^* = r + b\Pi_t$$

However, whereas in the basic Fisherian equation, theoretical considerations had led us to expect that b should not be significantly different from 1,[7] in Equation 4 theoretical considerations lead us to expect that b [which now is an estimation of $1/(1 - T_t)$] ought to be greater than 1. More specifically our knowledge of the mean of the average tax rate for the 1952–75 period leads us to expect that, if individuals did not suffer from money and/or/fiscal illusions, then b should approximate 1.47 [i.e., $1/(1 - 0.32)$].[b]

If, over the period, the weighted average tax rate T_t had been constant and equal to the mean of 0.32, then we could test for the effect of taxes on interest rates by regressing directly interest rates against expected rates of inflation. In this case, we would simply test for the significance of the coefficients of the expectation variable, expecting them not to be different from 1.47. However, since the average tax rate T_t was not constant over the period, a more precise test involves adjusting, for each year, the expectation variables by dividing them by $1 - T_t$. In such a case, the independent variable Π would be corrected for the effect of taxes *before* estimating the regression equations. The variable Π_t would thus be replaced by $\Pi_t/(1 - T_t)$ so that the regression coefficients for this corrected variable would still be expected to be one.

As we have indicated, an empirical test of Equation 3 requires that a measure of the *expected* (rather than the actual) rate of inflation be available. Until recently, there was no other choice but to use distributed lags on actual changes in past prices, hoping that these would generate good proxies for *expected* rates of inflation. This approach suffers from the shortcoming that, when used, the theory that we wish to test is jointly tested with the theory that inflationary expectations depend completely on the behavior of prices in the recent past. However, when unusual events occur (for example, when OPEC raised the price of oil) past prices may not give a good estimate of current inflationary expectations. On the other hand, current inflationary expectations may lag behind recent price changes if they are still influenced by the behavior of prices in a relatively stable past; if individuals have been brought up in an environment of price stability, they may continue to believe that price stability is the norm even when they are faced by current price changes.[9] In spite of these shortcomings, several tests were conducted, using various versions of distributed lags, including Koyck transformations. However, in order to take into account the objections that one would raise to this method, a more direct approach was also tried.

Various tests were conducted, using a directly observed measure of price expectation. Such a direct test of the theory has recently become possible by the uncovering and publication of some series of observed price expectations obtained through survey methods. One of these series has been derived from a semiannual survey made by Joseph Livingston, a financial columnist, who now writes for the *Philadelphia Enquirer*. Since 1946, Livingston has, twice a year, been asking fifty influential economists, forecasters, and financial analysts their opinions about the level that the consumer price index would reach six and twelve months hence.[10] These opinions when averaged provide a series for a directly observed price expectation variable which can be used in a test such as ours.

All the tests conducted in relation to several financial instruments (commercial papers, Treasury bills of various duration, etc.) failed to discover any tax effect. When Π_t was used alone, its coefficient was often, though not always, close to one. On the other hand, when it was replaced by $\Pi_t/(1-T_t)$ in the various regression equations, its coefficient fell significantly below the expected value of one.

The inevitable conclusion is that individuals have, to a large extent, been able to see through the money veil and, thus, have not suffered from money illusion; however, they have failed to see through the fiscal veil and, thus, have suffered from fiscal illusion. Interest rates have not adjusted enough to compensate individuals for the combined effect of inflationary expectations *and* income taxes. That individuals were unable to see through the particular fiscal illusion is hardly surprising when it is realized that it has been "discovered" by economists only in recent years. Thus, since for most of the period covered by this analysis, the relevant theory ignored the effect of income taxes, the existence of fiscal illusion does not mean that the expectations held by investors were "irrational."[11] These results indicate that, over the period covered by the empirical analysis, there were no tax-push effects coming from interest rates. Of course one must not conclude that these results would remain valid in future years should the rate of inflation remain at high levels.

12

Inflation, indexation, and the wage-tax spiral

In Chapter 11, which dealt with interest incomes, it was found that the available evidence indicated that economic agents, at least over the period covered by the statistical analysis, suffered from fiscal illusions. This meant that the market rates of interest did not adjust enough for the effects of inflation *and* taxation to leave lenders with unchanged real incomes and borrowers with unchanged real costs. Borrowers were definitely the gainers from inflation. This result was not considered surprising, because it was associated with a type of distortion – that of the taxable base – that has not been obvious, until very recently, even to economists.

For wages, however, the basic tax-related distortion is strictly the result of the progressivity of the income tax. In Chapters 2 and 3 of this study we saw that the distortions caused by progressivity (1) are far simpler to understand than those in the bases, (2) have been known for a long time, and (3) have been dealt with by many countries – through indexation or tax-cut policies. In view of this, it would be strange if wage earners – especially members of national unions with research staffs – suffered widely from progressivity-related fiscal illusions; or, if they did not, if they made no attempt at protecting themselves from the effect of higher marginal tax rates by bargaining on the basis of net-of-tax wages. Yet the existence of these fiscal illusions, on the part of workers, or, putting it differently, the lack of forward shifting of inflation-caused increases in personal income taxes, seems to be widely accepted in the literature in spite of its irrationality and growing evidence to the contrary. For example, the Brookings Conference on Inflation and the Income Tax hardly touched upon this issue which, in the final volume of 350 pages, was allocated a single, short paragraph.[1] And the issue, while recognized, did not fare much better in Laidler and Parkins' lengthy survey of the literature on inflation. In that survey its total treatment is limited to one sentence which states that: ''As to direct taxes, the work of Gordon and (with a bargaining theoretical justification) Johnston and Timbrell suggests that they play an important role."[2]

This reluctance on the part of many economists to recognize that increases in personal income taxes may, under particular circumstances, be shifted forward is due, first, to the public-finance literature on tax shifting, which assumes no shifting of personal income taxes; second, and more importantly, personal income tax shifting gives results inconsistent with the fiscal policy recommendation that one would get from the application of orthodox Keynesian analysis. In that analysis, increases in personal income taxes decrease disposable income. Since consumption is positively related to disposable income, the latter falls also. This fall is then magnified by the multiplier leading to a larger fall in income. The conclusion is that the increase in personal income taxes must be deflationary in real terms. However, while this conclusion might be valid within a comparative static Keynesian framework, it may not hold in a dynamic setting.[3] This recognition has led Blinder and Solow to "conclude then that tax raising may not be the best way to curb inflation."[4]

The reluctance on the part of economists to accept the possibility of a wage–tax spiral[5] is particularly strange, inasmuch as there have been many instances in various countries in which income tax reductions have been traded for lower wage demands in wage settlements. Or, at least, where inflation-induced marginal tax increases have been specifically used by unions to justify higher wage increases.[6]

The mechanics of the wage-tax spiral
Basic theory
If personal income taxes were truly proportional, the marginal and the average tax rates would be the same and these rates would not change with inflation (ignoring distortions of capital incomes or collection lags). However, these taxes are progressive and are levied on nominal, rather than real, tax brackets. As a consequence, any wage increase that a worker receives, whether real or purely nominal, is taxed at higher tax rates. In an inflationary situation, this leads to an increase in the average tax rate on total wage income, and, if the wage increases just compensate for inflation, it leads to a fall in real disposable income. How does a worker react to such a tax increase?

As an individual, and assuming that he has some control over the supply of labor that he (as well as his household) makes available to employers or to those who demand his services (if he is a free professional), he may be led to substitute (at the margin) some income (i.e., some work) for more leisure, especially if the marginal tax rates are high. This reaction is unrelated to the structure of the market,[7] although it is highly related to institutional constraints which may specify the number of hours that the worker must work. If the worker is a dependent worker, he may decline working overtime. If he is a professional, he may reduce the length of his workweek or increase the length of his annual vacation. And in both cases, there could be an effect on whether additional family members (wife, children, etc.) take or retain a job, or whether he decides to migrate. These effects could be important if the marginal tax rate is far above the average tax rate. In this case the substitution effect, which would push for less work, is likely to overwhelm the income effect, which is related to the average tax rate and which will push for more work.[8] The empirical evidence on these effects seems to indicate that work effort has in fact been reduced by high marginal tax rates, but the reduction may not be very important.[9]

As a member of a union, however, the individual may have the option of a more direct forward shifting of the tax increase if the union takes net-of-tax real wages as the basis for its wage.[10] This option is not available in a competitive labor situation in which, by definition, unions would not exist; and thus wage negotiations would be individual rather than collective affairs; and, it may be less plausible when unions represent only small groups of workers in fragmented labor negotiations.

It was Erik Lundberg who, in 1953, first hypothesized the possibility of a direct forward shifting of personal income tax increases on the income of workers.[11] His hypothesis can be outlined as follows. Assume that at a given moment, when the average price index is P_0, a worker receives a total wage income equal to Y_0. That income is taxed at an average rate equal to t_a so that his disposable income is $Y_0 (1 - t_a)$. Let us now assume that over the following period, the rate of inflation is such that the price level rises at an annual rate of Π from P_0 to P_1; what increase in his nominal wage income will leave the worker with the same real after-tax income? The reply to this question depends on the tax rate at which the increase in income is taxed. The absolute increase in nominal wage income, ΔY, necessary to leave the wage earner with an unchanged real after-tax income must be such that:

$$\frac{Y_0 (1 - t_a)}{P_0} = \frac{Y_0 (1 - t_a) + \Delta Y (1 - t_m)}{P_1} \tag{1}$$

where t_m is the marginal rate at which the increase in income is levied. It follows that, if Π is the rate of inflation, t_a is average tax rate applicable to the income before the increase, t_m is the marginal tax rate at which the increase is taxed, then the percentage increase in the nominal wage that will leave the wage earner with the same real after-tax income, $\dot{Y}$, must be:[12]

$$\dot{Y} = \Pi \frac{(1 - t_a)}{(1 - t_m)} \tag{2}$$

Given the average tax rate, t_a, the required percentage increase in nominal wages will be larger, the larger the rate of inflation and the marginal tax rate t_m. Thus, it is not the level of the average tax rate that determines the required wage increase but rather the relationship between average and marginal tax rates.[13] As was shown in Chapter 8 under "Determinants of the elasticity. . . ," the absolute difference between marginal and average tax rate depends on the income level. This difference will be small at low income levels, then it will increase at an increasing pace, reaching a maximum, and then it will start to decrease once again. Fig. 5 measures wage income on the horizontal axis and average tax rate on the vertical axis. The *ATR* curve depicts the behavior of the average tax rate. At an income level equal to Y_0, the *ATR* curve reaches the highest slope. This is a point of inflection at which the second derivative of the *ATR* curve is zero. Thus if the wage income of workers should be equal to Y_0, the tax-push effect will be most accentuated. Therefore, the same statutory income tax and the same rate of inflation could be associated with different tax-push effects, depending on the level of wages.

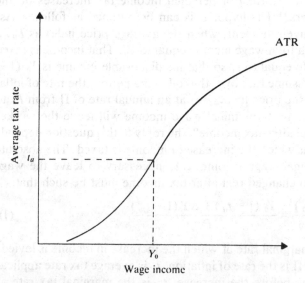

Figure 5

Equation 2 has been solved for a situation in which the rate of inflation is 10 percent per year and the average and marginal tax rates range from zero to maximum levels of 40 and 65 percent, respectively. These rates have been chosen to cover the situation prevailing in most OECD countries. The results, shown in Table 24, indicate that in some situations the required wage increases may have to be considerably higher than the rate of inflation. For example, a worker who had hitherto not paid any tax (due to various exemptions and deductions) and who faces a marginal tax rate of 30 percent on the wage increase would have to receive a wage increase of 14.3 percent to be left with the same disposable income. If enterprises do in fact accommodate these requests, labor costs will increase in real terms. Faced by these heavier wage bills, a likely response on the part of the enterprises will be to try to maintain their real profits by marking up the prices of their products. This markup process, if not interrupted, is likely to result in an inflationary spiral that could be associated with stagflation if other incomes are not adjusting accordingly.

Before leaving this section, we ought to mention one possible criticism of Lundberg's theory. Because tax increases are often accompanied by increases in public spending, one could argue that workers have no justification in retaliating against the tax increase by asking for compensatory wage increases. The fall in disposable income would be compensated by increased benefits derived from public spending, so

Table 24. *Percentage increases in nominal wages needed to compensate workers for a 10 percent inflation and for higher marginal tax rates*

Marginal tax rate (t_m)	Average tax rate (t_a)								
	0	5	10	15	20	25	30	35	40
0	10.0								
5	10.5	10.0							
10	11.1	10.6	10.0						
15	11.8	11.2	10.6	10.0					
20	12.5	11.9	11.3	10.6	10.0				
25	13.3	12.7	12.0	11.3	10.7	10.0			
30	14.3	13.6	12.9	12.1	11.4	10.7	10.0		
35	15.4	14.6	13.8	13.1	12.3	11.5	10.8	10.0	
40	16.7	15.8	15.0	14.2	13.3	12.5	11.7	10.8	10.0
45	18.2	17.3	16.4	15.5	14.5	13.6	12.7	11.8	10.9
50	20.0	19.0	18.0	17.0	16.0	15.0	14.0	13.0	12.0
55	22.2	21.1	20.0	18.9	17.8	16.7	15.6	14.4	13.3
60	25.0	23.8	22.5	21.3	20.0	18.8	17.5	16.3	15.0
65	28.6	27.1	25.7	24.3	22.9	21.4	20.0	18.6	17.1

that total workers' welfare might even increase. Thus, the decline of fiscal illusion on the tax side must be accompanied by an introduction of fiscal illusion on the expenditure side if Lundberg's theory is to have validity. As long as the workers (or their union leaders) recognize the value of public spending, they should not retaliate through the wage-tax spiral.

This argument has some validity. However, there are some elements that make it less convincing than it appears. First, workers, like most other taxpayers, may not see the connection between the taxes they pay and the benefits they receive from the government. Second, they may question the productivity of public spending, especially when the public sector has become very large. Third, and most importantly, additional spending has in recent years often been of a redistributive type, mainly from productive workers to other population groups.

Some qualifications

The theory of a wage-push spiral presented above must not be applied mechanically to a real-world situation, as various other factors as well as lags in the adjustment process may bring about results which may appear inconsistent with the theory. For these reasons, as well as for some other reasons yet to be discussed, the quantitative testing of this theory is very difficult. In the real world, Equation 2, if interpreted as a description of workers' behavior, must be amended to take into account the following factors:

1. On the basis of past productivity changes, workers may not be satisfied with maintaining constant their after-tax disposable income but may demand real increases. The higher have past increases been, the higher will probably be the increases that they will expect.

2. As various "wage equations" have shown, the industry level of profit will affect the firms' willingness to comply with the workers' demand.

3. The unemployment rate will have an impact on the workers' demands, as well as on the employers' willingness to accommodate them.

Even if we limit our discussion to the tax factor only, there are still difficulties in using Equation 2 in empirical studies of real situations. In the first place, Equation 2 assumes an immediate adjustment process. Thus, all that one needs to know is the average tax rate on the initial income and the marginal tax rate at which the wage increase is taxed. However, wage negotiations are not annual events and adjustments may not be immediate. Thus, in most cases, it would be important to know whether the average tax rate had been constant for some time or had changed in the immediate past.

Another and, perhaps, more basic difficulty in using Equation 2 to explain the behavior of wages is that the average and marginal tax rates are not the same for all workers but vary according to their incomes, which, in turn, depend on seniority, type of work, industry, and so on. Therefore, if the wage level should adjust for some "typical" group of workers, it will be too high for some and too low for others. For example, assume that the "typical" worker has an average tax rate of 20 percent and a marginal rate of 30 percent. Table 24 shows that the required wage increase, when the rate of inflation is 10 percent, will be 11.4 percent. For workers with, say, an average tax rate of 25 percent and a marginal tax rate of 40 percent, this wage increase will be too low. This is the same problem that was encountered with the required rate of interest.

The argument often heard that indexation of the tax system is not needed if gross-of-tax incomes adjust for inflation ignores the redistributional and efficiency effects of these adjustments. The redistributional effects are more obvious and are the ones described in the preceding paragraph. The efficiency effects are less obvious. If general wage negotiations bring about a uniform percentage increase for all wage levels that is adequate for the "average" wage, some groups of workers will find their disposable income falling, so that discontent, unrest, and, possibly, wildcat strikes will result. However, one important difference between interest rates and wage levels is that the first must be uniform throughout the economy (ignoring risk and term structure), whereas wages do not have to be. But if different groups of workers, with different wage levels, manage to receive wage increases that are adequate for their particular situations, the tax-push effect will be different among industries. Thus, while leaving unchanged the disposable incomes of the workers, the adjustment would bring about a distortion of the cost structure of industries. The conclusion is again the same as for interest incomes. Without indexation, the progressivity of the tax will bring about inevitable, but possibly important, welfare costs.

Income taxes and wages in OECD countries
The level of personal income taxation

For most OECD countries, the ratios of personal income taxes to gross domestic products have achieved high levels in recent years. For 1975, a ranking of countries according to these ratios would put Denmark first, with a ratio of 23.86; followed by Sweden, 21.17; Finland, 18.10; Norway, 17.09; New Zealand, 16.45; the United Kingdom, 14.29; Belgium, 13.24; Australia, 13.12; and so forth. Furthermore, for most of these countries, the increase in the ratio between 1965 and 1975 has been very high, implying that dynamically the marginal tax rates have far exceeded the average tax rates. Table 25 gives these ratios for the OECD countries for the 1965–75 period. Interestingly enough, the countries where income taxes have been reported to have played a role in the determination of wages are generally the same ones where revenues from income taxes are a high share of gross national products, and where these shares have been growing.

As discussed in the material on the mechanics of the wage–tax spiral, the spiral is not so much related to average tax levels for a country as to the difference between the marginal tax rates and the average tax rates for wage earners. Data compiled by OECD allow us to form an impression of this difference in relation to the level of gross earnings of an average production worker for 1972–6. This information is provided in Table 26. The information in this table, used jointly with Table 24, indicates that the countries where, over the 1972–6 period, the tax factor should have been of greatest importance in wage determination should have been Sweden, Australia, Finland, Austria, Belgium, Denmark, New Zealand, and a few others.

Evidence from wage negotiations

Is there any evidence that the problem caused by the progressivity of income taxes did in fact play a role in wage negotiations in some countries? Or, putting it differently, is there any evidence that workers bargained on the basis of net-of-tax wages? A perusal of the literature and of published documents reveals that this practice was relatively common, especially in the countries where one would have expected such a decline in tax illusions.

For *Australia,* various statements by the Department of Labor and Immigration, by the Australian Council of Trade Unions Special Conference of Affiliated Unions, and by other organizations clearly indicate an awareness of the problem. Typical is a statement by the Special Conference "that until indexation of taxation is introduced, there can be no adequate protection against the erosive effects of inflation on real after-tax income. This effect has continued to be a significant factor in the level of wage and salary demands."[14] In *Austria,* in 1971 and 1972, trade unions succeeded in negotiating income tax reductions as counterpart to lower wage settlement.[15] These reductions are obvious from Table 26. In *Canada,* in 1970, the Economic Council reported that "an increasing number of groups are taking not only price changes but also tax changes explicitly into account in their approaches to income bargaining."[16] In *Denmark,* the wage-tax spiral was one of the basic

Table 25. *Personal income taxes as percentages of GDP*

Country	1965	1966	1967	1968	1969	1970	1971	1972	1973	1974	1975
Australia	8.42	8.51	9.04	8.78	9.53	9.64	10.25	9.75	10.82	12.85	13.12
Austria	6.98	7.54	7.60	7.01	7.27	7.62	7.92	8.53	8.66	9.15	8.37
Belgium	6.31	7.05	7.53	8.06	8.25	8.58	9.06	9.78	10.30	11.33	13.24
Canada	5.98	6.52	7.42	8.05	9.34	10.39	10.37	10.93	10.51	11.52	11.32
Denmark	13.46	14.92	15.51	16.94	16.61	21.09	24.49	24.25	24.41	27.22	23.86
Finland	10.97	11.83	12.58	13.00	13.16	13.87	14.80	15.40	16.12	16.56	18.10
France	3.76	3.66	3.79	4.23	4.27	4.06	3.86	4.16	4.01	4.30	4.58
Germany	8.15	8.60	8.44	8.46	8.85	8.63	9.23	10.04	10.93	11.41	10.60
Greece	1.50	1.83	2.04	2.27	2.34	2.45	2.64	2.17	2.25	2.82	2.27
Ireland	4.32	4.94	5.39	5.23	5.12	5.72	7.42	7.07	7.44	7.46	8.39
Italy	3.25	3.32	3.35	3.53	3.62	3.33	3.62	3.95	3.54	4.97	4.95
Japan	3.99	3.80	3.85	3.97	4.11	4.27	4.65	5.16	5.83	5.35	5.07
Luxembourg	7.88	8.40	8.32	8.00	7.32	7.68	9.35	9.65	9.67	10.37	12.78
Netherlands	9.78	10.64	11.18	10.33	10.61	10.64	11.33	11.92	12.00	12.47	12.66
New Zealand	10.17	10.75	10.47	10.58	10.87	11.79	13.04	13.14	14.75	17.34	16.45
Norway	13.31	13.63	14.18	14.86	15.16	13.82	14.57	15.99	16.48	17.16	17.09
Portugal	...	1.20	1.24	1.29	1.44	1.74	1.75	1.63	1.63	1.88	2.20
Spain	2.29	2.11	2.18	2.12	2.05	1.97	2.09	2.15	2.26	2.43	2.95
Sweden	17.21	17.35	17.86	18.49	19.20	20.18	18.96	20.18	19.17	19.84	21.17
Switzerland	6.65	7.22	7.33	7.47	7.71	7.91	7.89	8.01	8.89	9.34	10.52
Turkey	3.52	3.65	3.93	3.96	4.15	4.52	5.25	5.14	5.55	5.56	6.55
United Kingdom	9.58	9.89	10.28	10.63	11.44	11.91	11.66	10.84	10.78	12.43	14.29
United States	8.10	8.39	8.76	9.22	10.70	10.59	9.68	9.96	9.86	10.27	9.99

Source: OECD, *Revenue Statistics of OECD Member Countries* (Paris, 1977).

Table 26. *Average and marginal personal income tax rates levied on the level of gross earnings of an average production worker, 1972–6 (single man)*

	Average tax rate					Margin tax rates				
	1972	1973	1974	1975	1976	1972	1973	1974	1975	1976
Australia	18	21	21	22	22	33	36	45	35	35
Austria	12	11	13	9	10	32	26	26	20	21
Belgium	11	11	12	13	14	21	23	26	30	34
Canada	20	19	19	19	19	29	31	33	33	33
Denmark	35	38	39	34	34	55	58	56	49	51
Finland	28	30	31	32	31	40	43	48	53	45
France	7	7	8	8	8	14	17	17	16	19
Germany	16	17	19	16	17	28	31	33	32	34
Greece	2	2	2	2	1	8	7	5	4	10
Ireland	19	20	20	23	25	26	28	35	38	39
Italy	8	9	5	8	7	17	17	12	15	13
Japan	11	12	10	—	—	18	21	17	—	—
Luxembourg	14	15	16	17	17	28	29	32	34	34
Netherlands	13	14	15	15	15	28	—	—	27	26
New Zealand	19	21	25	25	27	32	35	42	44	45
Norway	24	25	25	25	25	39	39	39	39	39
Portugal	2	3	2	4	5	2	3	12	14	5
Spain	1	2	3	4	6	9	9	9	12	12
Sweden	33	33	36	37	38	60	62	62	59	63
Switzerland	10	11	12	11	12	20	22	20	24	23
Turkey	—	—	—	22	21	—	—	—	30	31
United Kingdom	21	22	25	27	28	31	30	33	35	35
United States	19	19	20	20	19	29	26	26	27	26

Source: Committee on Fiscal Affairs, *The Treatment of Family Units in OECD Member Countries under Tax and Transfer Systems* (OECD: Paris 1977); and OECD, unpublished data.

reasons for the introduction of indexations. In *Finland,* the 1974 wage settlement specifically required an adjustment of the rates of the personal income tax. Furthermore, since 1973, the general income policy annual discussion between unions, employers, farmers, and government has always included taxation policy. In *Germany,* too, some unions have expressed their wage demands in terms of net-of-tax wages although this practice is not widespread.[17] In *New Zealand,* the Federation of Labor at the end of 1977 was arguing that inflation and productivity gains, per se, would justify wage increases of 17 percent, but when the progressivity of the income tax rates was taken into account, the increase ought to be at least 26 percent. In *Norway,* in 1976, the government explicitly contributed to the wage settlement between the employers' federation and the trade unions by lowering income taxes. In *Sweden,* in 1975, reduction in personal income taxes were explicitly tied, by the government, to lower wage demands. In the *United Kingdom* income tax reductions have also played a role in wage negotiations.[18] This role was explicitly recognized by the Chancellor when in 1976 he stated that "in my view, the key to achieving a rate of inflation which is well below 10 percent by the end of 1977 is to relate our tax policy in the coming year to the next policy for incomes."[19] As a result, increased personal reliefs in the income tax were tied to lower pay demands by Trades Union Congress.

The countries mentioned above have, by and large, three common characteristics: (1) they all have high and growing ratios of personal income tax revenue to gross domestic product; (2) they all have very progressive income taxes; (3) they have wage negotiation processes more or less unified at the national level.

Evidence from empirical analysis

In a growing number of countries, the hypothesis of forward tax shifting of personal income taxes has been supported by empirical studies. A complete survey of these studies and the theoretical models behind them is beyond the scope of this book. However, a brief mention of some of the results obtained might not be out of place.

Canada. Three studies have analyzed the possibility of forward tax shifting for Canada. Two of these, by Auld,[20] and by Taylor et al,[21] found some support for the hypothesis but the results were not definitive or highly significant. On the other hand, a study by C. J. Bruce concluded that "rates of change of Canadian money wage rates have been positively correlated with changes in the average rate of tax incidence."[22] All of these studies dealt with the period before the indexation of income taxes in Canada.

Netherlands. Studies carried out by the Netherlands Central Planning Bureau have found a high degree of tax shifting for that country.[23]

United Kingdom. At least two studies have tested the hypothesis of personal income tax shifting for the United Kingdom. One by Johnston and Timbull used the ratio of disposable wage income to gross wage income ("the retention ratio") as a variable designed to capture the effect of taxes on gross wages.[24] A weighted average of this ratio over the past three years was shown to play a role in the determination of the current wage level. Another study by Wilkinson and Turner provides an exhaustive support to the tax shifting hypothesis.[25]

United States. For the United States, the hypothesis of tax shifting has been supported by work by Robert J. Gordon and, to some extent, by Otto Eckstein and Roger Brinner. Gordon's work suggests that about one-fifth of any increase in personal income taxes is shifted forward in higher wages.[26] Eckstein and Brinner found that one-fourth of the tax increase may have been shifted forward in higher wages.[27] However, they also found that "subsequent adjustments . . . reduce this effect,"[28] so that over the long run, the workers bear the burden of the personal income tax.

The hypothesis of income tax shifting has also received substantial backing for many OECD countries in yet unpublished work carried out by OECD.

13

Some general conclusions on indexation

This book has analyzed in some detail the effects of inflation on the personal income tax and, to a lesser extent, the effects of inflation-induced increases in personal income taxation on the rate of inflation. It has also discussed various adjustment mechanisms aimed at neutralizing those effects, as well as their use in various countries. The purpose of this chapter is not to summarize the arguments presented in the previous chapters but to draw a few basic conclusions. These will be organized around three sections dealing respectively with political and stabilization, equity and efficiency, and administrative aspects. Particular issues may, of course, involve more than one of these aspects.

Political and stabilization aspects

The basic political argument related to the indexation of income taxes concerns the "proper size of the public sector" and thus has divided liberals from more conservative writers. As we saw in earlier chapters, in the absence of indexation and of substantial lags in collection, an increase in nominal income – whether due to inflation or growth – will increase the ratio of tax revenue to national income. Governments will have more money to spend without having to raise taxes. As a consequence the public sector is likely to be, or become, larger when no indexation is present.[1] An individual's attitude toward this expansion is likely to depend on his political views. Liberals are likely to favor it while conservatives are likely to oppose it.

In some cases, an increase in the size of the public sector has been justified on the ground that the prices of the goods and services bought by governments increase faster than those bought by the private sector. Consequently, an increase in nominal government expenditures in relation to GNP is required to maintain the real value of these expenditures. Of course, as long as there is growth, and prices are not falling, indexing for inflation alone would still be accompanied by an increase in the ratio of taxes to national income.

Another often-voiced political argument against indexation is that it represents a declaration of defeat on the part of the government that could have important psychological effects on the population. The defenders of this point of view argue that the fight against inflation will become more difficult once indexing is accepted, since some of the pains of inflation would be removed from it, and people may accept the view that inflation has become a way of life. The other side of this argument is that on the contrary, indexing will make it easier for the government to pursue the kind of policies that will put a stop to inflation.

Those who argue that indexation will facilitate the pursuit of stabilization policy point out that during an inflationary situation, many contracts – wages, interest payments, rents, and so on – reflect the expected rate of inflation. Thus, if many companies have, for example, agreed to new labor contracts that will increase *money* wages at the rate of, say, 15 percent per year over the next several years, on the expectation of an inflation rate of 12 percent, they would face serious difficulties if inflation should fall much below 12 percent. In such a case, the sharp increase in the *real* wage bill at the current level of employment would force these companies to lay off some of their employees. The increased unemployment might, then, induce the government to reverse its policy. The same argument applies to borrowers who have borrowed money at high rates of interest, and for long terms, expecting prices to continue rising, If prices cease rising, the real cost to them will be high. It is, thus, argued that, in the absence of indexation, the real costs associated with a stabilization policy become so great that the governments are no longer free to pursue such policies.[2]

The government itself may be caught in the process we have described in a variety of ways. In the first place, if the public sector is unionized, as it is in many countries, wage contracts will come to incorporate expected inflation, and perhaps even the effect of the progressivity of the income tax, so that the pursuit of a stabilization policy may be associated with (or made difficult by) increases in real wages. Second, the refinancing of the debt in an inflation situation will commit the government to the payment of nominally high future rates of interest once inflationary expectations have been incorporated in the rate of interest. To take an extreme example, over the past couple of years, the government of Argentina has been financing its deficit with the selling of bonds carrying nominal rates of interest of well over 100 percent. If the rate of inflation should be sharply reduced through a successful stabilization policy, the *real* rate of interest on those bonds could become extraordinarily high and so would the cost of the public debt to the government.[3] Third, comes the budgetary process itself. When various agencies – ministries, public enterprises, and so forth – present their budgetary requests, they are likely to incorporate inflationary expectations even when they are told to present these requests in prices of a given moment. The budgets themselves, which are expenditure plans for the future, are never in real prices but in nominal prices. As long as one thinks of the government as of a monolithic entity no problem arises when prices fall. But in the real world, governments are made up of many entities which compete for the limited resources; it would be very difficult to tell all of these public bodies that their budgetary appropriations are being reduced because of a sharp decline in the rate of inflation.

Much of the controversy related to indexation has evolved around the issue of stabilization. Some writers as, for example, Walter Heller and Albert Fishlow, have maintained that "putting income tax liabilities on an indexed basis reduces the automatic stabilizing effect of inflationary increases in governmental revenues and thus requires more discretionary fiscal action."[4] And the (Canadian) Carter Commission had concluded that "a tax system that taxed only increases in real purchasing power would irreparably damage the built-in stability of the system."[5] On the other hand, Milton Friedman has argued that "obstacles to ending inflation can be substantially reduced through . . . indexation."[6] The truth probably lies somewhere between these extremes and may depend on factors that differ among countries.

There can be no argument that indexing for price changes will reduce the built-in flexibility – that is, the responsiveness of income tax receipts to a change in income. In fact, this is really the main point about indexation, and this reduction will come about because purely inflationary changes in income will no longer affect the average tax rate for the country; because of this, the marginal tax rate for the country will not grow but will remain the same as the average rate.[7] However, there is now considerable controversy on whether this reduction implies a fall in the "automatic stabilizing effect" of the personal income that will "require more discretionary fiscal action" or that it will be inherently destabilizing as argued by Heller and Fishlow. This particular position has been challenged in different ways among which the most important are the following.

Size of discretionary changes. It should be emphasized that indexation of personal income taxes does not exclude the use of discretionary fiscal policy. Many writers on the subject seem to assume that once indexation of income taxes is introduced, there will not be any more use of, or any more need of, discretionary tax changes. This assumption is, of course, neither necessary nor warranted and it is perhaps useful to think of indexation as just one additional instrument of policy. In other words, a useful and fair comparison would be one between a choice that involves indexation *and* occasional discretionary changes and one that involves only discretionary changes. The latter option may require much larger ad hoc tax cuts. And the very size of these cuts might introduce a destabilizing element in the economy.[8] On the other hand, too frequent but smaller cuts would take too much time on the part of the politicians or experts involved. Thus indexation may reduce the need for large and/or frequent ad hoc changes and thus it may introduce an element of stability in the economy. The issue is somewhat similar to the one encountered in the choice of a fixed exchange rate with infrequent but substantial devaluation, and one which continuously adjusts for the differential rate of inflation between the domestic economy and the rest of the world. Many observers would agree that the higher the rate of inflation, the more attractive the latter policy becomes.

Autonomous nature of public expenditure. The traditional argument about the usefulness of built-in flexibility is highly dependent on the assumption that, in the short run, public expenditure is autonomous with respect to tax revenues. This assumption is probably valid for some countries, but it is less so for others where additional revenues may simply give rise, with very little lag, to additional expenditures. If this happens, the combination of higher taxes and higher public expenditure could make the inflationary situation more serious. Thus, once again, if taxes are indexed so that inflation does not bring about an increase in the average tax rate, public expenditure would not increase in relative terms and there would not be the expansionary stimulus associated with more taxes and public expenditure.

Built-in flexibility in recession. Indexation will lower the built-in flexibility of the personal income tax. By doing so, it might reduce the ability of the tax to stabilize the economy in downswings and in genuine upswings but might also restrain its negative influence during a recovery by reducing the size of the fiscal drag at less than full employment. The argument of the built-in flexibility suffers also by the fact that stagflation has brought about situations where real tax revenue may keep increasing (due to inflation) even when a country is in the middle of a serious recession.

The tax-push argument. In tax incidence theory, it is generally assumed that taxes on personal incomes are not shifted. However, as was argued in Chapter 12, changes in personal income taxes may bring about changes in the wage level – in other words, they may be shifted. Such a possibility has been exclusively discussed in connection with wages, but it may be equally applicable in connection with taxes on interest income and, perhaps, on other incomes. In an inflationary situation, workers who do not have money and fiscal illusions may be expected to bargain to maintain constant, or to increase, their real disposable incomes rather than their pretax incomes.

Given the income of the majority of the workers, the higher the marginal tax rate in relation to the average tax rate – in other words, the more progressive is the tax at that particular level of income (at the modal level) – the greater will the wage increase have to be to appease the workers. But, of course, the increase in wages above the price level – and above the productivity gain – will lead to, or assist the process of, cost-push inflation. The more important are wages in the determination of the price level, and the greater the difference between marginal and average tax rate for the average worker, the greater will be this induced price change, or tax-push effect.

If the previous discussion is correct for a given country – and of course one should not generalize, because this depends on factors which differ among countries – indexation may help by reducing the wage increases that workers would ask. Indexation would eliminate the progressivity related to nominal price changes, leaving only that related to changes in real incomes. Thus, the autonomous price increase associated with the process we have described would be reduced or even eliminated. For this reason, it has been argued that indexation is part of an incomes policy.[9]

The structural argument. In the discussion of the effects of indexation on stabilization, it is often not specified whether one is talking about stabilization of prices, output, employment, or what. The argument about indexation being destabilizing is simplest if one assumes that the price level, output, and employment move in unison without leads or lags. If this assumption does not hold, the issue of whether indexation does reduce or increase the stabilizing capacity of the tax on the economy is very complex. Prices in particular may lead or lag changes in output and employment, and taxes may lag significantly behind changes in prices. A perusal of the literature seems to support the contention that the first impact of an inflationary shock – say, an increase in export prices – might be (1) in developing countries, to increase the general price level and then, with considerable lag, perhaps to increase output, but (2) in some industrialized countries, to increase output rather quickly and then, some quarters later, to increase prices.[10]

If one considers the situation described in (2) where a given inflationary shock will increase output rather quickly and then, much later, will lead to price changes, indexing may be cutting taxes when output growth is slowing down. If this is the case, it may be stabilizing as was found in an econometric study dealing with Canada.[11] On the other hand, if the situation described in (1) prevails, then indexing may decrease taxes just when inflationary pressure is greatest.[12]

Equity and efficiency aspects

Equity. In earlier chapters it was seen that issues of equity arise in connection with various inflation-induced distortions. Some of these are caused directly by the progressivity of the tax; others, however, are caused either by the differential effect of inflation on various types of taxable incomes, or by nonuniform lags in the collection of taxes; others still are caused by the fact that different groups of taxpayers anticipate inflation differently, and some are more capable than others of protecting themselves against it. In all cases, the magnitude of these distortions are likely to be directly related to the rate of inflation and possibly to its variability.

Provided that the index used for the escalation is correct, and that the rate of inflation is not too erratic, the indexation of brackets and exemptions will go a long way toward eliminating some of the inequities caused by progressivity; however, it would do little toward the elimination of others. For example, the inequities associated with the distortion of taxable bases, or those due to collection lags, would not be eliminated. For these, additional and more complex adjustments would be required than for those due to progressivity.

Efficiency. Issues of efficiency arise in connection with many inflation-induced distortions. The ones that perhaps should be mentioned are the following:

1. A nonindexed personal income tax will often lead to an increasing ratio of tax revenue to national income. Unless other revenues are reduced, or the government allows the development of a budget surplus, the size of the public sector will increase. As resources allocated through the public sector do not go through a market test of profitability, the expansion of the public sector could be taken to imply a loss in efficiency for the economy as a whole. This potential inefficiency would be eliminated by indexation.

2. As more and more individuals, because of inflation, are shifted towards higher marginal tax rates, work effort and the labor supply are likely to be affected. Indexation will prevent individuals from being shifted into higher marginal tax rates strictly as a result of inflation.

3. Perhaps more important are the distortions that arise in the relative cost of labor as a result of nonuniform reactions of workers when faced with prospective reduction in their net-of-tax wage increases. As shown in the relevant chapter, the wage-tax spiral may be associated with substantial distortions in the structure of labor cost. Indexation would reduce or eliminate these effects.

4. Finally, the various distortions of taxable bases will inevitably be accompanied by welfare costs which could be reduced if these taxable bases are adjusted for inflation.

Administrative aspects

Don Patinkin has commented that "the demand for indexation is an increasing function of the rate of inflation".[13] Just how right he is can be seen from the following information.

In 1960, only one country had indexed the nominal structure of the personal income tax. By 1970, seven or eight countries had done so, and by the second half of the decade of the seventies, when double-digit inflation had become commonplace, no less than sixteen countries were indexing their income taxes. Whatever one's view of indexation, this is a phenomenon that is definitely acquiring popularity and that is likely to stay with us and acquire more followers. Table 27 lists the countries which at the beginning of 1979 were following this practice. The table shows the year when indexation becomes effective, the index used, and whether a discretionary element existed. This information relates just to bracket and exemption indexation and thus ignores the adjustments in the bases introduced by various countries.

Of the countries shown, nine indexed for inflation alone, while six used indexes not directly tied to the rate of inflation.[14] Seven of these countries had reserved some discretionary element in their indexation. Thus, the belief that indexation implies the total abandonment of any discretion is not supported by the evidence. Furthermore, all countries always have the choice of ad hoc or discretionary adjustments in the tax system, and many of the countries that have adopted indexation have also from time to time followed discretionary policies. What indexation did was probably to reduce the size of, and the need for, the discretionary adjustments.

A few general conclusions can be drawn from these experiences. First, indexing the rate structure, that is, the escalation of the

Table 27. *Countries that index personal income tax: January 1979*

Country	Year indexing introduced	Discre- tionary element	Index used
Argentina	1974, 1976	No	Wholesale price index
Australia	1976	No	Consumer price index
Brazil	1961	Yes	Minimum wage or consumer price index
Canada	1974	No	Consumer price index
Chile	1954	Yes	Basic tax unit
Denmark	1970	No	Hourly earnings of industrial workers
France	1969	Yes	Consumer price index
Iceland	1966	Yes	Change in nominal income
Israel	1976[a]	Yes	Consumer price index
Luxembourg	1968	No	Consumer price index
Netherlands	1971	Yes	Total population index
Peru	1973	Yes	Minimum wage
Sweden	1979	No	Consumer price index
Switzerland	[b]	[b]	[b]
United Kingdom	1978	No	Retail price index
Uruguay	1968	No	Consumer price index

[a] No data available for previous indexing.
[b] In Switzerland indexation was introduced in different years in the various cantons. It also varies from canton to canton.
Source: See text in Chapters 2 and 3.

exemptions and bracket limits, does not present any particular administrative problem. Taxpayers do not have difficulties in using new tax tables and authorities in producing them. Furthermore, as long as the rate of inflation is relatively low and stable, some index can be devised and used that will be satisfactory in solving the problems related to the rate structure, even though it would never be the theoretically perfect one.

More importantly, the countries that have indexed the rate structure have done so without paying much attention to the tax bases. The administrative problems associated with adjustments of the bases (for capital incomes) are more serious; governments have, thus, generally refrained from even attempting them.[15] If equity considerations were important in the original decision to introduce an indexation rule, this means that inequities will continue to exist among different *types* of income, even when they are eliminated among different *levels*. Thus, the popular literature has been misleading in arguing that indexation of the nominal structure would remove inequities introduced by inflation. The inequities that are removed are those associated with the rate structure. Those produced by distortions of the bases remain. At times the latter could be the more serious ones.

Several countries have taken advantage of the adjustment process in trying to redistribute the tax burden in favor of lower income groups. This process was most evident in Brazil and France, although it existed in other countries as well.

Finally, when the rate of inflation becomes very high, and particularly when it becomes unstable, several problems appear that are not obvious when inflation is low and stable. In particular (1) the indexes that are inevitably based on the recent past may become very inadequate; and (2) the differential lags in the payment of taxes (for example, those withheld as compared with those paid a long time after income has been earned) introduce additional inequities that are in no way reduced by indexation.

Notes

Chapter 1. Inflation and personal income taxation: an introduction to the main issues

1 Colin Clark, "Public Finance and Changes in the Value of Money," *Economic Journal* 55 (Dec. 1945): 371–89. A restatement of that thesis is found in Colin Clark, *Taxmanship,* Hobart Paper 26 (London: Institute of Economic Affairs, 1964), Chap. 4. Also J. A. Pechman and T. Mayer, "Mr. Colin Clark on the Limits of Taxation," *Review of Economics and Statistics 34* (Aug. 1952): 232–42; and Richard Goode, "An Economic Limit on Taxation: Some Recent Discussion," *National Tax Journal 5* (Sept. 1952): 227–33.

2 From this it should not be deduced that the effects of prices on taxes were never discussed before, but only that there was never much attention paid to this aspect. For a few examples of earlier worker which dealt with this relationship, see, J. Viner, "Taxation and Changes in Price Levels," *Journal of Political Economy 131* (Aug. 1923): 494–520; R. S. Weckstein, "Fiscal Reform and Economic Growth," *National Tax Journal 17* (Dec. 1964): 325–30; V. Tanzi, "A Proposal for a Dynamically Self-Adjusting Income Tax," *Public Finance/Finances Publiques 21,* no. 4 (1966): 507–19.

3 As the Meade report indicates, there are two possible definitions of economic income based on alternative principles. In the first, "a taxpayer's income in any one year is the value of what he could have consumed during the year without . . . diminishing [the real value] of his capital wealth in the process." In the second, income is defined as "the amount which he could consume in any one year and yet be left with the resources and expectations at the end of that year which would enable him to maintain that same level of consumption indefinitely in the future." See J. E. Meade, *The Structure and Reform of Direct Taxation,* Report of a Committee Chaired by J. E. Meade (London: Allen & Unwin, 1978) [referred to hereinafter as above: *Meade Report*], p. 31. Meade, as well as most public finance experts, favors the first concept for taxation purposes. That concept is consistent with the Schanz-Haig-Simon definition. See Richard Goode, "The Economic Definition of Income," in Joseph A. Pechman, ed., *Comprehensive Income Taxation* (Washington, D.C.: Brookings Institution, 1977), Chap. 1.

4 On the other hand, enterprises may find that inflation reduces the real value of their liabilities and may thus gain on that score.

5 See, for example, Henry J. Aaron, "Inflation and the Income Tax: An Introduction," in Henry J. Aaron, ed., *Inflation and the Income Tax* (Washington, D.C.: Brookings Institution, 1976), p. 24.

6 One could argue that the legislators based their judgment on some expected rate, perhaps based on historical experience. But this would raise the issue of the relevant period over which the expected rate applies.

7 This conflict was very much in evidence at the Brookings Conference on Inflation and the Income Tax (held in Washington, D.C. on Oct. 30–1, 1975), which resulted in the volume edited by Aaron, *Inflation and the Income Tax*. That conflict led Professor Fellner to comment somewhat tartly that the problem faced by the participants was similar to that faced by a plastic surgeon who is going to operate on the badly damaged face of a car-accident victim. He has pictures of the person taken before the accident but he does not know how good the pictures are. Does he try to operate on the face following the images in the pictures? Or rather should he try to follow his own aesthetic sense and make the patient as handsome as he can? Since different people will have different conceptions of what beauty is, Fellner argued that the first alternative was the only feasible one.

8 Of course, even a low rate of inflation can result in serious distortions over the long run, especially when the tax burden of the country is high.

9 For the time being, we are assuming that inflation leads to increases in real tax revenue. This, of course, is not always the case, as we shall show in later chapters.

10 Of these, Japan is the only one to have followed a discretionary *annual* "tax-cut policy." This policy was more the result of fast growth in real incomes than of inflation. See Chapter 9, this volume.

11 This, for example, was the main reason for the strong political opposition from social democrats and communists against the government bill of October 20, 1977, which indexed the income tax rates in Sweden.

12 See, for example, Thomas J. Sargent and Neil Wallace, "Rational Expectations and the Theory of Economic Policy" *Journal of Monetary Economics* 2 (Apr. 1976): 169–85.

13 Actually, if the problem of defining the base for the tax could be solved, another practical alternative would be to levy a strictly proportional income tax.

14 One important objective of this indexation is to hold down the roll of the taxpayers.

15 That is if a proportional rate was levied on the whole income without exemptions.

16 The terms "bracket indexation" and "indexation for capital-income adjustment" are used in the *Meade Report,* p. 100.

17 John Bossons and Thomas A. Wilson, "Adjusting Tax Rates for Inflation," *Canadian Tax Journal 21* (May–June 1973): 185–99. James L. Pierce and Jared J. Enzler, "The Implication for Economic Stability of Indexing the Individual Income Tax" in Aaron, ed., *Inflation and the Income Tax,* pp. 173–93.

18 U.S. Department of Health, Education, and Welfare, *Social Security Programs Throughout the World, 1975* (Washington, D.C.: U.S. Government Printing Office, 1976).
19 OECD, *Revenue Statistics of OECD Member Countries, 1965–1975* (Paris: OECD, 1977), pp. 84–5. See also Kenneth C. Messere, "Impact of Inflation on Tax Structure," International Institute of Public Finance XXIX Session, *Inflation, Economic Growth and Taxation* (Barcelona, 1973), 187–213.
20 Recently, the United Kingdom changed to a proportional tax on incomes below ceiling.
21 In time, if the rate of inflation is correctly anticipated, the return on the financial assets may adjust, but the demand for real balances will remain low as long as the anticipated rate of inflation remains high.
22 See Meade *Report,* p. 101.
23 J. S. Flemming and I. M. D. Little have recently proposed a wealth tax for the United Kingdom with characteristics somewhat similar to the Argentine tax but with many more brackets and much higher rates. See their *Why We Need a Wealth Tax* (London: Methuen, 1974).
24 See Meade *Report,* p. 101.

Chapter 2. Inflation and the real progression of the rates: problems and solutions

1 Of course whether higher *gross* incomes are also taxed with higher average tax rates depends also on the existence of loopholes.
2 It must be recalled throughout this discussion that we have ruled out other distortions (such as those due to lags, capital incomes, etc.).
3 Vito Tanzi, *The Individual Income Tax and Economic Growth* (Baltimore, Md.: Johns Hopkins Press, 1969), Tables III-5 and III-6, pp. 32–3.
4 It should be understood that it is not necessary for a taxpayer whose income has already become taxable to be pushed into a higher income bracket to experience an increase in the average tax rate. Such an increase would take place even if there were no progressivity in the income tax besides the one provided by the existence of the exemptions.
5 For more detail on this point, see Chapter 8, this volume.
6 Taxation Review Committee, *Preliminary Report* (Canberra: June 1, 1974), p. 75.
7 George Vukelich, "The Effect of Inflation on Real Tax Rates," *Canadian Tax Journal 20, no. 4* (July–Aug. 1972): 327–42; Gregory Jarvis and Roger S. Smith, "Real Income and Average Tax Rates: An Extension for the 1970–75 Period," *Canadian Tax Journal 25,* no. 2 (Mar.-Apr. 1977): 206–15.
8 Richard Allen and David Savage, "Indexing Personal Income Taxation," in T. Leisner and M. A. King, eds., *Indexing for Inflation* (London: Institute for Fiscal Studies, 1975), pp. 41–60.
9 C. J. Goetz and W. F. Weber, "Intertemporal Changes in Real Federal Income Tax Rates, 1954–70," *National Tax Journal 24,* no. 1 (Mar. 1971): 51–63; George M. von Furstenberg, "Individual Income Taxation and Inflation," *National Tax Journal 27,* no. 1 (Mar. 1975): 117–25; Emil M. Sunley,

Jr., and Joseph A. Pechman, "Inflation Adjustment for the Individual Income Tax," in Henry A. Aaron, ed., *Inflation and the Income Tax* (Washington, D.C.: Brookings Institute, 1976), pp. 153–66.

10 Alberto Majocchi, "Effetti Distorsivi dell'Inflazione nel Quadro dell'Imposizione Progressiva sul Reddito delle Persone Fisiche," in Emilio Gerelli, ed., *Imposte e Inflazione* (Milan: Franco Angeli, 1976), pp. 110–54.

11 It should also be pointed out that these studies have not tried to estimate the distorting effects of inflation among taxpayers with different *types* (and not just levels) of incomes and subjected to different methods of tax assessment and collection. Thus, they have dealt with only part of the problem.

12 This is often the case when the income tax structure is indexed in relation to the legislated minimum wage, which over the long run, is likely to reflect price and productivity changes as well as political considerations.

13 This alternative is similar to that suggested by A. R. Prest in "Inflation and the Public Finances," *Three Banks Review*, no. 97 (Mar. 1973), p. 26.

14 For earlier descriptions of some of these schemes and for their use in several countries, see A. H. Petrei, "Inflation Adjustment Schemes Under the Personal Income Tax," IMF *Staff Papers 22* (July 1975): 539–64; David R. Morgan, *Overtaxation by Inflation* (London: Institute of Economic Affairs, 1977).

15 No practical and general adjustment scheme can satisfy this specific requirement. See on this, P. A. Diamond, "Inflation and the Comprehensive Tax Base" in *Journal of Public Economics 4*, no. 3 (Aug. 1975): 227–44.

16 A variation of this alternative would leave unchanged the nominal income tax structure but would adjust the annual tax bills on a formula basis. See R. S. Weckstein, "Fiscal Reform and Economic Growth," *National Tax Journal 17* (Dec. 1964): 325–30. Both the scheme itself and Weckstein's variation were first proposed as far back as 1923 by Jacob Viner, in "Taxation and Changes in Price Levels," *Journal of Political Economy 31* (Aug. 1923): 494–520.

17 See, for this proposal, Douglas Adie and Svetozar Pejovich, "Inflation and Taxes: A Case for the Taxpayer" (Mimeo., Ohio University, Mar. 1973).

18 In July 1975, a comprehensive tax reform abolished this system and replaced it by one similar to the fourth scheme discussed further on. See Chapter 3, this volume.

19 This scheme was suggested in Amotz Morag, *On Taxes and Inflation* (New York: Random House, 1965), p. 169.

20 In the United States, this adjustment mechanism is usually associated with the name of Milton Friedman who backed it in his *Newsweek* column on March 3, 1969. A later elaboration is found in Milton Friedman, "Monetary Correction" in American Enterprise Institute, *Essays on Inflation and Indexation* (Washington, D.C.: AEI, 1974).

21 For a proposal and discussion of such a superindexation scheme, see Chapter 9, this volume. The mechanics for the application of this superindex is similar to that for the fourth scheme. The limits of the taxable income brackets and the exemptions and deductions expressed in fixed nominal amounts could, for example, be increased annually at a rate equal to the nominal growth of per capita income or of some similar concept such as

hourly earnings. Obviously, the revenue loss associated with this superindex is greater than under a scheme that indexes only for prices. This loss depends on the rate of growth of per capita income or hourly earnings in addition to the rate of inflation.

22 It must be recalled that for the time being, we are assuming that capital incomes have already been adjusted for inflation; furthermore, the problems associated with collection lags are also being ignored.

23 If the objectives are multiple, perhaps no index will ever be able to make possible their simultaneous achievement. For example, no index could achieve the objective of keeping constant the ratio of income tax revenue to GNP while leaving unchanged the relative tax burdens on groups of taxpayers. For an exhaustive discussion of the index to be used, see Edward F. Denison, "Price Series for Indexing the Income Tax System" in Aaron, ed., *Inflation and the Income Tax*, Chapter 9. Good discussions are also contained in the Meade report [J. E. Meade, *The Structure and Reform of Direct Taxation* (London: Allen & Unwin, 1978], pp. 115–20, and in the Report on Inflation and Taxation by the Australian Committee of Inquiry into Inflation and Taxation, R. L. Mathews, Chairman (Canberra: Australian Government Publishing Service, 1975) [hereinafter referred to as the *Mathews Committee Report*], pp. 230–35.

24 Several studies have dealt with these aspects in a few countries. Inter alia, see D. C. Tipping, "Price Changes and Income Distribution," *Applied Statistics 19*, no. 1 (1970): 1–17; J. Muellbauer, "Prices and Inequality: the United Kingdom Experience," *Economic Journal 84* (Mar. 1974): 32–55; Ryotaro Iochi, *Measurement of Consumer Price Changes by Income Class* (Tokyo: Kinikuniyo Book Co., 1964); Y. Manzly, "Price Changes in the Consumption Basket of Various Income Groups in Israel," *Bank of Israel Economic Review*, no. 41 (Apr. 1974): 35–55; E. M. Snyder, "Cost of Living Indexes for Special Classes of Consumers," in National Bureau of Economic Research, *The Price Statistics of the Federal Government*, General Series 73 (New York: NBER, 1961).

25 Incidentally, the assumption in these discussions is that the tax is fully shifted forward.

26 Statistiske Efterretninger [Statistic news], "Konjunkturoversigt" [Economic trends], *No. 1* (Copenhagen: Apr. 1975), p. 89.

27 Of course, it is assumed that the government will not spend the extra real tax revenue that it receives.

Chapter 3. Inflation and the real progression of the rates: countries' experiences

1 Good descriptions of these adjustment schemes are contained in International Fiscal Association, 31st Congress, *Inflation and Taxation* (Vienna, 1977).

2 See Chapter 2, section on effects of inflation on personal income tax liability.

3 For 1978, the cumulative Federal government revenue losses due to indexing are estimated at Can$4 billion. The losses due only to the indexing for

1978 (i.e., to the escalation by 7.2 percent) are estimated at Can$850 million.

4 Over the period referred to above, the actual change in the cost of living index was 14 percent but one percentage point increase was attributed to changes in indirect taxes. The *Mathews Committee Report* had not recommended that the consumer price index be adjusted to remove the effects of changes in terms of trade or in indirect taxes.

5 At the end of 1977, the wholesale price index replaced the consumer price index for purposes of indexation in the whole tax system (see Law No. 21734 of January 19, 1978).

6 See "Taxation Without Misrepresentation," *Economist,* July 30, 1977, p. 70.

7 See Ministère de l'Economie et des Finances, *Statistiques et études financières.* Deuxième Rapport du Conseil des Impôts, 26è année (Novembre 1974).

8 In 1977, the brackets were raised 7.5 percent at the bottom and 5 percent at the top.

9 Luxembourg, Income Tax Law of December 4, 1967 (Article 125).

10 The index used was described in Chapter 2 in the section on changes in indirect taxes.

11 See the statement by Joseph Gabbay in Henry J. Aaron ed., *Inflation and the Income Tax* (Washington, D.C.: Brookings Institution, 1976), p. 228. See also Yoram Ben-Porath and Michael Bruno, "The Political Economy of a Tax Reform," *Journal of Public Economics 7* (June 1977): 285–307.

12 Interesting analyses of various aspects of Brazilian indexation are contained in M. Eshaq Nadiri et al, "Indexation, the Brazilian Experience," National Bureau of Economic Research, *Occasional Papers, vol. 4,* no. 1 (Winter 1977).

13 This was normally that of the State of Guanabara.

14 See Jack D. Guenther, "Indexing Versus Discretionary Action—Brazil's Fight Against Inflation," *Finance and Development 12* (Sept. 1975): 24–9.

15 Decreto Ley No. 824 modified by Decreto Ley No. 910. These two decrees were published in Diario Oficial No. 29.041 (Dec. 31, 1974) and Diario Oficial No. 29.092 (Mar. 1, 1975).

16 The schedules and rates in the 1969 law were the following: the first DKr17,000 of taxable income was taxed at 18 percent; the next DKr13,000 was taxed at 30 percent; the next DKr40,000 was taxed at 40 percent; the part of income above DKr70,000 was taxed at 45 percent. The basic exemption was DKr5,000.

17 The new schedule for 1975 was the following: the first DKr9,000 was exempt; the next DKr41,000 was taxed at 16 percent; the next DKr40,000 was taxed at 32 percent, and the income above DKr90,000 was taxed at 44 percent. As shown, the basic exemption is now incorporated in the schedule itself. In 1975, these rates were applied at 90 percent of their value (i.e., 14.4, 28.8, and 39.6 percent, respectively).

18 The index to be used is the change in the hourly earning of an individual worker between the latest March before the tax year and the previous March.

Chapter 4. Inflation and the taxation of capital gains: problems and solutions

1 However, other definitions of income may lead to the exclusion of at least some capital gains. See, for example, Nicholas Kaldor, *An Expenditure Tax* (London: Unwin University Books, 1955), pp. 41–6.
2 Richard Goode, *The Individual Income Tax,* rev. ed. (Washington, D.C.: Brookings Institution, 1976), p. 184.
3 See ibid., pp. 183–6; Department of the Treasury (Australia), *Capital Gains Taxes,* Treasury Taxation Paper No. 10 (Canberra: Nov. 1974), pp. 11–13.
4 House of Commons Debates (Canada), January 29, 1975, 2710.
5 Joseph A. Pechman, *Federal ̅ , Policy,* 3rd ed. (Washington, D.C.: Brookings Institution, 1977), pp. 111–2; and Martin J. Bailey, "Inflationary Distortions and Taxes," in Henry J. Aaron, ed., *Inflation and the Income Tax,* (Washington, D.C.: Brookings Institution, 1976), pp. 299–302.
6 Leif Johansen, *Public Economics* (Amsterdam: North-Holland, 1965), p. 233; and Goode, *Individual Income Tax,* pp. 185–8.
7 The wholesale price index was lower in 1945 than in 1865.
8 However, it would be practically impossible to extend the adjustments to protect the holders of cash balances.
9 Criticisms of this approach can be found in: Taxation Review Committee, *Preliminary Report,* June 1, 1974 (Canberra: Australian Government Publishing Service), Ch. 9; Roger Brinner, "Inflation and the Definition of Taxable Personal Income," in Aaron, ed. *Inflation and the Income Tax,* Chapter 4; and, Meyer W. Bucovetsky, "Inflation and the Personal Tax Base: The Capital Gains Issue," *Canadian Tax Journal 25,* no. 1 (Jan.–Feb. 1977): 79–107.
10 See Brinner, "Taxable Personal Income," for a formal proof of this point. Especially Table 4-1, p. 128.
11 The most detailed description of this method can be found in Brinner, "Taxable Personal Income." A good description with an example of a table of inflation factors can be found in the *Meade Report* [J. E. Meade, The Structure and Reform of Direct Taxation (London: Allen & Unwin, 1978)], p. 131. See also John G. Watson and Michael F. O'Reilly, "A Scheme for the Indexation of Capital Gains Tax," *British Tax Review* (1978), no. 1, pp. 4–19. As it will be shown in the section dealing with actual experiences, this method is used by several countries.
12 Brinner, "Taxable Personal Income," p. 123.
13 Much of the discussion on the choice of the index has related to adjustments of brackets for real progressivity. There has been almost no discussion related specifically to the index to be used for adjusting tax bases. It is not obvious that both types of adjustment require the same index.
14 See Aaron, ed., *Inflation and the Income Tax,* p. 267.
15 Edward F. Denison, "Price Series for Indexing the Income Tax System," in Aaron, ed., *Inflation and the Income Tax,* p. 248.
16 To simplify the issue, it is assumed that interest payments are rebated against incomes generated by the assets.
17 Commission d'Etude d'une Imposition Généralisée des Plus-Values, *Rapport* (Paris, 1975), vol. I, p. 9.

18 The United States is also likely to introduce such a system. See "Indexing for Capital Gains But Not Ordinary Income Tax," *Tax Notes 7*, no. 5 (July 31, 1978): 99–100.
19 Up to 1968, the updating was on a yearly basis.
20 Gains on the sale of principal residences, or secondary residences where the taxpayer does not own the house he lives in, are exempt.
21 Thus the indexation of the base is combined with an inclusion ratio system.

Chapter 5. Inflation and the taxation of interest income: problems and solutions

1 Roger Brinner and Alicia Munnell, "Taxation of Capital Gains: Inflation and Other Problems," *New England Economic Review*, (Sept./Oct. 1974), p. 7 (italics added).
2 For earlier references to the problem discussed in this chapter see, in particular, P. Baffi, "Savings in Italy Today," pp. 137–8, and F. A. Lutz, "Inflation and the Rate of Interest," p. 116, both in Banca Nazionale del Lavoro *Quarterly Review*, no. 109 (June 1974); Edward M. Bernstein, "Indexing Money Payments in a Large and Prolonged Inflation," and Herbert Giersch, "Index Clauses and the Fight Against Inflation," both in American Enterprise Institute, *Essays on Inflation and Indexation* (Washington, D.C.: AEI; 1974), pp. 15 and 82; R. I. G. Allen and D. Savage, "Inflation and the Personal Income Tax," *National Institute Economic Review*, no 70, (Nov. 1974): 61–74. A more basic reference is John Bossons, "Indexing Financial Instruments for Inflation," *Canadian Tax Journal 22*, no. 2 (Mar.–Apr. 1974): 107–17.
3 Many outstanding economists of the past, including Mill, Marshall, Pigou, Einaudi, etc., have sustained the thesis of the "double taxation of saving," The prevailing modern view does not support that thesis. See Richard Goode, *The Individual Income Tax* (Washington, D.C.: Brookings Institution, 1964), pp. 25–8 for a concise summary of the arguments.
4 The return to money – defined here as cash plus demand deposits – in this context is in kind, and namely the *utility* derived from holding it.
5 See, for an empirical backing of this thesis, my papers "Demand for Money, Interest Rates and Income Taxation," Banca Nazionale del Lavoro *Quarterly Review*, no. 111 (Dec. 1974): 319–28; and "Income Taxes and the Demand for Money: A Quantitative Analysis" Banca Nazionale del Lavoro *Quarterly Review 128* (Mar. 1979): 55–72.
6 The literature on this point is considerable. Inter alia, see Colin Wright, "Saving and the Rate of Interest" in A. C. Harberger and M. J. Bailey, eds., *The Taxation of Income from Capital* (Washington, D.C.: Brookings Institution, 1969); and Michael J. Boskin, "Taxation, Saving, and the Rate of Interest," *Journal of Political Economy 86*, no. 2, part 2 (Apr. 1978): S3–S27.
7 For Fisher's seminal contribution, see Irving Fisher, *The Rate of Interest* (New York: Macmillan, 1907), pp. 270–80; see also his later work, *The Theory of Interest* (New York: Macmillan, 1930).
8 See, inter alia, James E. Pesando, "Alternative Models of the Determination of Nominal Interest Rates, The Canadian Evidence," *Journal of*

Money, Credit, and Banking 8, no. 1 (May 1976): 209–18; for the United States, William E. Gibson, "Interest Rates and Inflationary Expectations: New Evidence," *The American Economic Review 62* (Dec. 1972): 854–65; for Argentina, Mario I. Blejer, "Money and the Nominal Interest Rate in an Inflationary Economy: An Empirical Test," *Journal of Political Economy 86,* no. 3 (June 1978): 529–34.

9 A soon-to-be-published study by the author shows that the real rate of interest is itself affected by fluctuations in economic activity. This complication is ignored here. See Vito Tanzi, "Inflationary Expectations, Economic Activity, Taxes, and Interest Rates," *American Economic Review* (in press.).

10 This term depends on the compounding period. It disappears if one assumes continuous compounding in which case the formula $r^n = \Pi + r$ will be exact.

11 This is true because we are ignoring the term Πr in Equation 2 above. Strictly speaking, the real value of $50 has fallen, so that he is somewhat worse off. When the rate of inflation becomes high, the term Πr should no longer be ignored. In our example, consideration of Πr would require that r^n rises to 15.5, so total interest income rises to $155.

12 In fact, this rate may be higher if inflation, by increasing the overall nominal income of the taxpayer, pushes him into a higher income bracket, provided that the structure of the income tax has not been corrected through bracket indexation.

13 Obviously, one who had borrowed at the lower rate of interest prevailing before inflation got under way would gain even more.

14 *Meade Report* [J. E. Meade, *The Structure and Reform of Direct Taxation* (London: Allen & Unwin, 1978], pp. 136–7.

15 This formula can also be used to determine taxable interest income for a lending institution which makes a large number of nonmarketable loans. In this case Ar^n would be the total interest income received by the institution in one year, r^n the average nominal interest rate charged, and A the average outstanding balance.

16 See Albert Goltz and Desmond Lachman, "Monetary Correction and Colombia's Saving and Loan System," *Finance and Development 11,* no 3 (Sept. 1974): 24–6.

17 This legal distinction would become significant in the determination of what are called "tax expenditures." If the portion was "exempted," it would increase "tax expenditures." If it was not considered an income it would not.

18 See Alexander Kafka, "Indexing for Inflation in Brazil," in *Essays on Inflation and Indexation,* pp. 90–1. On the Brazilian experience, see also M. Eshaq Nadiri et al, "Indexation, The Brazilian Experience," National Bureau of Economic Research, *Occasional Papers 4,* no. 1 (Winter 1977). On indexed loans see also J. Whitley, "Index-Linked Mortgages," in Thelma Liesner and Marvyn A. King, eds., *Indexing for Inflation* (London: Institute for Fiscal Studies, 1975), pp. 77–91.

19 H. J. Hofstra, *An Inflation Adjusted Tax System,* A Summary of Dutch Report (The Hague: Government Printing Office, 1978), p. 61.

20 See *Meade Report* [J. E. Meade, *The Structure and Reform of Direct Taxation* (London: Allen & Unwin, 1978)], p. 136.

21 This example is adapted from Henry J. Aaron, "Inflation and the Income Tax: An Introduction," in Henry J. Aaron, ed., *Inflation and the Income Tax* (Washington, D.C., Brookings Institution, 1976), pp. 8–9.

22 Index-linking was discussed in the United Kingdom by the Committee to Review National savings headed by Sir Harry Page. See Sir Harry Page, "The Saver of Slender Means," *Three Banks Review*, no. 114 (June 1977): 3–27. For a more general discussion see OECD, *Indexation of Financial Assets* (Paris: OECD, 1975).

Chapter 6. Inflation and the taxation of business income

1 For analyses related more specifically to the impact of inflation on corporations see, inter alia, *Inflation Accounting*, Report of the Inflation Accounting Committee, Chairman F. E. P. Sandilands (London: H.M.S.O., 1975); William T. Baxter et al, *Economic Calculations Under Inflation* (Indianapolis: Liberty Press, 1976); M. F. Morley, *The Fiscal Implications of Inflation Accounting* (London: Institute for Fiscal Studies, 1974); A. J. Merrett, "Indexing Company Accounts," in Thelma Liesner and Mervyn A. King, eds., *Indexing for Inflation* (London: Institute for Fiscal Studies, 1975), pp. 61–76; J. A. Kay, "Inflation Accounting—A Review Article," *Economic Journal 87* (June 1977): 300–11; and papers by T. Nicholas Tideman and Donald P. Tucker, by Sidney Davidson and Roman L. Weil, and by George E. Lent, all in Henry J. Aaron, ed., *Inflation and the Income Tax* (Washington, D.C.: Brookings Institution, 1976).

2 Of course, the higher the inflation rose, the lower will be the present value of that stream.

3 This appears to be Brinner's option; see Roger Brinner, "Inflation and the Definition of Taxable Personal Income," in Aaron, ed., *Inflation and the Income Tax,* pp. 131–2.

4 It must be recognized that the gains we are talking about are, in fact, *capital* gains. This seems to be the ground on which some accountants would prefer to ignore gains on liabilities. They would prefer to report these gains only when the debt is paid off and the gain is thus realized.

5 The indexation in this case is only for tax purposes and not part of the contract between lender and borrower.

6 But these streams were chosen on purpose to emphasize the basic point.

7 H. J. Hofstra, *An Inflation Adjusted Tax System,* A Summary of Dutch Report (The Hague: Government Printing Office, 1978), p. 40.

8 Ibid., p. 41. The same recommendation is implicit in William Fellner et al, *Correcting Taxes for Inflation* (Washington, D.C.: American Enterprise Institute, 1975), pp. 31–3.

9 This method values inputs at historical costs and treats any increase in input prices as realized profits.

10 For a good survey of countries' practices see Dorothea Stromberg, "How to Eliminate Inflation from Inventory Accounting, A Comparison of Stock Valuation in West European Industrial Countries," *Intertax* (1977/8): 287–99.

11 In the United States the additional tax liability due to inventory profits has been estimated to amount to many billions of dollars. See Fellner et al, *Correcting Taxes for Inflation,* pp. 28–31.

12 W. T. Baxter, in Baxter et al, *Economic Calculations Under Inflation,* floor discussion, p. 193.

13 Ibid., response, pp. 90–1.

14 This is less true for inventories.

15 See W. T. Baxter, "Inflation Accounting: A British View," in Baxter et al, *Economic Calculations Under Inflation,* pp. 159–89. See also W. T. Baxter, "Accountants and Inflation," *Lloyds Bank Review,* no. 126, (Oct. 1977): 1–16; and J. M. Renshall "Current Cost Accounting in the U.K. – A Short Survey of Its History, Reception and Prospects," *Intertax* (1976/9): 314–24.

16 See Robert F. Sprouse, "Inflation, Accounting Principles, and the Accounting Profession," in W. Baxter et al, *Economic Calculations Under Inflation;* pp. 114–15.

17 See for a detailed description of these experiences: George Lent, "Adjustment of Taxable Profits for Inflation," IMF *Staff Papers 22,* no. 3 (Nov. 1975): 641–79.

18 For details on these schemes see: Milka Casanegra de Jantscher, "Taxing Business Profits During Inflation: The Latin American Experience," *International Tax Journal 2* (Winter 1976): 128–46.

Chapter 7. Inflation, lags in collection, and the real value of income tax revenue

1 And by the same token, the real value of revenues would not be affected by inflation if the elasticity were one. Thus, if indexation of the tax succeeded in making the price elasticity equal to one, there would not be, in this lagless world, any inflation-induced increase in the ratio of income taxes to national income. But, of course, this theoretical situation is not practically possible.

2 During this whole discussion, the underlying legal structure is assumed to remain unchanged. We are thus talking about automatic, or built-in, elasticity, which excludes the effects of discretionary changes.

3 To simplify the analysis and emphasize the impact of price changes, real growth during the inflationary period is assumed to be either zero or insignificant.

4 Even with zero inflation, the taxpayer gets some advantage due to the postponement of taxes. The higher the rate of discount, the greater the advantage related to a given lag.

5 Even in this case, real revenue would be affected to the extent that inflation distorts the taxable bases (i.e., capital gains, interest, profits, etc.). However, the change in real revenue would not be induced by the lag.

6 It must be emphasized that in this analysis we are measuring only the effect of the collection lag. Other inflation-induced effects – distortions of bases and so on – are being ignored.

7 In the United States, in 1975 the proportion of wages and salaries in total

reported gross income fell consistently from about 95 percent for incomes less than $5,000 to about 10 percent for incomes above $1 million.

8 In most countries, income taxes, except for those withheld at the source, are collected with considerable lags.

9 See Chapter 2, this volume.

10 To my knowledge, there is no literature dealing with "optimal" lags.

11 Argentina, Brazil, Chile, and some other countries index the unpaid taxes.

12 Milton Friedman, "Discussion of the Inflationary Gap," *American Economic Review 32* (June 1942): 308–14; republished in Friedman's *Essays in Positive Economics* (Chicago: University of Chicago Press, 1953), pp. 251–62. Martin J. Bailey, "Welfare Cost of Inflationary Finance," *Journal of Political Economy 63* (Apr. 1956): 93–110. More than five decades ago Keynes had also been interested in the issue of inflationary finance: see John M. Keynes, *A Tract on Monetary Reform* (London: Macmillan, 1923), Chap. 2, pp. 37–60.

13 For an analysis of this issue see Vito Tanzi, "Inflation, Real Tax Revenue, and the Case for Inflationary Finance: Theory With an Application to Argentina," IMF *Staff Papers 25,* no. 3 (Sept. 1978): 417–51.

Chapter 8. Sensitivity of personal income tax yield to incomes changes: theory and measurement

1 However, when there is inflation, it may also depend on the distortions of the tax bases.

2 To simplify the analysis, it has been assumed that there is only one basic exemption. Problems concerning the treatment of families have therefore been ignored.

3 However, whether the increase is real or just due to inflation could make a difference and thus change the value of K unless capital-income indexation is adopted.

4 This ratio is low for some countries but extremely high for others.

5 Namely, it depends on how wide and how steep is the rate structure.

6 See Richard Musgrave, *The Theory of Public Finance* (New York: MacGraw-Hill, 1959), p. 507.

7 It must be reemphasized that if there is inflation, this will require the indexation of tax bases.

8 R. Goode, *The Individual Income Tax* (Washington, D.C.: Brookings Institution, 1964); Wilfred Lewis, Jr., *Federal Fiscal Policy in the Postwar Recessions* (Washington, D.C.: Brookings Institution, 1962).

9 E. Cary Brown and Richard J. Kruizenga, "Income Sensitivity of a Simple Personal Income Tax," *Review of Economics and Statistics 41* (Aug. 1959): Alan Prest, "The Sensitivity of the Yield of Personal Income Tax in the United Kingdom," *Economic Journal 72* (Sept. 1962): 576–96.

10 W. H. Waldorf, "The Responsiveness of Federal Income Taxes to Income Change," *Survey of Current Business 47* (Dec. 1967): 32–45; Joseph Pechman, "Responsiveness of the Federal Individual Income Tax to Changes in Income," *Brookings Papers on Economic Activity 2* (1973): 385–427.

11 Goode, *Individual Income Tax*, p. 346.
12 E. J. Mishan and L. A. Dicks-Mireaux, "Progressive Taxation in an Inflationary Economy," *American Economic Review 48* (Sept. 1958): 590–606.
13 J. O. Blackburn, "Implicit Tax Rate Reductions with Growth, Progressive Taxes, Constant Progressivity, and a Fixed Public Share," *American Economic Review 57* (Mar. 1967): 162–9.
14 There are twenty-four such classes so that one gets twenty-four estimates of *t* and *y*.
15 This method was also used by Alan Prest in connection with United Kingdom data. See "Personal Income Tax . . ." cited above.
16 Adjusted Gross Income (AGI) results after gross income, from all sources subject to tax, is adjusted to reflect allowances for business expenses. AGI less personal deductions (for outlays such as taxes, medical expenses, charitable contributions, and so on) and less personal exemptions gives Taxable Income, TI.
17 See Internal Revenue Service's *Statistics of Income*, 1972 (Washington, D.C.: GPO, 1975), Table 1.4, pp. 15–24.
18 Joseph Pechman, "Responsiveness," pp. 385–427.
19 This method was first suggested and applied to U.S. data in Vito Tanzi, "Measuring the Sensitivity of the Federal Income Tax from Cross-Section Data: A New Approach," *Review of Economics and Statistics 5*, no. 2 (May 1969): 206–9. It has since been applied to data for Denmark and Canada. See Palle S. Andersen, "Built-in Flexibility and Sensitivity of the Personal Income Tax in Denmark," *Swedish Journal of Economics 75* (Mar. 1973): 1–18; and Michel Boucher, "L'Impôt Canadien sur le Revenu des Particuliers: Sa Contribution à la Stabilisation de l'Economie," *Public Finance/Finances Publiques 32*, no. 21 (1977): 159–67.
20 See Simon Kuznets, "Quantitative Aspects of the Economic Growth of Nations," *Economic Development and Cultural Changes 6*, no. 4, part II (July 1958):1–128; D. I. Verway, "A Ranking of States by Inequality Using Census and Tax Data," *Review of Economics and Statistics 18* (Aug. 1966): 314–21.
21 See for more detail Emil M. Sunley, Jr. and Joseph A. Pechman, "Inflation Adjustment for the Individual Income Tax" in Aaron, ed., *Inflation and the Income Tax* (Washington, D.C.: Brookings Institution, 1976), pp. 153–66; and Vito Tanzi, "The Sensitivity of the Yield of the U.S. Individual Income Tax and the Tax Reforms of the Past Decade," IMF *Staff Papers 23*, no. 2 (July 1976): 441–54.

Chapter 9. Indexing the personal income tax for inflation and real growth

1 This increase will not be evenly distributed among taxpayers in different income classes. As was shown in the material on the determinants of elasticity, Chapter 8, this volume, the rate of increase will be particularly high for taxpayers whose incomes puts them near the inflection point.
2 This might be the case for many developing countries. A government that expects to remain in power for a long time and that wants to increase the tax

burden of the country would find attractive an elastic income tax. Provided that nominal incomes are growing (because of real growth or inflation), the government can expect to receive progressively higher revenue without having to go through the politically embarrassing process of increasing tax rates.

3 See especially Council of Economic Advisers, *Economic Report of the President*, July 1962 (Washington, D.C.: GPO, 1962). The advent of stagflation has made this concept somewhat less attractive than it appeared at the time it was developed. This concept played a large role in the United States in the "New Economics" of the Kennedy–Johnson era.

4 Richard S. Weckstein, "Fiscal Reform and Economic Growth," *National Tax Journal 17* (Dec. 1964), p. 325.

5 Over this period prices rose by 13.9 percent, while real per capita income rose by 20 percent.

6 The effects of inflation alone on the distribution of the tax burden for the 1954–63 period have been calculated by C. J. Goetz and W. F. Weber in "Intertemporal Changes in Real Federal Income Tax Rates, 1954–70," *National Tax Journal 24*, no. 1 (Mar. 1971): 51–63. The effects of inflation *and* growth have been calculated by John J. Dittrick, Jr., *The Interrelationship Between the U.S. Personal Income Tax Structure and Inflation*, Ph.D. dissertation (American University, 1975).

7 See Vito Tanzi, *The Individual Income Tax and Economic Growth* (Baltimore, Md.: Johns Hopkins University Press, 1969), Chapter VII.

8 Frederick G. Reuss, *Fiscal Policy for Growth Without Inflation, The German Experiment* (Baltimore, Md.: Johns Hopkins University Press, 1963), Chapter 7. In time, as the rate of growth slowed down, German tax policy became less dynamic and tax changes less frequent.

9 The ratio of this tax to GNP was 5.14 in 1958 but had increased to 7.55 by 1963. By 1975 that ratio had reached 10.6 percent.

10 Furthermore, unless these changes are annual, the problem of the effect of the fiscal drag on the upswing of a cycle will still exist.

11 See Alan S. Blinder and Robert M. Solow, "Analytical Foundations of Fiscal Policy," in *The Ecomomics of Public Finance* (Washington, D.C.: Brookings Institution, 1974).

12 Thus, for example, the top quintile of personal income will continue to pay a constant proportion of its income in taxes and a constant proportion of the total income tax burden.

13 For a discussion of this proposal, see *Inflation and Taxation*, Report of Committee of Inquiry into Inflation and Taxation (Canberra: Australian Government Publishing Service, 1975), 123–28; and Lars Matthiessen, "Index-Tied Income Taxes and Economic Policy," *Swedish Journal of Economics 75* (Mar. 1973): 49–66. See also Gilberto Murano, "Imposta Personale e Inflazione: Un 'analisi Macroeconomica" in Emilio Gerelli, ed., *Imposte e Inflazione* (Milano: Franco Angeli, 1976).

14 When a tax system is indexed for increases in prices alone, the curve in Figure 2 will not shift to the right because of price changes but will still shift because of real income changes.

15 See *Meade Report* [J. E. Meade, *The Structure and Reform of Direct Taxa-*

tion (London: Allen & Unwin, 1978)], pp. 117–8; *Mathews Committee Report* [Report of Committee of Inquiry into Inflation and Taxation, *Inflation and Taxation*, (Canberra: Australian Government Publishing Service, 1975)], pp. 123–8. Of related interest also is Theo Stevens, "The Impact of Growth and Inflation on Taxation" in Institut International des Finances Publiques, *Inflation, Economic Growth and Taxation*, XXIX Session, Barcelona Congress, 1973, 99–126.

16 *Meade Report*, p. 118.
17 Such a proposal was first made in my paper "A Proposal for a Dynamically Self-Adjusting Personal Income Tax," *Public Finance 21*, no. 4 (1966): 507–19.
18 Thomas F. Dernburg, *Indexing the Individual Income Tax for Inflation: Will This Help to Stabilize the Economy?* Joint Economic Committee of U.S. Congress, Studies in Fiscal Policy, Paper no. 2 (Dec. 27, 1976).
19 Ibid.
20 See John J. Dittrick, Jr., "The Interrelationship Between the U.S. Personal Income Tax Structure and Inflation," (Ph.D. dissertation, American University, 1975).
21 He made no adjustment to the deduction allowances. Thus, he continued to take a basic exemption of 10 percent of adjusted gross income with a maximum of $1,000.

Chapter 10. Inflation, income taxes, and the equilibrium rate of interest: theory

1 For seminal contributions, one ought to consult Irving Fisher, *The Rate of Interest* (New York: 1907, Macmillan, 1907), pp. 270–80, and a later revision, *The Theory of Interest* (New York: Macmillan, 1930). A good description can also be found in J. Hirshleifer, *Investment, Interest, and Capital* (Englewood Cliffs, N.J.: Prentice-Hall, 1970), Chap. 5.
2 See, especially: Thomas J. Sargent, "Anticipated Inflation and the Nominal Rate of Interest," *Quarterly Journal of Economics 86* (May 1972): 212–25; Ignazio Visco, "Inflation and the Rate of Interest, *Quarterly Journal of Economics 89* (May 1975): 303–10; F. A. Lutz, "Inflation and the Rates of Interest," Banca Nazionale del Lavoro, *Quarterly Review*, no. 109 (June 1974): 88–117; Eugene F. Fama, Short-Term Interest Rates as Predictors of Inflation," *American Economic Review 65* (June 1975): 269–82; Martin Feldstein and Otto Eckstein, "The Fundamental Determinants of the Interest Rates," *Review of Economics and Statistics 52* (November 1970): 363–75. William E. Gibson, "Interest Rates and Inflationary Expectations: New Evidence," *American Economic Review 62* (Dec. 1972): 854–65; Kajal Lahiri, "Inflationary Expectations: Their Formation and Interest Rate Effects," *American Economic Review 66* (Mar. 1976): 124–31; Vito Tanzi, "Inflationary Expectations, Economic Activity, Taxes and the Rate of Interest," *American Economic Review*, in press.
3 More recently several authors have begun to realize the possible effects of income taxes on the rate of interest. On this see, for example, Michael R. Darby, "The Financial and Tax Effects of Monetary Policy on Interest Rates," *Economic Inquiry 13* (June 1975): 266–76; Vito Tanzi, "Inflation,

Indexation and Interest Income Taxation," Banca Nazionale del Lavoro, *Quarterly Review 29* (Mar. 1976): 64–76; Martin Feldstein, "Inflation, Income Taxes, and the Rate of Interest: A Theoretical Analysis," *American Economic Review 66* (Dec. 1976): 809–20.

4 This is the production possibility curve for the individual rather than for the whole economy. It is determined by the resources available to the individual at time 0 and by the real investment opportunities open to him.

5 For the rest of the chapter we shall ignore this term.

6 Of course these shifts do not reflect any changes in physical terms – merely the fact that we are now measuring the physical quantities in these curves in period 1 prices, which are assumed to be higher.

7 However, if individuals' expectations of future inflation differ from the average Π, even in this case there may be distortions introduced by inflation. See below for an elaboration of this point.

8 As pointed out in note 3, this chapter, a few recent studies have begun to consider the effects of taxes.

9 In other words, the principal A would need to grow by $A\Pi$ in order to retain its real value.

10 This implies that in a situation where the income tax is progressive, those with higher total incomes (regardless of the size of interest income itself) will be subjected to higher taxes on illusory interest income.

11 If the actual rate of inflation turns out to differ from the expected rate, even the required rate of interest will not leave the lender with an unchanged real rate of interest.

12 For many countries this information is available from the tax authorities. For the United States, it is found in Internal Revenue Service, *Statistics of Income*, various issues. For estimates of the average tax rate on interest income for the United States for the period 1913–65 see Vito Tanzi, "Demand for Money, Interest Rates and Income Taxation," Banca Nazionale del Lavoro, *Quarterly Review*, no. 111 (Dec. 1974): 325. The method was devised for another purpose by Colin Wright in "Saving and the Rate of Interest" in Arnold C. Harberger and Martin J. Bailey, eds., *The Taxation of Income from Capital* (Washington, D.C.: Brookings Institution, 1969).

13 Since individuals buy different baskets and because the prices of particular commodities fluctuate more than the general price index, individuals would have been differently affected by past inflation.

14 An empirical analysis of this point for the United States is made in the next chapter.

15 James Tobin, "Money and Economic Growth," *Econometrica 33* (Oct. 1965): 671–84. Taxes on interest income reduce the opportunity cost of holding money. See on this Vito Tanzi, "Income Taxes and the Demand for Money: A Quantitative Analysis," Banca Nazionale del Lavoro *Quarterly Review*, no. 128 (March 1979): 55–72.

16 Robert A. Mundell, "Inflation and Real Interest," *Journal of Political Economy 71* (June 1963): 280–3.

17 Vito Tanzi, "Inflation, Real Tax Revenue, and the Case for Inflationary Finance: Theory with an Application to Argentina," IMF *Staff Papers 25*, no. 3 (Sept. 1978): 417–51.

18 See Michael J. Boskin, "Taxation, Saving, and the Rate of Interest," *Journal of Political Economy 86,* no. 2, Part 2 (Apr. 1978): S-3–S27.
19 See Feldstein, "Inflation."
20 Ibid.
21 That is, if economic operators suffered from neither money nor fiscal illusions.
22 See Erik Lundberg, *Instability and Economic Growth* (New Haven: Yale University Press, 1968), pp. 199–201. Original statement is in Erik Lundberg, *Business Cycles and Economic Policy* (London: Allen & Unwin 1957); the Swedish edition appeared in 1953. Lundberg's argument about wages is that wage earners may try to maintain constant their real disposable income during an inflationary situation. When faced with progressive income taxes, they may require wage increases that exceed the rate of inflation, thus contributing to a cost-push – or tax-push – inflation. This argument is discussed in more detail in Chapter 12, this volume.
23 In the United States, mortgage interest accounted for 3.75 percent and 3.7 percent of the consumer price index in December 1971 and December 1972, respectively. Data from U.S. Department of Labor, Bureau of Labor Statistics. A quantitative study has concluded that the direct impact of changes in interest rates on price changes in the United States in recent years has been relatively small. However, during the period covered by the study – 1955 to 1969 – the change in the rate of interest was also quite small. Higher increases could have had more significant effects. See Steven A. Seeling, "Rising Interest Rates and Cost-Push Inflation," *Journal of Finance 29,* no. 4, (Sept. 1974): 1049–61. Furthermore, the indirect effects might be far more important. For example, a substantial increase in the rate of interest may bring about an inflow of capital into the country which might affect the money supply and thus the rate of inflation.
24 Economic theory is unable to provide an answer to what they would do in such a situation. However, the hunch among many observers has been that the effect on the propensity to save would be negative. That hunch has recently received some empirical support. See Boskin, "Taxation, Saving, and Interest."
25 See Milton Friedman, "Monetary Correction" in American Enterprise Institute, *Essays on Inflation and Indexation* (Washington, D.C.: AEI 1974), p. 41. This process is facilitated by the existence of legal ceilings on the rates of interest that some of these intermediaries are allowed to pay.

Chapter 11. Inflation, income taxes, and interest rates: some empirical results

1 Following much of the literature on this subject, we shall assume that r, the real rate, is constant. However, the author has shown elsewhere that r is very much influenced by fluctuations in real output. See "Inflationary Expectations, Economic Activity Taxes, and Interest Rates," *American Economic Review* (in press).
2 If the individual suffers from money illusions his subjective evaluation of the situation would differ from the objective one, so that he may feel better

or worse off. Also it must be understood that these statements concern the individual only in relation to his lending and borrowing activities. Inflation will obviously affect him in other ways, so that the *total* effect of inflation may be beneficial or damaging to him.

3 Obviously, to provide a positive real rate, the nominal rates should have been higher.

4 Obviously, these conclusions apply to classes as a whole. Within each class some taxpayers are net debtors and some net creditors. Therefore, the above conclusions are not necessarily applicable to each individual.

5 As the rates vary at which the incomes of the various classes are taxed, whether the government gains or loses depends to a large extent on where the interest incomes and the interest deductions accrue.

6 It should be emphasized that these conclusions relate strictly to the tax treatment of interest income.

7 For this reason, the *b* was dropped from Equation 3, Chapter 10, this volume.

8 Actually the value might have to be even higher as discussed in Chapter 10, dealing with the equilibrium rate of interest.

9 See Milton Friedman, "Factors Affecting the Level of Interest Rates, Part I," *Savings and Residential Financing, 1968 Conference Proceedings* (Chicago: Savings and Loan League, 1968): 10–27; and Robert J. Gordon, "Interest Rates and Prices in the Long Run, A Comment," *Journal of Money, Credit and Banking 5* (Feb. 1973), 460–3.

10 This directly observed inflationary expectation variable has been published in John A. Carlson, "A Study of Price Forecasts," *Annals of Economic and Social Measurement 1* (June 1977), Table 1, pp. 33–4.

11 See J. F. Muth, "Rational Expectations and the Theory of Price Movements," *Econometrica 29*, (July 1961): 315–35.

Chapter 12. Inflation, indexation, and the wage-tax spiral

1 See Henry J. Aaron, ed., *Inflation and the Income Tax* (Washington, D.C.: Brookings Institution, 1976), p. 193.

2 D. E. W. Laidler and J. M. Parkin, "Inflation – A Survey," *Economic Journal 85*, no. 340 (Dec. 1975): 741–809. The sentence cited above is on p. 765.

3 See on this A. T. Peacock and G. K. Shaw, "Is Fiscal Policy Dead?" Banca Nazionale del Lavoro *Quarterly Review*, No. 125 (June 1978): 107–22; Alan S. Blinder and Robert M. Solow, "Analytical Foundations on Fiscal Policy" in Alan S. Blinder et al, *The Economics of Public Finance* (Washington, D.C.: Brookings Institution, 1974), pp. 3–115, especially pp. 101–1; and Alan S. Blinder, "Can Income Tax Increases be Inflationary? An Expository Note," *National Tax Journal 26* (June 1973): 295–301.

4 Blinder and Solow, "Analytical Foundations," p. 101. They propose cuts in public expenditures.

5 George Perry, for example, described this possibility as "extremely remote." See Aaron, ed., *Inflation and the Income Tax*, p. 193.

6 See on this Committee on Fiscal Affairs, *The Adjustment of Personal In-come Tax Systems for Inflation* (Paris: OECD, 1976), pp. 25–26; *Mathews Committee Report* [Report of Committee of Inquiry into Inflation and Taxa-tion, *Inflation and Taxation* (Canberra: Government Publishing Service, 1975)]: pp. 91–107; Thomas F. Dernburg, "The Macroeconomic Implica-tions of Wage Retaliation Against Higher Taxation," IMF *Staff Papers 21*, no. 3 (Nov. 1974): 758–61.

7 It would exist in purely competitive markets.

8 See Richard Musgrave, *The Theory of Public Finance* (New York: McGraw-Hill, 1959), pp. 232–49; Committee on Fiscal Affairs, *Theoretical and Empirical Aspects of the Effects of Taxation on the Supply of Labor* (Paris: OECD, 1975); also *Meade Report* [J. E. Meade, *The Structure and Reform of Direct Taxation* (London: Allen & Unwin, 1978)], pp. 7–11.

9 OECD, *Effects of Taxation*, pp. 7–11.

10 Union members are less likely to have money or fiscal illusions when unions have capable research units performing an educational role. In any case, the wage negotiations are conducted by the union leaders rather than by the workers themselves.

11 Erik Lundberg, *Instability and Economic Growth* (New Haven: Yale Uni-versity Press, 1968), pp. 99–201. The original statement is in Lundberg's *Business Cycles and Economic Policy* (London: Allen & Unwin, 1957); the Swedish edition appeared in 1953.

12 See Lars Mathiessen, "Index-Tied Income Taxes and Economic Policy," *Swedish Journal of Economics 75* (Mar. 1973): 60–3; and Richard Mus-grave, "Tax Structure, Inflation, and Growth" in Institut International des Finances Publiques, XXIX Session, *Inflation, Economic Growth and Taxa-tion* (Barcelona Congress, 1973), pp. 15–16.

13 As long as marginal and average tax rates are equal, the tax factor will not play a role regardless of the level of taxation.

14 Mathews' report, *Inflation and Taxation*, p. 98.

15 Committee on Fiscal Affairs, *Personal Income Tax Systems*, p. 25.

16 Ibid.

17 Cited from Deutscher Gewerkschaftsbund, *Welt der Arbeit*, Sonderdienst, January 1972. Committee on Fiscal Affairs, *Adjustment of Personal Income Tax Systems*, p. 25.

18 See especially Frank Wilkinson and H. A. Turner, "The Wage–Tax Spiral and Labour Militancy," in Dudley Jackson, H.A. Turner, and Frank Wil-kinson, *Do Trade Unions Cause Inflation?* 2nd ed. (Cambridge: Cambridge University Press, 1975), pp. 63–103.

19 Hansard Col. 272 6th April 1976.

20 D. A. L. Auld, "The Impact of Taxes on Wages and Prices" *National Tax Journal* (Mar. 1974): 147–50.

21 L. Taylor, S. Turnovsky, and T. Wilson, *Inflationary Prices in North American Manufacturing* (Ottawa: Prices and Income Commission, 1973).

22 C. J. Bruce, "The Wage–Tax Spiral: Canada 1953–70," *Economic Journal 85*, no. 338 (June 1975): 372–6.

23 See C. A. van der Beld "The Growth of Employment in the Public Sector

and in the Private Sector," paper presented to the Expert Conference on the Structural Determinants of Employment and Unemployment, OECD 1977.
24 J. Johnston, and M. Timbull, "Empirical Tests of a Bargaining Theory of Wage Rate Determination," *Manchester School* (June 1973): 141–67.
25 Frank Wilkinson, and H. A. Turner, "The Wage Tax Spiral and Labour Militancy" in Dudley Jackson, H. A. Turner, and Frank Wilkinson, *Do Trade Unions Cause Inflation?* 2nd ed. (Cambridge: Cambridge University Press, 1975).
26 Robert J. Gordon, "Inflation in Recession and Recovery," *Brookings Papers on Economic Activity, 1* (1971), Table 1, pp. 118–9.
27 Otto Eckstein and Roger Brinner, *The Inflation Process in the United States,* (Washington, D.C.: G.P.O., 1972).
28 Ibid., p. 17.

Chapter 13. Some general conclusions on indexation

1 Of course, through discretionary tax cuts the government can prevent the expansion of the public sector. But, tax cuts are expensive in terms of the time of legislators and policymakers, so that some countries might prefer to rely on a rule such as indexation.
2 On the issue of wage indexation, see, inter alia, Richard Jackman and Kurt Klappholz, "The Case for Indexing Wages and Salaries," in Thelma Liesner and Mervyn A. King, eds., *Indexing for Inflation* (London: Institute for Fiscal Studies, 1975); Anne Romanis Brown, "Indexation of Wages and Salaries in Developed Economies," IMF *Staff Papers 23,* no. 1 (Mar. 1976): 226–71; Morris Goldstein "Wage Indexation, Inflation and the Labour Market," IMF *Staff Papers 22,* no. 3 (Nov. 1975): 680–713; D. A. Peel, "On the Case for Indexation of Wages and Salaries," *Kyklos 30,* Fasc 2 (1977): 259–70.
3 In the particular case of Argentina, two factors protect the government from the problem discussed above: (1) the fact that most borrowing is for relatively short periods (up to six months); (2) the fact that interest rates are themselves indexed, so that a fall in the rate of inflation would be accompanied by a fall in nominal rates.
4 *News Letter,* National City Bank of Minneapolis, June 20, 1974.
5 *Report of the Royal Commission on Taxation* (Ottawa: Queen's Printer, 1966), 2: 23.
6 "Using Escalators to Help Fight Inflation," *Fortune,* July 1974, p. 94.
7 Of course a change in real income would still lead to an increase in the average tax rate, and as long as inflation is accompanied by growth, the marginal tax rate will still exceed the average tax rate. Only if the index is tied to the growth of per capita income will this not happen.
8 This will be particularly true if because of the size of the change, more time is needed for analysis and for legislative approval, so that, by the time fiscal policy exerts its influence, the situation may have changed and the effect of the policy may thus be destabilizing.

9 See Lars Mathiessen, "Index-Tied Income Taxes and Economic Policy," *Swedish Journal of Economics*, 75, no. 1 (Mar. 1973).

10 For the United Kingdom, this may not be so. The recent Cambridge "fiscal view of the balance of payment" implies that in the United Kingdom at least, an autonomous fiscal deficit affects prices far more than output. This view has been promoted by Lord Kaldor and members of the Department of Applied Economics at Cambridge University.

11 John Bossons and Thomas A. Wilson, "Adjusting Tax Rates for Inflation," *Canadian Tax Journal 21*, (May/June 1973): 185–99. For the United States, James L. Pierce and Jared J. Enzler have argued that "indexing the income tax system will not produce significantly greater economic instability than already exists." See their paper "The Implication for Economic Stability of Indexing the Individual Income Tax," in Henry J. Aaron, ed., *Inflation and the Income Tax* (Washington, D.C.: Brookings Institution, 1976), pp. 173–87. The quote is on p. 187.

12 In a more recent econometric analysis of the Canadian indexation, Grady and Stephenson found results slightly different from those obtained by Bossons and Wilson. Their conclusion was that indexing has reduced built-in stability with respect to certain types of shocks (persistent volume shocks) and increased it with respect to others (persistent price shocks). See Patrick Grady and Donald R. Stephenson, "Some Macroeconomic Effects of Tax Reform and Indexing," *Canadian Journal of Economics 10*, no. 3 (Aug. 1977): 378–92.

13 Don Patinkin, "What Advanced Countries Can Learn from the Experience with Indexation," In M. Eshaq Nadiri et al, *Indexation, the Brazilian Experience*, National Bureau of Economic Research *Occasional Papers 4*, no. 1 (Winter 1977), p. 178.

14 Switzerland is ignored.

15 But as we saw in the relevant chapters, some countries have attempted to adjust capital incomes.

Index